THE SUBJECT OF ADDICTION
PSYCHOANALYSIS AND THE ADMINISTRATION OF ENJOYMENT

THE SUBJECT OF ADDICTION

PSYCHOANALYSIS AND THE
ADMINISTRATION OF ENJOYMENT

by

Rik Loose

LONDON   NEW YORK

First published in 2002 by
H. Karnac (Books) Ltd.
6 Pembroke Buildings, London NW10 6RE
A subsidiary of Other Press LLC, New York

Copyright © Rik Loose, 2002

All rights reserved. No part of this publication may be reproduced, stored in a retrieval system, or transmitted, in any form or by any means, electronic, mechanical, photocopying, recording, or otherwise, without the prior written permission of the publisher.

British Library Cataloguing in Publication Data

A C.I.P. for this book is available from the British Library

ISBN 1 85575 299 9

10 9 8 7 6 5 4 3 2 1

Edited, designed, and produced by The Studio Publishing Services Ltd, Exeter
Printed and bound in Great Britain by Biddles Ltd. *www.biddles.co.uk*

www.karnacbooks.com

*For
Jean
and
F. F.*

ACKNOWLEDGEMENTS

I would like to specifically thank Paul Verhaeghe for his support, encouragement and outstanding capacity to inspire. I want to express my gratitude to Julien Quackelbeen for installing a true passion for psychoanalysis in me. I want to thank Oliver Rathbone from Karnac Books for helping to realise this project and stimulating me till the very end. I would like to thank Cormac Gallagher and Jean Kilcullen for having given me the opportunity to work in academia (and more than that).

I would like to express my gratitude to the many colleagues I met, and friends I made, through the Department of Psychoanalysis of the University of Gent, namely, Lieven Jonckheere, Katrien Libbrecht, Dany Nobus, Els Vandenbussche, Filip Geerardijn, Hubert van Hoorde, Karin Temmerman, Pat Jacobs, Tom De Belie, Francine Danniau, Frederic Declerck, Iris De Groot, Annick De Coninck, Roel De Cuyper, Luc Vander Vennet, Erik Broekaert and many others.

I want to thank Henk Dits for his genuine interest and enthusiasm, Gerry Sullivan for all his help, (his contribution for this book cannot be over-estimated), Geert Bisschop for his fort-da behaviour and art work and Helen and Garrett Sheehan for being there when most necessary.

Further I want to thank all those friends and colleagues in Ireland and England who have meant a lot to me in various ways both personally and in terms of my work, namely, David (you'll never do it) Slattery, Maeve Nolan, Patricia McCarthy, Barry O'Donnell, Helena Texier, Bernard Burgoyne, Alan Rowan, Leena Häkkinen, Kirsty Hall, Andrew (many problems) Honeyman, Siobain O'Donnell, Susan Cassidy, Marie Fogarty, Martin Daly, Aisling Campbell, Mark Maguire, Brian Hughes, Olga Cox, Patricia Stewart, Rob Weatherill, Stephen Costello, Aurelie Olivier, Terry Ball, Marek McGann and all (the other) staff members at DBS School of Arts. Last but not least I want to thank the psychoanalysis and MA in Addiction Studies students (past and present) at DBS School of Arts (LSB College) for their interest and critical approach.

CONTENTS

ACKNOWLEDGEMENTS — vii

FOREWORD by Professor Paul Verhaeghe — xi

PREFACE — xv

PART I:
CLASSICAL FOUNDATIONS FOR A THEORY ON
ADDICTION: THE ENERGETICS OF LIBIDO AND
THE ECONOMICS OF DESIRE

Introduction — 3

CHAPTER ONE
The place of cocaine in the work of Freud — 7

CHAPTER TWO
Freud's pre-analytical period — 23

CHAPTER THREE
A limit to Freud's dream — 35

CHAPTER FOUR
Freud's war during the "inter-bellum":
the death-drive and the extermination of happiness — 61

Conclusion — 85

PART II:
THE POST-FREUDIAN REDUCTION OF A FIELD AND
THE FRUITS OF A CONFRONTATION

Introduction — 95

CHAPTER FIVE
Between drive and ego: the ascent of the subject — 99

PART III:
ELEMENTS FOR A LACANIAN THEORY (AND TREATMENT)
OF ADDICTION — THE ADMINISTRATION OF TOXICITY

Introduction — 133

CHAPTER SIX
The pleasure before death: the symbolic, the imaginary
and jouissance — 137

CHAPTER SEVEN
The death of pleasure: the real, the body and jouissance — 167

CHAPTER EIGHT
Science, addiction and diagnosis: a question of administration — 195

CHAPTER NINE
Addiction and discourse: a moral question and the ethics of
treatment — 235

Conclusion — 271

REFERENCES — 285

INDEX — 297

FOREWORD

Addiction, like prostitution, is a phenomenon as old as the human race. Evidently they have something in common—their relationship to desire and enjoyment—and both form a problem for the society in which they take place. It is not too difficult to find a reason for this. A society is a perfect example of an institution consisting of a collection of people held together by a number of commonly shared rules and conventions. This applies to every institution, be this a family, a school, an association, or a psychiatric institution. The rules and conventions that we find in these institutions, no matter how private they may be, always have the same aim: the regulation of enjoyment on the basis of a number of collectively developed and often legally binding agreements. Hence, every institution also presents an ideal, precisely through which that regulation is articulated.

Like prostitution, addiction has escaped these conventions, which is exactly why they form a problem for society as an institution. This does not detract from the fact that they are fundamentally different. Prostitution evades conventional solutions concerning the sexual relationship (and its impossibility), but in doing so it manages to maintain the convention. Both ordinary regulation—the one subject to the norm—and prostitution, emphasize phallic enjoyment and the exchange between partners. This is not the case with addiction. Lacan's reflections on this issue evinced a particular characteristic which he sensed only latently: the addict abandons the detour via the Other, abandons phallic enjoyment and chooses radically for immediate access to jouissance. This is precisely why he or she places him or herself outside the conventions of the group and, as such, forms a threat to this convention. The addict acts alone, the Other is excluded. The reaction of the Other is always of a master-discourse type: you will enjoy according to the rules! The ideal is commanded, and its failure predictable and well known.

That is why a particular opportunity is missed, not least because something is not heard or observed. The addict acts alone, that's true, but it is remarkable that time and again attempts at group formation reveal themselves in and through addictive use. Alcoholic brothers-in-arms stay together glued to the bar the hour at which they have to go home alone delayed as long as possible. The same can be recognised in many different forms of use: a near desperate attempt to install nonetheless a collective, a group, through which the jouissance and unbearable real are shared. Something similar emerges in the treatments of addiction, in which therapeutic communities and AA groups promise a changing of the guards.

The addict cannot do without the Other, it is just that he or she has a totally different relationship to the Other than the ordinary divided subject. Here we can refer to a differential-diagnostic distinction which Freud introduced very early on in his work: the actual neuroses versus the psychoneuroses. The former patients remain stuck in the process of becoming subject with an Other who does not respond to the appeal which emanates from the body as a result of which the processing of this appeal continues at the level of the body. The latter do indeed get a response, which subsequently, via secondary elaboration and the Oedipal structure, is turned into meaningful symptoms.

The distinction between these two concerns above all the relationship to the Other. The first group remain stuck on the threshold of the Other, whilst the second group live inside the house of language. The consequence of this for the later therapeutic relationship is extremely far-reaching, both on a technical and on an ethical plane. There are hardly any signifying symptoms, therefore classic interpretation does not work. The relationship—the response of the Other—is demanded but its reception is extremely problematic because the basis for such a reception is lacking. Hence, therapeutic work is predominantly characterized by ethics: how to install a workable relationship with a subject on the basis of which the existential problem concerning enjoyment can be treated via words. This is literally not at all self-evident. An over-hasty focus on prohibition and the ideal will not work because of the actual neurotic structure—after all, there is no sound basis.

It is a real merit of this book that it does not focus on attempts like that to resolve things. It is a real merit of this book that it does not focus on the illusion of hasty and simple approaches to the problem of addiction. Instead, what we get is a thorough study of the *subject* who uses (drugs or alcohol), in contrast to the everuseless focus on the product or the use of it. This study is unique—I don't know of any other study, which traces so thoroughly the thoughts on addiction to be found in both Freud's complete works and the post-Freudians. This fact alone is sufficient to turn this book into a classic. Moreover, Rik Loose has applied the same impressive rigour to the challenge of a similar interpretation of the work of Lacan.

All of this amounts to a lot more than a mere summary. The result is a creative conceptualisation which converges nicely with a number of empirical facts. On the one hand, we have a new theory of addiction as a phenomenon by understanding it as "flood-gates" in the subject regulating what Freud called the "toxic substance", and which was developed further by Lacan as "jouissance". With this theory Rik Loose introduces a new concept: "administration". Without a doubt this concept will acquire a place in psychoanalytic thinking on addiction in the future. On the other hand, he puts all emphasis on the relationship between the addicted subject and the Other, specifically with a view to treatment possibilities. This relationship is not an a priori given like it is in "ordinary" psychopathology; rather it has to be created in and through—the treatment. This relationship has to allow a situation such that the subject can carry out an exploration of his or her relationship to jouissance via a protected and safe relationship with the Other.

Instead of the classic response—"do (and enjoy) like us!"—the possibility for a demand has to be created. Perhaps then the addicted subject will also be able to hear a number of answers.

Professor Paul Verhaeghe

PREFACE

> Oh, who will tell us the entire history of narcotics?—It is nearly the history of "culture", our so-called higher culture!
>
> F. Nietzsche, The Gay Science, 2001, p. 87.

The earliest evidence of psychoactive drug use and knowledge of hallucinogenic plants dates back some 13,000 years (Rudgley, 1999). Most early forms of religion used drugs in an attempt to gain divine knowledge. Drugs and drug use are an integral part of human culture. Yet, we know hardly anything about drugs, at least not the kind of knowledge that would help us to understand how drugs affect people and how people become addicted to drugs. This is most surprising in light of the vast amount of knowledge that has been accumulated in the sciences.

So, what should we expect from science concerning the effect of drugs and the pathology of addiction? What this book will argue is that while science has devoted considerable time and resources to the question, (for instance, the American National Institute of Drug Abuse (NIDA) allocates $600,000,000 a year to research into drug abuse), we still have not established a satisfactory scientific basis for an explanation of addiction. On the other hand, although psychoanalysis has yet to seriously and systematically address the problem of addiction, it is my contention that psychoanalysis has a unique contribution to make.

In psychoanalysis, little work has been done on addiction compared to what has been done in the sciences. Indeed, within psychoanalysis itself little has been done in comparison to the work that has been done on other psychopathologies. It is certainly possible to accuse psychoanalysis of not taking responsibility in this area: a fine contrast with the proclamation of the ethics of psychoanalysis, which exhorts the suffering subject to assume responsibility; and psychoanalysts themselves are certainly not excluded from that responsibility (neither in relation to their patients, nor in relation to themselves). Yet, a psychoanalytic theory on addiction that includes the subject (and his or her responsibility) is something that psychoanalysts have only recently become interested in.

Psychoanalysis might not be an obvious choice for the treatment of addiction. It is a well-known fact that most addicts do not wish to spend the time (or the money) on such a slow and painstaking process as psychoanalysis; their preferred solution to the problems of life would be something that takes immediate effect and that, therefore, doesn't require them to take responsibility. Moreover, a lot of addicts who are in need of treatment cannot afford the time for a long therapeutic process, precisely because the urgency of their need for treatment is in direct proportion to the time they have left. Psychoanalysis is nevertheless in an excellent position to make a contribution to a problem that has so far defied much of our understanding. By inviting people to speak about themselves, their lives, death, pleasure, pain, relationships, sex, work, and family, psychoanalysis has established an unique way of collecting clinical material, a material that surely must be immediately relevant coming as it does from the horse's mouth. Also, addiction is on the increase and that fact alone justifies the necessity for a different approach. This book does not argue that all addicts should undergo a "classical analysis" for many years in order to live happily ever after with or without drugs or alcohol (although it is suggested that an analysis can be enormously beneficial, not to say interesting, especially for addicts). Instead, this book argues that aspects of the ethics, method of treatment, and experience of psychoanalysis should be seriously considered and, where possible, incorporated into the treatment of addicts, irrespective of whether this treatment takes place on an individual, group, community or institutional basis. The main aim of this book is to provide a theoretical foundation for this argument. People who work with addicts often express the sentiment that they don't know exactly what they are dealing with, nor indeed what they are (or should be) doing. The theory put forward in this book can serve as an orientation in the confrontation with a clinic of addiction.

Part I will look for evidence in Freud's work of the existence of a classical foundation for a psychoanalytic theory on addiction; all of Freud's remarks on addiction will be investigated with reference to their theoretical context, with special emphasis on possible ethical and clinical implications. *Part II* will investigate the post-Freudian literature on addiction. It has been said that the usual post-Freudian method consists of explaining pathologies on the basis of whatever concept or period in Freud is in fashion at the time the explanation is sought. It is nevertheless hoped that it is possible to cut a path through the post-Freudian world which will eventually lead to a body of knowledge that will be satisfied neither with one or two aspects of Freud's work, nor even with the opinion that Freud's thinking was infinitely more rigorous and open than most post-Freudian thinking. This is the kind of knowledge that interrogates established forms of knowing. Hence, we end up with Lacan in *Part III*, because his return to the Freudian field allowed him to pierce through this field and move beyond Freud's thinking. In this part it will be argued that Lacan's concepts and theories lend themselves well for investigating the problems of addiction in our time in a manner that avoids reductionism and that is relevant to the clinic of addiction, to treatment and to its current impasses.

A note on terminology is appropriate here. This book focuses on the addiction to so-called toxic substances, also known as the toxicomanias, as distinct from other addictions such as, compulsive gambling, sex addiction or the addiction to computer games. The term addiction has interesting etymological connections. The word addict comes from the Latin *addictus*, which is the past principle (pp) of *addicere*, which means to adjudge or to assign to. The former meaning refers to the making of a decision, whilst the latter refers to a bond or a bind with something or someone. These connections are highly relevant to the particularities of the pathology of addiction. But there is another interesting connection. Etymologically, addiction also relates to diction, meaning to announce or to say. A central argument in this book is the importance of speech and language for an understanding of addiction. There is a fundamental antagonism between speech or diction and addiction: addiction is a-diction.[1]

For some of the readers, especially those not familiar with Lacan's thought, aspects of this book might perhaps come across as unnecessarily dense and difficult. However, it is important to keep in mind that addiction is an object of study which is enormously complex, but which nevertheless appears to provoke the tendency to gross over-simplifications and banal explanations for a variety of reasons. This book is an attempt to understand that tendency and to break away from it.

Note

1. A-diction is a term that was introduced by Nestor Braunstein (1992, p. 257).

PART I:
CLASSICAL FOUNDATIONS FOR A THEORY ON ADDICTION: THE ENERGETICS OF LIBIDO AND THE ECONOMICS OF DESIRE

Introduction

"... why isn't everyone a drinker?"
de Mijolla and Shentoub, *Pour une Psychanalyse de L'alcoolisme*, 1973, p. 33

It is a remarkable fact that there is no substantial psychoanalytic theory of addiction, especially given that Freud had some clinical experience of working with addicts.[1] This fact is even more remarkable in light of the fact that one of Freud's first attempts to cure someone was his clinical intervention with his friend and colleague, Ernst von Fleischl-Marxov. Freud had hoped that cocaine could help his friend to lose his addiction to morphine. This attempt failed and eventually von Fleischl-Marxov died from a cocaine addiction.[2] Surely these clinical encounters must have aroused Freud's interest in the problem of addiction and provoked questions regarding its metapsychology? Freud's theory and metapsychology were always developed on the basis of his clinical work with patients and, after all, his mind was uncommonly predisposed to curiosity. There are numerous interesting and important references to addiction in his writings, ranging from his pre-analytical period to the end of his life, but it is nonetheless strange that he never wrote an article dealing exclusively with addiction. Despite the many references, it is still possible to speak of a relative silence in Freud's work with regard to the clinical problem of addiction. He developed elaborate theories on neurosis, perversion, and psychosis, so why is there no such elaborate theory on addiction in his work? Could it be that there were deep-rooted psychological motives in Freud himself that contributed to this neglect? These questions have been taken up by various authors and will not be dealt with here.[3] It is well known that Freud's relationship to drugs was ambiguous. When Freud came across cocaine in 1884 he was immediately fascinated by it, particularly its therapeutic properties and he used it himself sporadically for about 10 years. He was not really interested in alcohol and only occasionally drank wine. He was irritated by problems of addiction in his practice and social environment. He was hopelessly addicted to smoking and nicotine. He smoked about 20 cigars a day. He needed cigars to work and lack of nicotine plunged him into bad moods. When he was diagnosed as having cancer of the mouth he was informed that his smoking habit would kill him and on several occasions he was strongly advised by his physicians to stop smoking but, despite this medical advice, he was unable to stop (Gay, 1988, pp. 426–427). From Freud's biographer, Ernest Jones, we know that for a long time Freud refused to take analgesics against the excruciating pain produced by the cancerous growth in his mouth. He likened taking drugs to embracing death. Freud's personal and professional ambiguities toward addiction perhaps contributed to the fact that there is no proper theoretical development in relation to addiction in his work. One can therefore not depend on a coherent theoretical foundation in Freud in order to construct a psychoanalytic theory and clinic of addiction. Nevertheless an exploration of remarks on, and references to, addiction throughout Freud's work show that there is a lot of material to work with and on which to reflect. Chapter 1 is devoted to his papers on cocaine. These papers are so central to the development of his work and so important for an understanding of a psychoanalytic approach to addiction, that they warrant a separate investigation. The aim in Part I will be to analyse in detail all of Freud's remarks on addiction.

Chapters 2–4 on Freud all use the work of Yorke (1970), de Mijolla and Shentoub (1973) and Magoudi (1986). But I have opted to do a detailed analysis of the theoretical and clinical context in which Freud's references to addiction occur rather than compile and review the written material, so my point of reference to the above writing is, largely, taken from where I depart from them. The choice for this approach was made for two reasons: firstly, to demonstrate the theoretical complexities and lack of uniformity involved in Freud's thinking on what is often considered to be an uniform or relatively straightforward clinical problem, and secondly, to indicate that these clinical and theoretical complexities have been largely ignored by most post-Freudian writers.

Notes

1. For instance Peter Gay in his biography of Freud mentions that Freud analysed Jones' mistress Lou Kann who was a morphine addict (1988, pp. 186–187). Also, the famous analyst Ruth Mack Brunswick, was addicted to morphine and a whole series of other drugs. Freud had understood that her addiction should be treated. She was in analysis with him, with interruptions, from 1922 to 1938.
2. For more details about this important period in Freud's life see again Peter Gay (Ibid., p. 45).
3. In an article on Freud's relationship to cocaine Ali Magoudi argues that factors and events which contributed to Freud's "cocaine episode", as Jones called it, resulted in a theoretical position which led to a tendency in Freud and psychoanalysts after him, to exclude addicts from psychoanalytic treatment. Magoudi highlights the blind spots in Freud's self-analysis and theory in order to show how they functioned as obstacles to analysis of addicts and addictions (1995). For a further exploration of these questions the reader is referred to the following two authors: Peter Gay (1988, op. cit., p. 427) and Didier Anzieu (1975, pp. 75 & 78).

CHAPTER ONE

The place of cocaine in the work of Freud

"This is the malady in them all for which law must find a pharmakon. Now it is a sound old adage that is hard to fight against two enemies at once—even when they are enemies from opposite quarters. We see the truth of this in medicine and elsewhere"

Plato, *Laws*, 919b

"There is no such a thing as a harmless remedy. The pharmakon can never be simply beneficial"

J. Derrida, "The Pharmacon", p. 99

A "side interest"

In *An Autobiographical Study* Freud described his involvement with the drug cocaine as "a side interest though it was a deep one..." (Freud, 1925d, p. 14). In the short passage he dedicated to this period of his life, he referred only to the missed opportunity of discovering cocaine as a local anaesthetic. Freud seemed to marginalize this aspect of his work, as indeed others have as well. When it is not marginalized by others, it is often used as a way of

7

denigrating his work. It has been argued, for instance, that Freud was addicted to cocaine and that the founding texts of psychoanalysis were a result of grandiose delusions that were induced by cocaine.[1] On occasions, serious studies of this period in Freud's work have been done.[2] These studies insist on the importance of returning to this aspect of Freud's work and conducting a thorough exploration. The aim of these works is to reassess the problematic relationship that existed between the addictions and psychoanalysis from the very beginning. A return is fruitful if we come back with something new. If not with new answers, at least with new questions concerning the ongoing problem of situating addiction within the theoretical and clinical field of psychoanalysis.

In this chapter a reading of Freud's *Cocaine Papers* is proposed as the beginning of the Freudian adventure.[3] A detailed exploration of his subsequent pre-analytic trajectory (till the so-called birth of Psychoanalysis with *The Interpretation of Dreams* from 1900) in Chapter 2 will allow us to establish a relationship between these papers by Freud and concepts such as the sexual toxins, libido and the actual neuroses.

Freud's *Cocaine Papers* are interesting reading, but they become especially relevant when we read them in the context of his work; that is, not as a side interest of Freud's, nor as an allotrion, which is the term he used to classify his interest in cocaine in a letter to Wittels. Allotrion is an interesting word. It can be defined as a rupture which consists of the introduction of a foreign idea amongst the body of ideas within a certain scientific discourse or doctrine. Geberovich makes the interesting observation that a closely associated French term allotriophagie signified the following during Freud's time: "the deprivation of appetite due to the incorporation of non-alimentary substances" (Geberovich, 1984, pp. 158–159, my translation). Freud's choice of words might not have been accidental, but motivated unconsciously. On the rare occasions he wrote about this episode in Freud's life, Jones referred to his forgetfulness, his mistakes and his lapses (Byck, 1974, p. 200). We know that it is precisely parapraxes such as these which reveal an unconscious desire that has been unsuccessfully censored. In other words, it is possible that Freud had repressed something concerning this so-called "episode" in his life, as Jones called it. In seminar XI Lacan says: "The truth is perhaps simply one thing, namely the desire of Freud himself, the fact that something in Freud was never analysed" (Lacan, 1979, p. 12). He continues:

> What I had to say on the Names-of-the-Father had no other purpose, in fact, than to put into question the origin, to discover by what privilege Freud's desire was able to find the entrance into the field of experience he designates as the unconscious. It is absolutely essential that we should go back to this origin if we wish to put analysis on its feet (Ibid.).

On the next page, Lacan asserts that this question of Freud's desire is not to be considered on a psychological level, that is, as a trait of his individual personality. Freud's desire concerns desire in the position of an object and as caused by an object. This object is the unconscious and so, therefore, Freud's unconscious. Freud's life and his work cannot be considered as separate entities. One of the first objects of Freud's interest was the drug cocaine. In fact, we know from certain letters he wrote to his then fiancee Martha, and from reading *Über Coca* (1984e; the first of these papers), that he was very passionate about cocaine.[4] It seems reasonable to assume that Freud's relationship to the drug cocaine could be one of the areas of research that might open the door to an understanding of his discovery of the unconscious, the nature of the object in psychoanalysis and, possibly, the virtual exclusion of the problem of addiction from this field of research.

At this point an observation will be introduced which seems to be paradoxical. In his post-script to *The Question of Lay-Analysis*, Freud wrote that he was never a doctor in the proper sense of practising medicine and that he was never aware of any craving to help suffering humanity, because his innate sadistic disposition was not strong enough. When prompted by fresh influences, he became interested in the neuroses, though he felt that his lack of medical temperament was no obstacle to the treatment of his patients; on the contrary... (Freud, 1926e, pp. 253–254).

However, in a letter from 25 May, 1884 to Martha Bernays, Freud referred to the role cocaine played in the discovery of his medical vocation. He wrote: "It is only now I feel like a doctor, because I have been able to help a patient and I hope to help others" (Byck, 1974, p. 7). In other words, Freud wanted to medically cure patients from their suffering and he hoped he had found a panacea in the form of cocaine with which he would be able to do this.

The difference between this earlier position and his later position is that in the later one his desire was to cure analytically via psychological methods and without depending on a pharmaceutical object, whilst in the former position he had placed all his hopes on the drug cocaine.

But there is more. Freud had also realized that a conscious wish to help can be the transformation of an unconscious sadistic impulse or desire. It might perhaps have been this unconscious impulse that played a role in his relationship with his friend and colleague, Ernst von Fleischl Marxov. He was Freud's ego-ideal and great rival at the same time. Fleischl died of a cocaine overdose after Freud had intervened in order to wean him off a morphine addiction.

The real difference between Freud's earlier and later positions is that, in the interim period, he had not only discovered unconscious desire, but also that the object which causes this desire is an object that is lost forever. This is the object of psychoanalysis as opposed to the object cocaine as a therapeutic instrument.

Vera Ocampo summarizes the consequences of Freud's encounter with cocaine as follows:

> The encounter with the drug awakens in Freud the desire not only to cure others but also to cure himself (his neurasthenic and neurotic symptoms), and from the beginning, these desires emerge as two sides of the same coin; the first other of this Freudian desire is an addict—Fleischl. The problematic nature of addiction gives rise to a therapeutic act which leads Freud to question his own desire for the first time and, further into the heart of his intellectual adventure, to address the question of desire itself. But if addiction is the first object of Freud's desire to cure, it also constitutes his first obstacle and his first therapeutic failure (Vera Ocampo, 1989, pp. 115–116, my translation).

What was the consequence of Freud's impasse, his failure with cocaine? In an attempt to answer this question some of Freud's steps in his work on cocaine will be considered.

Having arrived at this crossroads, the choice has been made to explore Freud's work, rather than take the path of investigating his personal life. As such, it is possible to avoid the risk of reducing the implications of the *Cocaine Papers* to a mere moment in Freud's personal history, "The Cocaine Episode". As with all of Freud's scientific moments, there has always been more involved than his personal history. That is why it is more rewarding to study his work than to study his personal life, if one's aim is to follow Freud in the discovery and development of psychoanalysis as a science. Jean Allouch seems to suggest that when we consider Freud's relationship to the drug cocaine as a symptom, then the necessity of this symptom will be reflected in his writings about it (Allouch, 1984, p. 28). Freud's symptom "ceased to write itself"; he dropped his passionate relationship with cocaine and this opened up the possibility of other pathways. A detailed study of Freud's writings on cocaine is therefore crucial to an understanding of these pathways.

The Cocaine Papers

The text *Uber Coca* which came first in the series and was published in July 1884, is a curious mixture of objective scientific writing and subjective writing, which reflects a passionate belief in the magical properties of the drug cocaine. This text begins with a botanical description, an historical overview of its usage in Peru and its reception in Europe. It continues with a look at the effects of cocaine on animals and the human body before ending with the mention of several therapeutic possibilities. The properties of cocaine, which initially attracted Freud to the drug, were its ability to increase the capacity to work, to allow people to do without food for long periods, and to increase physical strength. He even wrote in response to Poeppig's description of physical and intellectual decadence as a result of habitual cocaine use that "...all other observers affirmed that the use of coca in moderation is more likely to promote health than to impair it, and that the coqueros live to a great age" (Freud, 1884e, p. 52).

When Freud referred to experiments with cocaine on himself and others, he mentioned that individuals react differently to the drug. He realized that there was no uniform effect. Freud would come back to this in his other papers. In his last paper on cocaine, *Craving for and Fear of Cocaine*, he related these different effects of cocaine to individual variations in excitability and "a factor of individual predisposition." This lack of uniform effect will later come to shatter Freud's medical–pharmacological fantasy of being able to find a universal panacea for human suffering. Initially Freud's thinking was very much determined or influenced by physics, energetics, and thermodynamics.

Pharmacology relies on two related factors. Firstly, the predictability of the effects of drugs and secondly, the lack of difference in reaction to them between individuals and within individuals. Freud's emphasis on the instability of the effect of cocaine contradicts the suggestion by the editor of the *Cocaine Papers*, Robert Byck, that one should read these as written by someone who was interested in the science of pharmacology and who could be considered as one of its founders (Byck, 1974, p. xvii). This is not to say that Freud was not interested in cocaine as a therapeutic instrument. This fact was referred to before when it was mentioned that the last section of *Über Coca* deals with the various therapeutic possibilities of cocaine. There he collated the various recommendations and these clearly show Freud's interest in therapy and in cocaine as its instrument. Freud hoped to explain the "facts" of cocaine within the parameters set by the sciences of physics and energetics in order to guarantee scientifically that the effects of cocaine are uniform, predictable, and above all, good. Freud tried to locate a formal or scientific cause for the effect of cocaine. His interest in therapy would last. Concerning cocaine as an instrument for therapy, his very first scientific observations already subverted his personal and medical fantasy about cocaine being the ideal pharmacological instrument for therapy.

It will be shown that, through his own scientific work on cocaine, Freud continued to subvert his fantasy and that this "working-through" of the fantasy resulted in the abandonment of cocaine as an object. To do this it is necessary to follow Freud step by step through his writings on cocaine.

When writing about the psychic effects of cocaine in *Über Coca*, Freud mentioned that the exhilaration and lasting euphoria did not appear to differ from the normal euphoria of a healthy person. The kind of mood induced by cocaine gave Freud the impression that cocaine did not stimulate in a direct way, but that in fact it seemed to affect those elements in our general state of well-being which lead to depression. He wrote, somewhat enigmatically: "One may perhaps assume that the euphoria resulting from good health is also nothing more than the normal condition of a well-nourished cerebral cortex which is "not conscious" of the organs of the body to which it belongs" (Freud, 1884e, p. 60).

In this euphoric state, produced by the effect of cocaine, long-lasting, intensive mental and physical work can be performed without fatigue and without the need for much food and sleep. Freud would come back to this as well.

In the last section of *Über Coca*, Freud wondered why and how cocaine has this stimulating effect. Through various authors, he considered the possible relationships between cocaine and three interrelated elements to determine where the effect of cocaine takes place. These elements were: (1) the system or organism into which the cocaine is incorporated; (2) a vital energy operating within this organism which can be affected by this incorporation, and; (3) the conversion of this energy into work. Where does cocaine intervene? How does it intervene? These questions emerged within the theoretical framework of 19th century energetics, which was based on the principle (or law) that the total amount of energy in an isolated system (or organism) is constant. Freud was attempting to answer these questions within that framework. One consideration is that cocaine can be a "source of savings". He wrote:

> A system which has absorbed even an extremely small amount of cocaine is capable, as a result of the reaction of the body to coca, of amassing a greater store of vital energy which can be converted into work than would have been possible without coca. If we take the amount of work as being constant, the body which has absorbed cocaine should be able to manage with a lower metabolism, which in turn means a smaller intake of food (Ibid., p. 68).

The effect of cocaine indicated here is that it is able to accumulate disposable energy in the organism and that if this energy is not being used, this organism will need less food and sleep. Freud wrote that this did not necessarily contradict the law of conservation of energy. He explained this as follows: "For labour which draws upon food or tissue components involves a certain loss, either in the utilization of assimilated food or in the conversion of energy into work; this loss could perhaps be reduced if certain appropriate steps were taken" (Ibid.).

Freud did not explain what these steps were or how they worked. It seems as if he had to force himself in his thinking here to stay within the limited theoretical framework of 19th century energetics. As long as Freud continued to work within the path paved by masters such as Fechner, Brücke, Helmholtz and Du Bois-Reymond, and as long as he wished to build neurology on the basis of physics, energetics would remain a problem for him (Quackelbeen, 1991, p. 104).

As a next step, Freud considered the possibility that the influence of cocaine resulted in a better availability of materials already stored in the organism, which produced more working power and necessitates less food. Freud considered this next step because experiments on animals had refuted the conception of cocaine as a "source of savings". Animals which had been given cocaine succumbed quicker to inanimation (or energy loss) than those who had received no cocaine. Then, Freud said, that an experiment from history seemed to contradict this last conclusion. In the year 1781 the city of La Paz was under siege. Only those inhabitants who had taken cocaine survived starvation. Why? Is there a difference between animals and human beings in terms of their reaction to cocaine? And if so, what is that difference?

Freud had arrived at an impasse, he was unable to answer these questions, yet he said (probably to buy himself some more time): "The therapeutic quality of coca which we took as our argument at the onset does not (...) deserve to be rejected out of hand" (Freud, op. cit., p. 69).

It would be some time before Freud rejected cocaine as a therapeutic instrument. He was not yet prepared to give up on his fantasy, even though within the conceptual framework of 19th century energetics, he was still not able to answer the questions as to how and where cocaine affects the relationship between the three aforementioned elements; organism, vital energy, and work. There seemed to be a factor missing which, for instance, could explain the difference between animals and humans and the reason for the survival of those starving people of La Paz who took cocaine. In relation to this Freud said the following: "In this connection one might recall the fact that the human nervous system has an undoubted if somewhat obscure, influence on the nourishment of tissues; psychological factors, after all, cause a healthy man to lose weight" (Ibid.).

Were these psychological factors a first indication of a way out of the deadlock of a thinking which took place within the theoretical framework of energetics? Possibly, but Freud's work on cocaine had not yet reached this point.

In the Addenda to *Über Coca*, Freud wrote that the only constant effect of cocaine he had found was an increased capacity for work (Freud, 1885f, p. 107). This had led him to conduct a series of experiments in which he wanted to demonstrate the effect of cocaine by comparing the variations in certain measurable quantities in living beings. In his paper, *Contribution to the Knowledge of the Effect of Cocaine*, Freud wrote that he expected a greater uniformity in the action of cocaine when an objective method of measurement could be found (Freud, 1885a, p. 98). Freud wanted to investigate the motor power of certain muscle groups and psychic reaction time as operations of the action of cocaine. For this he used, respectively, a dynamometer and a neuroamoebimeter. He carried out these experiments on himself, because he said he had such a regular reaction to cocaine, unlike most other people. Freud continued to experiment over a period of weeks. It is important to follow these experiments step by step and not just to concentrate on the general conclusions Freud had drawn from these.

The first experiments showed that cocaine caused a marked increase in motor power. He also noticed something else, namely that, in terms of motor power, there were not just fluctuations on a daily basis, but fluctuations during the course of one day. In other words, there was another variable at work. This changed the situation, because then it seemed to have become impossible to measure the effect of cocaine independently, that is, without the interference of (yet) another unknown factor. Freud continued his measurements in motor energy. This time, however, without the influence of cocaine. He was struck by two facts: "Firstly, the figures for the motor energy of a muscle group reveal a regular fluctuation in the course of a day; secondly, the same figures reach quite different absolute values on different days" (Ibid., p. 101).

This appeared to confirm his previous findings and he squeezed in the remark that these results might not have had much to do with cocaine, but that they were worth mentioning nevertheless. In fact, they were crucial. They made it clear to him that the variations in motor energy are an expression of a "general state of well-being", and not so much an effect of cocaine. The magical properties of cocaine were beginning to break down. Freud continued by saying that he did not consider the action of cocaine to be a direct one, but that he considered it to be indirect and affected by an improvement of the state of well-being. This was supported, according to Freud, by two factors: "Muscular energy increases most obviously after taking cocaine when cocaine euphoria has developed, but before the total quantity can be absorbed into the circulation; and motor power increases considerably if the cocaine takes effect when the general condition is poor and motor power diminished" (Ibid., p. 102).

Freud had experimentally proved here what he had already briefly mentioned in *Über Coca*, namely, that the mood induced by cocaine was not so much due to direct stimulation as to the disappearance of those factors in our "general state of well-being" which caused depression (Freud, 1884e, p. 60). Cocaine had an optimum effect when the condition was poor (depression) and its effect was less when the condition was normal (a good mood). The effect came about via a state of euphoria and not as a result of the direct effect of the substance on the organism. Cocaine affected those factors which made the difference between a good mood and a bad mood. Now, a fourth element could be added to the aforementioned three elements from *Über Coca* (organism, vital energy and work): a factor (or factors) which caused variations in a "general state of well-being". Cocaine, when incorporated by the organism, resulted in more muscular energy (and work capacity) via a factor which caused variations in a "general state of well-being". According to Allouch the action of cocaine does not intervene on a constant, but on something which is variable (Allouch, 1984, p. 41). So, the effect of cocaine is dependent on a variable, and not on a constant factor, which Freud had tried to isolate with his experiments. This is extremely interesting when one keeps in mind that "energy is not a substance, which, for example, improves or goes sour with age; it's a numerical constant that a physicist has to find in his calculations, so as to be able to work" (Lacan, 1987[1974], p. 22). The energy produced by cocaine, ideally speaking, should be measurable (or calculable) in relation to a constant factor. Yet what happened was that this factor—Freud did not know what it was—was not constant but unpredictable. Something kept raising problems in relation to being able to find out exactly how the effects of cocaine came about in the human being.

Towards the end of this paper on his experiments, Freud wrote that similar conclusions could be drawn from his experiments on the influence of cocaine on reaction time. These later experiments confirmed his earlier findings. What followed then was very important. He wrote: "I often noticed that under cocaine my reaction times were shorter and more uniform than before taking the drug; but sometimes, in a more cheerful and efficient mood, my psychic reactions were just as good" (Freud, 1885a, p. 104).

In other words, certain psychic conditions such as "feeling well" or a "good mood" had the same effect as cocaine. In his experiments on motor energy, he had discovered exactly the same thing. A psychic condition of well-being, such as a good mood or euphoria, resulted in similar quantities of disposable motor energy as did the effect of cocaine.

On the basis of the results of Freud's experiments, it is possible to say that cocaine should have become less important to him as an object of scientific interest and research. He had discovered that it was nothing more than a remedy for a "weak psychic state" and as such it had lost its privileged place of being the only relevant factor which could explain the phenomena he wanted to investigate. This psychic state and its weakness would turn out to be the relevant variables. They would later become his objects of interest and research.

Meanwhile, however, the necessity of cocaine as a fantasy object for Freud had not yet ceased to write itself in his work, although the subversion of this fantasy does continue through the scientific advances in this work on cocaine.

In March 1885, about 3 months after the paper on his experiments, Freud read a paper before the Psychiatric Society of Vienna. In this paper, he summarized his findings so far. Before he discussed cocaine as being capable of weaning morphine addicts off their drug, he mentioned another use of the drug which, according to him, would be of direct interest to psychiatry. He said:

> Psychiatry is rich in drugs that can subdue over-stimulated nervous activity, but deficient in agents that can heighten the performance of the depressed nervous system. It is natural therefore, that we should think of making use of the effects of cocaine that we have described above in the forms of illness, that we interpret as states of weakness and depression of the nervous system without organic lesions. As a

matter of fact, cocaine has been used since its discovery against hysteria, hypochondria, etc. (Freud, 1885b, p. 116).

This passage clearly indicates that Freud wanted to hold on to the belief that cocaine could be useful. But this time as a psychopharmacological remedy against a state of psychic weakness, which is not caused by organic lesions. It did work, after all, because the general effect of cocaine in cases of psychic weakness was euphoria. Freud was still left with the question of why it worked in cases of psychic illness, of which hysteria is one. Jean Allouch writes that in Freud's relationship to hysteria, at this point in his work, cocaine was at the place where psychoanalytic treatment would come to be (Allouch, op. cit., p. 40). That is to say, for Freud, cocaine had come to function as a therapeutic solution to the problem of hysteria (amongst other problems), as well as a means via which he began to question the truth which structured it. A little later, Freud would abandon these two functions which cocaine served for his work. It is interesting to note however that the functions of therapy and scientific research (or theory) had already come together here in his work on cocaine. This was an ethical position he would maintain for the rest of his life.

It is important to notice something else. Freud talked about "states of weakness and depression without organic lesions". This seemed to indicate a shift in his thinking. In the years 1882–1885, Freud had received a thorough training in neuroanatomical and neurophysiological thinking from people like Nothnagel, Meynert and Brücke. In this theoretical framework, hysteria and other forms of "psychic weakness" are based on an organic lesion. This concept of organic lesion served to totally explain—and therefore unify—the whole field of the afflictions of the nervous system. In 1885, when speaking to the Psychiatric Society of Vienna about the general effect of cocaine, Freud referred to those afflictions of the nervous system not based on organic lesions. The implication of this statement was that he was now entertaining the idea of a psychic process (or lesion) as a basis for nervous illnesses. Did that mean that he had broken through the framework of organic–physiological thinking with its implicit reliance on the principle of conservation of energy as formulated by Helmholtz?[5] The answer had to be that Freud had not yet been able to change his thinking in relation to this. This change would have to wait another 35 years when he was to write about his discovery that there was a principle in people that operated beyond any kind of conservation or constancy in *Beyond the Pleasure Principle* (1920g).

But what did change at this stage was that Freud's passionate interest in cocaine and his ongoing scientific work led him to the discovery of psychic processes and a desire to know about their different ways of functioning, and this without losing his commitment to therapy, provoked in the first instance by his encounter with the drug cocaine. He would also deal with the problems of energetics by creating what he called his myth of libido in order to find a concept that would relate more adequately to human (sexual) energy. In Lacan's conceptual apparatus this would become jouissance. This concept plays a prominent role in a Lacanian theory on addiction and it will therefore be explored in detail further on in this work (see pages 174–177 and 214 also for an explanation of it, relationship to pleasure).

It is necessary to take one final step with Freud to account for his complete abandonment of cocaine as a therapeutic object and as his object of medical fantasy. In July 1887, 2 years after his last publication on cocaine, Freud wrote his final paper on the subject, entitled, *Craving for and Fear of Cocaine*. In the period between those two papers, Freud had become interested in hysteria and had visited Charcot in Paris. He had also been accused of contributing to the causation of cocaine addiction as "the third scourge" of mankind, next to alcohol and morphine addiction, by the German psychiatrist, Erlenmeyer (Freud, 1887d, p. 172). In the *Cocaine Papers*, as edited by Robert Byck, we are encouraged to read this final paper as a defence against this accusation. The danger of a reading of the paper from this angle is that we run the risk of missing out on a last and definitive shift in Freud's relationship to the drug cocaine: a shift which would establish a complete break of an epistemological nature and which would shatter his medical fantasy in relation to cocaine once and for all.

In this paper, Freud claimed that the value of cocaine for morphine addicts was lost because it became a substitute for morphine. In response to the mass hysteria concerning cocaine as a dangerous drug, he wrote the following:

All reports of addiction to cocaine and deterioration resulting from it refer to morphine addicts, persons who already in the grip of one demon are so weak in will power, so susceptible, that they would misuse, and indeed have misused, any stimulant held out to them. Cocaine has claimed no other, no victim on its own (Ibid., p. 173).

The implication of this statement was that it was not cocaine itself which caused addiction, but a factor in the person which made them susceptible to any addiction.[6] This is a conception of addiction which is more advanced than some contemporary theories on addiction.

Next, Freud wrote that cocaine affected people in different ways. Cocaine had become an unpredictable object. In some people a toxic effect would appear and it was not possible to know who would have a general reaction to it (p. 174). He continued:

> I suspect that the reason for the irregularity of the cocaine effect lies in the individual variations in excitability and in the variation of the condition of the vasomotor nerves on which cocaine acts. Since little attention has been paid to this factor of individual predisposition, and the degree of excitability generally cannot be known, I consider it advisable to abandon so far as possible subcutaneous injection of cocaine in the treatment of internal and nervous disorders (Ibid., p. 175).

This factor of individual predisposition, the lack of knowledge about the degree of excitability, and the consequent unpredictability of the object cocaine, could no longer be reconciled with neurophysiological thinking and the master-discourse of medical/pharmacological practice, in which symptoms should be immediately treatable and should represent a cumulative and predictable general knowledge (to be possessed by the doctor, who must be in a position of mastery over the diseased patients). The variable (and still unpredictable) factor of the (pre) disposition of the subject and the lack of knowledge about excitability had completely subverted the possibility of a medical, neurophysiological approach to the understanding and treatment of mental suffering and addiction. Nevertheless, Freud remained hopeful that one day thermodynamics and energetics would explain the "facts" of the psyche. Meanwhile, however, he did not get to know anything about cocaine as a drug. The drug did not contain a knowledge for Freud that he only needed to discover; a variable (subjective) element interfered.

Again, there had been no formal cause locatable in the drug, and there was no general knowledge available that could scientifically explain the effects of cocaine on people.

Having arrived at this impasse in Freud's work on cocaine it is possible to say that he had stumbled upon the impossible desire of the hysteric.

From this point on, it is clear that Freud's passionate interest in cocaine had "ceased to write itself". He had lost his object of fantasy, only to find a substitute for it, another object of interest which would open different pathways and eventually lead him to the discovery of the unconscious. This object was the desire of the hysteric. It had thrown a spanner in his work on cocaine and it would continue to do so in the subsequent trajectory of his work on more than one occasion. A spanner in the work of Freud always seemed to lead to a change in a new direction. A change that would eventually lead to a different kind of causation; a causation that is not situated in the object, but indeed elsewhere. Freud would announce a change in direction concerning the usefulness of narcotic drugs in the treatment of hysteria not long after his last paper on cocaine.

Notes

1. For a striking example of such an argument see E. M. Thornton's, *The Freudian Fallacy* (1986).
2. We can mention for instance, the excellent works by Fernando Geberovich, *Une Douleur Irrésistible: Sur la Toxicomanie et la Pulsion de Mort* (1984); Sylvie le Poulichet, *Toxicomanies et Psychanalyse: Les Narcoses du Désire* (1987); Eduardo Vera Ocampo, *L'Envers de la Toxicomanies: Un Idéal D'indépendance* (1989); and Jean Allouch, *Lettre pour Lettre: Transcrire, Traduire, Translittérer* (1984). The chapter "Freud coquero" in Allouch's book has especially been an invaluable source of inspiration for a reading of Freud's *Cocaine Papers*.
3. Freud's work on cocaine was collected by Robert Byck in a document called *Cocaine Papers* (1974). This document also contains commentaries, book chapters, historical information, letters by Freud, biographical information, literary references, all of which is related to Freud's work on cocaine or cocaine itself.
4. A number of letters which Freud wrote to his fiancée, Martha Bernays, were selected for inclusion in the *Cocaine Papers*. Some of these letters

indicate Freud's strong personal interest in cocaine (Byck, 1974, pp. 39–45). Freud's first article in the series on cocaine, "Über coca", is a bizarre blend of scientific endeavour and passion for cocaine as a fascinating object (1884e, pp. 48–73).

5. It was stated how this fundamental principle of energetics functioned as a conceptual straightjacket, when Freud tried to understand and explain, scientifically, the effects of cocaine on the human body and the results of his experiments on cocaine.

6. This factor is an early indication of the existence of what Lacan names the subject; an aspect of the psychic structure that psychoanalysis operates on and that science attempts to exclude by concentrating solely on objectivity and the object of study.

CHAPTER TWO

Freud's pre-analytical period

"What is the latter (phallic jouissance) if not the following, which the importance of masturbation in our practice highlights sufficiently—the jouissance of the idiot?"

J. Lacan, *Encore*, 1975a, p. 81

From an ideal material object to the disappointment of fantasy

I n 1888, the year after Freud wrote his last paper on cocaine, he published an article called *Hysteria*. He wrote:

As factors which produce outbreaks of acute hysterical illness may be adduced: trauma, intoxication (lead, alcohol), grief, emotion, exhausting illness—anything, in short, which is able to exercise a powerful effect of a detrimental kind (Freud, 1888b, p. 50).

Alcohol and other intoxicants were considered here by Freud to be potentially dangerous substances or "foreign agents" which could harm the psyche of the subject. Drugs were only one of a number of external factors which could cause hysteria. Five pages later he wrote:

23

To begin with, internal medication is to be disrecommended here and narcotic drugs are to be warned against. To prescribe a narcotic drug in an acute hysteria in nothing less than a serious technical mistake (Ibid., p. 55).

Four years previously, Freud thought he had found a narcotic drug which could function as an "universal panacea" against human suffering. In the previous chapter we saw how his investigations in relation to the drug cocaine led him to the conclusion that such a panacea was an illusion. Here he warned against using any kind of drug as a cure for hysteria. Nothing in this article refers directly to addiction. In a text from 1890 called *Psychical (or Mental) Treatment* Freud dealt with the question of hypnotic treatment. He wrote that hypnosis should not be employed as a last resort measure, but could be employed with all nervous diseases and morbid habits such as alcoholism, morphine addiction and sexual aberrations (1905[1890], p. 299). In his text *Hypnosis* from 1891(d), Freud wrote that hypnosis should only be used for "purely functional, nervous disorders, for ailments of psychical origin, and for toxic as well as other addictions and that in general it should be avoided for symptoms with an organic cause" (1891d, p. 106). This is interesting as it seems to suggest that for Freud the addictions belong to those symptoms which do not have an organic cause. In a letter to Fliess from 1895 on Paranoia and known as Draft H, Freud wrote the following:

> The alcoholic will never admit to himself that he has become impotent through drink. However much alcohol he can tolerate, he cannot tolerate this insight. So his wife is to blame—delusions of jealousy and so on (Freud, 1895, p. 110).

This is the first time that an association between alcoholism and sexuality comes to the surface in Freud's thinking. Another interesting aspect of this brief passage is the mechanism of denial in the alcoholic ("my sexual problem has nothing to do with drink") and its associated mechanism of not taking responsibility by blaming others ("my sexual problem has nothing to do with me, my wife is to blame"). It is important to note that Freud referred to alcoholism here in the context of paranoia. He would come back to the delusion of jealousy in the alcoholic in his text on Schreber. In a letter to Fliess from 1896, Draft K, Freud referred to drinking (dipsomania) as a secondary symptom which could arise if the compulsions of obsessional neurosis were transferred to motor impulses against the obsession (Freud, 1896, p. 166). That Freud here considered drinking to be a secondary symptom related to obsessional neurosis is not unimportant. It is interesting that according to Freud this could only happen if something of the ideational aspect of the obsessional neurosis was translated into a motor impulse. He seems to be suggesting that these motor impulses are ritual actions, protective behaviours, brooding and so on. In other words, drinking is something other than purely ideational or, one could say, drinking is not a symbolically structured formation of the unconscious. In *Further Remarks on the Neuro-Psychoses of Defence* from 1896, Freud considered dipsomania to be a numbing of the mind as a protective measure against obsessional affects. Once again, he placed drinking amongst the secondary symptoms in obsessional neurosis where it functioned as an anaesthetic (1896b, p. 173). In a letter to Fliess from 11 January 1897, he wrote, "dipsomania arises through the intensification or, better, substitution of the one impulse for the associated sexual one" (Masson, 1985, p. 222). He also wrote there that the same idea applied to the gambling mania of another patient. This was the first time that Freud had suggested that addictions like toxicomania or gambling could be substitutions for repressed sexual impulses. Thirty-one years later, in his paper on Dostoevsky, he would come back to his idea of gambling as a substitute satisfaction for unsatisfied sexual impulses. In this paper he linked the addiction of gambling to masturbation. This was not the first time that Freud had established a connection between addiction and masturbation. The first time Freud wrote about masturbation in the context of addiction was towards the end of 1897, a year in which he had made some of the most important discoveries in psychoanalysis through his self-analysis, such as unconscious fantasies being the falsification of the truth.

Important discoveries

In order to illustrate how crucial this period was, not only for the area of addiction, but for Freud's thinking as a whole, it might be helpful to look at some of the important discoveries from this year.

But before doing this it is necessary to step back a couple of years.

In 1895, Freud's Q-hypothesis, which concerns a quantity of affect or energy, helped him to establish the beginnings of a differential diagnosis.[1] In an article on anxiety neurosis, he explored the relationship between anxiety and sexuality in terms of the dynamic between the psyche, the soma and quantities of energy (Freud, 1895b, pp. 90–115). Normally, a quantity of energy originating in the soma reaches a certain threshold of intensity, with the result that it can be "picked up" and processed by the psyche in such a way that it is properly abreacted. This process can go wrong in three different ways, and thus lead to three different pathologies: (1) there is a conflict in the psyche which prevents the energy from being adequately abreacted, and it is therefore sent back to the soma where it leads to conversion symptoms; (2) there is a "psychical insufficiency" which prevents accumulated somatic energy from being psychically processed, it remains therefore somatic and subsequently becomes harmful; and (3) there is an "inadequate disburdening" of the somatic impulse, through, for instance, masturbation, with the result that a proper abreaction of the energy is again prevented, and again it becomes harmful. The first possibility indicates the mechanism at work in the psychoneuroses, whilst the second and third possibilities refer to anxiety neurosis and neurasthenia respectively, both of which belong to the category of the actual neuroses. In Chapter 7 the connection between actual neurosis and addiction will be further explored. The third possibility is particularly interesting here in light of the connection he would establish between masturbation and addiction for the first time towards the end of the year 1897.

It is possible to infer from what Freud wrote about the quantity of energy in his article on anxiety neurosis that this quantity exists in a somatic form and in a psychic form. The latter is the result of a psychic processing of the somatic form and is called sexual libido. The originally somatic or material form of energy is turned into a psychic or non-material kind of energy. Libido is the result of the transformation of somatic energy into a form of psychic excitation which becomes attached to psychosexual representations. Freud subsequently discovered that this quantum of psychic energy can be displaced over these representations. Displacement will later become one of the mechanisms of the primary process of the unconscious.

But before this, Freud was beginning to realize that this displacement of energy often concerns a wish or a psychosexual desire about which hysterics do not want to know and against which they vigorously defend themselves with symptoms. Paul Verhaeghe considers this discovery of Freud's to be the true point of departure for psychoanalysis. He writes:

> From that point on, hysteria was no longer determined by some mysterious trauma, but by an inarticulable desire that kept on being displaced. On 27 October 1897, Freud generalized this point and made it the most fundamental characteristic of hysteria: longing is the main character-trait of hysteria, just as a current anaesthesia (even though only potential) is its main symptom (Verhaeghe, 1997, pp. 15–16).

Before 1897 Freud believed that hysteria or neurosis was caused by a scene of sexual seduction in childhood which he considered to be traumatic for the infant. The infant cannot comprehend this scene and the trauma remains an inactive part of the child's psyche, until a second scene is experienced, in or around puberty, which activates this dormant part of the psyche with a deferred effect. Slowly, but surely, Freud began to realize that the hysterical symptoms contain an element of pleasure. This made him think that the first traumatic scenes might perhaps have been somewhat pleasurable for the infant. Freud had stumbled upon the elements of infantile sexuality. The infant must have experienced a conflict between the pain of trauma and something pleasurable. This was the moment when the cathartic method of abreaction began to disappear because the contradictory forces of conflict invalidate the idea of an unproblematic purging of a "toxic" quantity of energy. Or as Paul Verhaeghe writes:

> The failure of hysterical defence was not due to a failure of the process of discharging the memory of an external trauma. Hysterical defence fails because it has to make a compromise between a desire and the repression of this desire (Verhaeghe, op. cit., p. 25).

In a letter to Fliess from 6 April 1897, Freud mentioned for the first time that hysteria was caused by fantasies made up of things that children had heard at a very early age but were only understood later in life (Masson, 1985, p. 234). Freud's letter to Fliess from 2 May 1897 is a very important one. Here Freud indicated that the cause of hysteria was to be sought in fantasies which are related to infantile impulses and whose origins might also stem from masturbatory activity.

> In the first place, I have gained a sure inkling of the structure of hysteria. Everything goes back to the reproduction of scenes. Some can be obtained directly, others always by way of fantasies set up in front of them. The fantasies stem from things that have been heard, but understood subsequently and all their material is of course genuine. They are protective structures, sublimations of the facts, embellishments of them, and at the same time serve for self-relief. Their accidental origin is perhaps from masturbation fantasies. A second important piece of insight tells me that the psychic structures which, in hysteria, are affected by repression are not in reality memories—since no one indulges in memory activity without a motive—but impulses that derive from primal scenes (Ibid., p. 239).

The importance of these remarks about self-relief and masturbation lies in their clear hints at the possible connection between an "artificial" production of pleasure and something unpleasant or dangerous against which this pleasure forms a protection. The interesting aspect of this connection is that masturbatory sexual pleasure can be used against frightening sexual impulses. This is crucial for the development of a psychoanalytic theory of addiction and it will be discussed in more detail, along with Freud's remark about masturbation and addiction later in that year.

From here on, Freud will elaborate his idea that something painful or traumatic needs to be processed psychically by, for instance, fantasies. The letter to Fliess from 7 July 1897 is interesting, not only because Freud felt on the verge of something new, but also because he appeared to be making progress in his own self-analysis. His understanding of his own neurosis seemed to coincide with his idea that memories and fantasies can be falsifications of the past (and the latter also of the future) (Ibid., p. 255). The letter from 21 September 1897 is a crucial one. This is generally considered to be the letter in which Freud abandons the trauma theory. He wrote to Fliess that in the unconscious "there are no indications of reality" and he suggested that it was perhaps not possible to distinguish between truth and fiction in the unconscious (Ibid., p. 264). Freud had abandoned his belief in his "neurotica". In the very same letter, Freud wrote the following remark in brackets: "... there would remain the solution that the sexual fantasy invariably seizes upon the theme of the parents" (Ibid., pp. 264–265). Indeed it was four letters later (15 October) that Freud wrote to Fliess, (again in the context of his self-analysis), about the Oedipus Complex as "a universal event in early childhood" (Ibid., p. 272). In another famous letter to Fliess, from 14 November 1897, he wrote that fantasies and the repression of these fantasies had something to do with "sexual zones" (Ibid., pp. 279–281). This was Freud's first elaboration of a theory on infantile sexuality, a theory so far only hinted at. Almost hidden in the letter was an interesting throwaway remark: "...and the final outcome is consequently that a quota of libido is not able, as is ordinarily the case, to force its way through to action or translation into psychic terms, but is obliged to proceed in a regressive direction (as happens in dreams)." In other words, a certain quantity of energy cannot be psychically processed for some reason, and it therefore becomes disturbing. Something is excluded from language and consequently produces a traumatic effect. In 1898 Freud mainly concentrated on the analysis of his dreams and, in doing so, he very much relied on linguistic analysis. In his first letter of the next year (3 January 1899) he returned to fantasies and infantile sexuality, but this time he included the linguistic connection between them. He wrote:

> In the first place, a small bit of my self-analysis has forced its way through and confirmed that fantasies are products of later periods and are projected back from what was then the present into earliest childhood; the manner in which this occurs also emerged—once again by verbal link. To the question "What happened in earliest childhood?" the answer is, "Nothing, but the germ of a sexual impulse existed" (...). In the second place, I have grasped the meaning of a new psychic element which I conceive to be of general significance and a preliminary stage of symptoms (even before fantasy) (Ibid., p. 338).

The new psychic element is the unsymbolized aspect of the sexual impulse and Freud considers it to be a first stage in the formation of symptoms. Nothing needs to have happened. These impulses (in unprocessed form) are enough in themselves to cause trauma. It is only sometime later that they are retroactively understood with the help of fantasies which take shape with what Freud calls "verbal links" and which are what we can call elements of language. It is in this latter stage that the formation of symptoms takes place on the basis of these elements of language. For Freud, symptoms are therefore structured like a language and contain the "germ of a sexual impulse". This "germ" is something that is only retroactively and falsely understood. In other words, all symptoms ultimately relate to a disturbing element of pleasure (or satisfaction).

Those last couple of years had been very fruitful for Freud. He had discovered fantasy, infantile sexuality, the structuring effect of the Oedipus Complex and the importance of language for an understanding of the psyche. Above all, he had discovered that human suffering was not caused in the first place by a clearly locatable external trauma but by a disturbing element within the psychic economy of the subject which ex-ists like an unprocessed remainder. Neurotics are no longer innocent victims of an external cause; something disturbs them from within. It is now time to return to the end of that important year of 1897 when Freud made his remark on the connection between masturbation and addiction.

Masturbation and addiction:
from disappointment to the quest for something more

On 22 December 1897, he wrote the following to Fliess:

> The insight has dawned on me that masturbation is the one major habit, "the primary addiction", and it is only as a substitute and replacement for it that the other addictions—to alcohol, morphine, tobacco, and the like come into existence. The role played by this addiction in hysteria is enormous; and it is perhaps there that my major, still outstanding obstacle is to be found, wholly or in part. And here, of course doubt arises about whether an addiction of this kind is curable, or whether analysis and therapy must come to a halt at this point and content themselves with transforming hysteria in neurasthenia (Ibid., p. 187).

In this passage, Freud related the addictions to drugs, alcohol and other substances to neurasthenia via the "primary" addiction to masturbation. It was mentioned earlier that, according to Freud, the "inadequate disburdening" of the somatic impulse through masturbation could lead to a lack of proper abreaction of the somatic energy and would ultimately result in a harmful effect. What is an inadequate disburdening and what is a lack of proper abreaction? For Freud, (at that time), the former meant that the absence of "normal" sexual activity could result in an inadequate release of sexual tension or energy. The latter meant that, as a result of this inadequate release, there could not be the proper processing and wearing away by the psyche of a certain amount of this somatic energy, which would then become harmful or toxic and would cause neurasthenia. If the other addictions were substitutes for masturbation, then it seemed that Freud considered addiction to be related to "actual neurosis". Following on from his earlier connections between some of the addictions to other neuroses and mental problems, this must surely have been the beginning of the possibility of a differential diagnosis for addiction.

It was here, perhaps, that he encountered the limitations of his technique, but this is of such crucial importance that it needs to be explored and questioned separately. Freud's final comparatively extensive remarks before the turn of the century on addiction and again masturbation stem from an article from 1898 called *Sexuality in the Aetiology of the Neuroses*. He was predominantly concerned here with the related questions of how to break addictive habits and what it was that caused them. He wrote:

> To break the patient of the habit of masturbating is only one of the new therapeutic tasks which are imposed on the physician who takes the sexual aetiology of the neurosis into account; and it seems that precisely this task, like the cure of any other addiction, can only be carried out in an institution under medical supervision. Left to himself, the masturbator is accustomed, whenever something happens that depresses him, to return to his convenient form of satisfaction. Medical treatment, in this instance, can have no other aim than to lead the neurasthenic, who has now recovered his strength, back to normal sexual intercourse. For sexual need, when once it has been aroused and has been satisfied for any length of time, can no longer be silenced; it can only be displaced along another path. Incidentally, the same thing applies to all treatments for breaking an addiction. Their success will only be an apparent one, so long as the physician contents himself with withdrawing the narcotic substance from his patients, without troubling about the source from which their imperative need for it springs. "Habit" is a mere form of words, without any explanatory value. Not everyone

who has occasion to take morphia, cocaine, chloralhydrate, and so on, for a period, acquires in this way an "addiction" to them. Closer enquiry usually shows that these narcotics are meant to serve—directly or indirectly—as a substitute for a lack of sexual satisfaction; and whenever normal sexual life can no longer be re-established, we can count with certainty on the patient's relapse (Freud, 1898a, pp. 275–276).

It strikes one as funny that Freud proposed to treat masturbators (like other addicts) in an institutional setting under medical supervision. We are less concerned today with masturbation, but we are in a moral panic about addiction. Whatever image an institution full of masturbators under medical supervision conjures up for you, do not let yourself be distracted by it and do not ignore what is really at stake here. Masturbation and addiction have in common the fact that both activities are able to produce a pleasure which is completely independent of others. The encounter with others always implies an element of risk, of anxiety and, above all, of unpredictability. To be part of human culture and to take part in the social bond also implies that there is a price to pay. This price is the loss of total pleasure when castration cuts the child out of the unity with the mother and replaces it with an ordinary or limited kind of pleasure. Addiction creates the illusion that this total pleasure is attainable again and masturbation creates the illusion for the other that the masturbator might have access to this pleasure. But the masturbator knows only too well how limiting an orgasm can be. This "knowledge" of the masturbating subject is probably the reason why masturbation is less of a threat to culture than addiction and why these days we have treatment centres for addicts and not for masturbators.

When do we find masturbators in treatment centres? When the limited effects of their activities do not suffice anymore and are supplanted with, for instance, drugs or alcohol. When Freud made the connection between masturbation and neurasthenia, he did not take his place in an age-long cultural tradition of frightening people away from such an un(re)productive activity as masturbation by linking it with all kinds of imaginary diseases and ailments. When he posited that one of the causes of neurasthenia could be masturbation, he was more concerned with an inherent problem in human sexuality. His concern was with the possibility that some aspect of our sexuality could not be symbolized or psychically processed, and that this lack could lead to all kinds of disturbances such as neurasthenia or, as he suggested in the above quote, depression. He wrote that whenever something happened to the masturbator that depressed him, he might relapse into his convenient form of satisfaction. So perhaps the "primary addiction" was related to depression or neurasthenia in a much more problematic way than had so far been considered. Depression and neurasthenia could cause this "primary addiction", rather than just the other way around. In other words, Freud was opening up the possibility here that addiction and masturbation, as pleasure producing activities, could be related to mental pain as the cause of these activities. The rest of the quote substantiates this idea. He wrote that "habit" had no explanatory value and that not all people who take morphine or cocaine became addicts. In fact, he related the cause of addictions to a "lack of sexual satisfaction" by positing addiction as a substitute satisfaction. He even went so far as to suggest that, in itself, abstention from drugs and alcohol would never be sufficient to cure a patient, but that one needed to look at the cause of the addiction within the subject. In this sense, Freud was already way ahead of most modern addiction treatment ideologies which proclaim that there are no causes of addiction, and that this preoccupation with causes only diverts attention away from what should be the only and true therapeutic aim: abstention. The problem for Freud in 1898 was that the therapeutic solution he came up with was a "normal sexual life". His blind hope for a complete solution in the form of a normal sexuality or sexual satisfaction hid his inkling that "something-is-up" in the domain of human sexuality. With this blind hope of a normal sexuality, Freud was precisely at the same level as those modern treatment ideologies which proclaim abstinence as their aim and happiness as their object. Still, the connection that Freud made between masturbation and addiction would prove a productive one. Meanwhile, however, Freud had become interested in dreams, not least his own.

Note

1. This affect or energy is a quantity of something and Freud defines it, in 1894, in what is known as the Q-hypothesis: "I refer to the concept that

in mental functions something is to be distinguished—a quota of affect or sum of excitation—which possesses all the characteristics of a quantity (though we have no means of measuring it), which is capable of increase, diminution, displacement and abreaction, and which is spread over the memory-traces of ideas somewhat as an electric charge is spread over the surface of a body" (Freud, 1894a, p. 60). Freud's concept of quantity here is important. This quantity is something that cannot be measured but it can be changed and distributed. It is something that can be related to ideas or representations. It is clearly something which, according to Freud, can be harmful when it exists in isolated form or when it accumulates. Freud's initial psychotherapy of hysteria was an attempt to set this energy or quantity free from the clutches of the isolated or repressed group of representations by establishing a link between this group and the rest of the psyche and by allowing this energy to be worn-away via associations. Freud's idea of how this quantity functions is based on the constancy-principle from 19th century energetics referred to in Chapter 1.

CHAPTER THREE

A limit to Freud's dream

"Pain was it? No, but misery. Casual overcasting of sunshine was it? No, but blank desolation. Gloom was it that might have departed? No, but settled and abiding darkness"

T. De Quincey, *Confessions of an English Opium Eater*, p. 46

Toxicity

In 1900 Freud published his seminal work, *The Interpretation of Dreams*. He writes, "the interpretation of dreams is the royal road to a knowledge of the unconscious activities of the mind" (Freud, 1900a, p. 608). This sentence is very well known and often quoted in order to illustrate the importance of dreams for the therapeutic work of analysis. It is however crucial to keep in mind that this "knowledge of unconscious activities" is structurally incomplete. Freud asserted that not every dream can be interpreted, that dream-passages often have to be left obscure, and that there are tangles of dream-thoughts which cannot be unravelled. As mentioned before, Freud referred to this as "the dream's navel, the spot where it reaches into the unknown" (Ibid., p. 525). All dreams are wish-fulfilments, but the ultimate causes of these wishes remain unknown to the human psyche. In his investigation of dreams, Freud came to the same conclusion as he did with his investigation of (infantile) sexual impulses, namely, that there are parts of the psyche that are alien to the subject and cannot be reached with words. He did not write anything worthy of mention about addiction or alcoholism in this book.

Writing on the theme of thumb sucking in a paragraph on auto-erotism from the *Three Essays on the Theory of Sexuality*, Freud stated the following:

> It is not every child who sucks in this way. It may be assumed that those children do so in whom there is a constitutional intensification of the erotogenic significance of the labial region. If that significance persists, these same children when they are grown up will become epicures in kissing, will be inclined to perverse kissing, or, if males, will have a powerful motive for drinking and smoking (Freud, 1905d, p. 182).

In the *Three Essays on Sexuality*, Freud developed his theory on infantile sexuality. Briefly summarized, the theory states that the infantile sexual drive is put together from various factors and exists in components and it is only in adulthood that the impulses combine into a unit with a single aim. Children come into the world with elements of sexual activity and sexual enjoyment begins with nourishment. There is a connection between sucking at the breast and thumb sucking. This connection is established over a period of time in which a certain amount of sexual satisfaction is derived from the process of feeding. Eventually, the need for repeating this sexual satisfaction becomes independent of the process of feeding. In order to retrieve this satisfaction, infants resort to thumb sucking, and do so for two reasons: firstly, as an attempt to repeat the experience of satisfaction, it maintains a familiarity with the sucking of the feeding process; and secondly, it is a very desirable activity for infants as it allows them to function independently of an external world, a world which they are not yet able to master.

This second reason is very important because we will see that the desire to be independent of the external world is also an essential characteristic of addiction. Thumb sucking, as a repetition of the experience of sexual satisfaction is a very early manifestation of an infantile sexual drive. Freud considered thumb sucking to be a sexual activity because it is the rhythmic movement of a sucking by the mouth which requires complete attention, has nothing to do with nourishment, and can lead to something in the nature of an orgasm (Ibid., p. 180). Thumb sucking is a typical manifestation of the oral stage of sexual development. However, the ultimate source of any sexual excitation stems from processes in the organism and satisfaction comes from sensory excitation of erotogenic zones, whereby any part of the skin or indeed any organ can function as such a zone (Ibid., pp. 183–184).

At certain stages in the sexual development the infant will concentrate its efforts on certain erogenous zones in order to obtain sexual satisfaction in a masturbatory kind of way.[1] It is, however, very important to realize that Freud considered sexual development in dialectical terms. That means that sexual stages continue to exist and exert their influence after they have been passed through. The different drives belonging to the different regions of the body will continue to co-exist. Therefore the infantile sexual drives are not unified and, as they find satisfaction without an external object, they are also auto-erotic (Ibid., p. 233). From the very beginning the drives show a degree of organization, but problems can arise in the course of their development. If there is—as Freud states in the aforementioned quote—a fixation of sexual satisfaction to the labial region, the girl might become addicted to kissing when she grows up and the boy might have to face a drinking or smoking habit later on in life. The future prospects are clearly more favourable for the girl than for the boy, although we have to say, the boy is not entirely without hope when he experiences a sexual intensification of the labial region; Freud did suggest in the same quote that the fixation of this intensification is only "a powerful motive" for addiction. Therefore, addiction is neither an inescapable fate nor a hereditary necessity for the fixated boy. Freud indicated in this passage that addiction can be related to a fixation in the oral stage of libidinal development and, by implication, he hinted at a possible connection between addiction and perversion. Around this time Freud considered perversions to be the over-development and overpowering influence of certain of the component drives. The addictions can be the result of an excessive oral drive and they are (in that case) a form of oral perversion.

Another reference to addiction occurs in the *Three Essays on the Theory of Sexuality*. Freud wrote:

> It must suffice us to hold firmly to what is essential in this view of the sexual processes: the assumption that substances of a peculiar kind arise from the sexual metabolism. For this apparently arbitrary supposition is supported by a fact which has received little attention but deserves the closest consideration. The neuroses, which can be derived only from disturbances of sexual life, show the greatest clinical similarity to the phenomena of intoxication and abstinence that arise from the habitual use of toxic, pleasure-producing substances (alkaloids) (Ibid., pp. 215–216).

The neuroses that are derived from disturbances of sexual life are the actual neuroses. It was not the first time in Freud's work that he observed a connection between addiction and the actual neuroses. Freud suggested here that the habitual use of toxic substances for the purpose of producing pleasure leads to a similar malaise in the subject as the "inadequate" sexual practices for the subject who suffers from an actual neurosis.[2] The common factor between the actual neuroses and addiction is the element of toxicity. Certain sexual behaviours (such as masturbation and coitus interruptus) cause a sexual metabolism which produces substances that can cause the subject harm. These toxic substances have an effect on the subject, which is similar to the effect from the toxic substances of alcohol and drugs.[3] The connection between addiction, the actual neuroses and toxicity will be explored in greater detail in Chapter 8.

At the same time Freud was writing his book on the theory of sexuality, he was also working on another book concerning jokes or witticisms. In *Jokes and their Relation to the Unconscious* (published in 1905) Freud was very concerned with the question of the production of pleasure (via jokes) and how this question relates to the economy of expenditure of energy. In order to be able to resolve some of these "issues", Freud could not help noticing the crucial role of language for the production of pleasure and for the distribution of energy. He wrote:

> "Pleasure in nonsense", as we may call it for short, is concealed in serious life to a vanishing point. In order to demonstrate it we must investigate two cases—one in which it is still visible and one in which it becomes visible again: the behaviour of a child in learning,

and that of an adult in a toxically altered state of mind (Freud, 1905c, p. 125).

The first case that Freud investigated concerned the acquisition of language in children. He said that when children learn their mother tongue they like to experiment with words "without regard to the condition that they should make sense, in order to obtain from them the pleasurable effect of rhythm or rhyme" (Ibid., p. 125). Increasingly, the child will be forbidden this kind of enjoyment, but later there might be attempts to disregard the restrictions caused by the acquisition of language, and children and adults find pleasure in the nonsensical use of words and language. Freud was of the opinion that logical thinking and meaningful reality place huge demands on the individual. That is why children and adults alike are attracted by what is forbidden by reason and will indeed on occasions rebel against the demands of logic and reality. Therefore, people experience pleasure in nonsense, and jokes carry this element of nonsense within them. The second case Freud investigated concerned the perhaps more mature university student who, later on, might even attend some congresses. The drinking these students are capable of on "Rag-Day" is proof of the fact that they need to unburden themselves of the pressures of learning logic and reason. The same holds true when some of these students attend congresses later in life when after the meeting they lapse into a comic commentary on what was being discussed. Freud wrote:

> The Bierschwefel[4] and the Kneipzeitung[5] give evidence by their names to the fact that the criticism, which has repressed pleasure in nonsense, has already grown so powerful that it cannot be put aside even temporarily without toxic assistance. A change in mood is the most precious thing that alcohol achieves for mankind, and on that account this "poison" is not equally indispensable for everyone. A cheerful mood, whether it is produced endogenously or toxically, reduces the inhibiting forces, criticism among them, and makes accessible once again sources of pleasure which were under the weight of suppression. It is more instructive to observe how the standards of joking sink as spirits rise. For high spirits replace jokes, just as jokes must try to replace high spirits when possibilities of enjoyment are otherwise inhibited—among them the pleasure in nonsense—and then jokes can come into their own: "Mit wenig Witz und viel Behagen."[6] Under the influence of alcohol the grown

man once more becomes a child, who finds pleasure in having the course of his thoughts freely at his disposal without paying regard to the compulsion of logic (Ibid., p. 127).

Freud indicated here that alcohol disinhibits and saves the subject energy which would otherwise be used to repress the pleasure of nonsense. In other words, alcohol can form a relief from the demands of human reality. The essential part of this quote should not be overlooked though. Freud seemed to favour the act of joking over the state of high spirits. This is important, as it is an indication of Freud's ethical stance. Whereas high spirits is something that happens to—or overcomes—the subject, joking is an act and so the implication is that it is the subject him or herself who is responsible for the production of pleasure. Moreover, it is an act of speech or articulation, as joking is something that takes place within the realm of language; it is something that is spoken (or written) in language. To keep things within the realm of language and related to meaning is a crucial part of the ethics of clinical practice in psychoanalysis. Addiction is precisely the opposite movement from keeping things in language: it is the artificial creation of a mood of high spirits via the chemical route of the body.[7]

A "gross episode"

In three letters written by Freud in 1908 and addressed to Jung, references were made to the addiction of their colleague, the rebellious and burlesque Otto Gross.[8] It is most peculiar that these references are not mentioned in any of the surveys, reviews or texts dealing with Freud's ideas and theories on addiction. Freud's remarks on addiction in these letters, and indeed on the case of Otto Gross itself, are interesting enough to warrant (at least) a brief discussion. Gross was an assistant to the famous psychiatrist Kraepelin and a patient of Jung's. Freud knew Otto's father, Hans, who was a professor in criminology in Graz and Prague. Otto was a psychoanalyst and philosopher and he was also hopelessly addicted to cocaine and opium. At one point, Otto's addictive behaviour became so problematic for his environment that his father decided to have him locked away in a psychiatric institute. Needless to say, the already strained relationship between father and son was certainly not improved by the incarceration. Otto was, and remained, a troubled, rebellious character. He was freed after a while and then disappeared from the scene until his death, due to drug addiction, was announced in 1920.[9] In relation to Otto Gross's addiction, Freud wrote the following to Jung:

> However, we shall also have to talk about Otto Gross; he urgently needs your medical help; what a pity, such a gifted, resolute man. He is addicted to cocaine and probably in the early phase of toxic cocaine paranoia (McGuire, 1974, Letter 84, p. 141). I can imagine how much of your time he must be taking. I originally thought you would only take him on for the withdrawal period and that I would start analytical treatment in the autumn. It is shamefully egotistic of me, but I must admit that it is better for me this way; for I am obliged to sell my time and my supply of energy is not quite what it used to be (Ibid., Letter 94, p. 152). I have a feeling that I should thank you most vigorously—and so I do—for your treatment of Otto Gross. The task should have fallen to me but my egoism—or perhaps I should say my self-defence mechanism—rebelled against it. Now I have no reason to doubt your diagnosis, inherently because of your great experience of D.pr. (Dementia Praecox), but also because D.pr. is often not a real diagnosis. We seem to be in agreement about the impossibility of influencing his condition and about its ultimate development. But couldn't his condition be another (obsessional) psychoneurosis, with negative transference caused by his hostility to his father, which presents the appearance of absence or impairment of transference? (Ibid., Letter 99, pp. 157–158).

The first thing that strikes one about these remarks is that some sort of "deal" was done between Freud and Jung; Jung would support Gross through the withdrawal period (or detoxification period as we would call it these days) and Freud was to do the analytical treatment. This did not happen, because Freud—as he indicated himself—had no desire to analyse Gross. It is possible to speculate that it was Gross's addiction to cocaine that caused resistance in Freud.[10] However, what is certain is that Freud thought that the withdrawal from addiction should be separated from the analytical treatment; an analytical treatment being more directed towards an exploration of the addiction in relation to the clinical structure of this patient.

This raises a number of important questions which are still relevant today: (1) Do we need a dual treatment in the case of addiction: one aimed directly at the symptom of addiction and another that aims at the subject? (2) If a dual treatment is needed, can this treatment be done by the same person, or should one person (or institution) deal with the withdrawal phase and another with the analysis or therapy? (3) Is it possible to do therapy or analysis with someone who is under the direct influence of alcohol or drugs? These questions must be revisited, but it is interesting just to note here that some of these questions were already being considered in psychoanalytic circles at that time. Freud questioned Jung's diagnosis of Dementia Praecox, a Kraepelian diagnostic term, which designates a form (or aspect) of psychosis. Freud wondered whether Gross might be suffering from an obsessional neurosis. What is implied in this exchange between Freud and Jung is that Gross's addiction was thought to be a function of his psychosis or neurosis, that is to say, they thought that Gross's addiction had a function in relation to his subjective clinical structure. This touches upon the question of diagnosis in the clinical field of addiction: is addiction a separate clinical entity, or is it a symptom that functions in relation to the different clinical structures of the subject, or indeed can it be both? The question of diagnosis will be explored further in Chapter 8.

The issue of transference is also of interest here. It was clear from the last letter that it was near impossible to treat Gross. One can glean from Freud's words that the relationship between Gross and Jung was not very good. Freud suggested that there was negative transference on Gross's part and that this was a symptomatic repetition of the relationship with his father. But Freud said that it was a negative transference that expressed itself in an absence or impairment of it. A negative transference that impairs the therapeutic relationship makes sense because an impaired relationship is the very definition of negative transference. However, when the result of a negative transference is the absence of transference, is it is justified to speak of a transference relationship at all? Could it be the case that Gross had no transferential relationship with Jung because his transference was on to the object drug? Cocaine and opium might have functioned for Gross as the solutions to his problems, a function that could have been taken up or developed by Jung. The crucial question is: why did the transference not develop?

Before turning to this question, it is important to underline the fact that the management of the transference is very difficult in the treatment of addiction. Often addicts do not seek help because they have a "perfect" solution at hand. The following question then arises: how can the analyst or therapist create a demand (for therapy or analysis) in the addicted subject in a way that does not transgress the ethics of the speaking subject?[11] And once the transferential relationship or demand has been established, another question raises its ugly head: how can the transference be maintained such that the addicted subject does not "relapse" into a transference onto the object drug or alcohol? To maintain the transference in a way that is manageable is an enormous task for the therapist or analyst. It is an essential characteristic of the clinical condition of addiction that limits are transgressed and boundaries crossed, not just in terms of the search for comfort, pleasure or excitement, but also in terms of human relationships. The demand of the addict can be overwhelming once it has been established.[12] In therapy or analysis with addicts, one has to be prepared to work with extremes of positive and negative transference. To maintain the transference and to allow it to develop is, however, an ethical imperative and it is the only way out of a lethal impasse for the addict. It is not difficult to see how addiction can easily lead to counter-transference, especially when we take note of the fact that addiction, as a fundamental human problem, highlights the impasses of human existence and the shortcomings of the subject, including those of the therapist. Freud clearly did not want to work with Gross. When he used the words "self-defence" and "rebellion" to describe his aversion to analyse Gross we can be sure that something of his own desire was at stake.

Jung did not function as an object of Gross's demand for a solution, the transference did not take seed, much less grow. We know from letter 94, from the Freud/Jung correspondence, that Freud was to be Gross's analyst. That must mean that Gross wanted to be in analysis with Freud and that implies that they had discussed this. In other words, the transference went in Freud's direction and never developed in the relationship with Jung. In letter 85 one is told that Gross's father had pleaded with Jung to help his son and that Jung predicted that Otto would run away whenever he saw the chance, he was a real problem for Jung.[13] Nevertheless, in letters 95 and 98, Jung wrote that he had worked very hard with Gross and that he had helped him through the painful withdrawal process (pp. 153, 155, 156). In letter 156 Jung wrote that Gross had abandoned the treatment because he felt he had been cured.[14] Jung predicted a bad end for Gross and he wrote to Freud: "He is one of those whom life is bound to reject" (Letter 98, p. 156). Gross had remained in treatment with Jung only for a very brief period. Little over a week after Gross had left, Jung wrote to Freud: "I wish Gross could go back to you, this time as a patient, not that I want to inflict a Gross episode on you, but simply for the sake of comparison" (Letter 100, p. 161). It is clear from these statements that Jung was glad to see the back of Gross and that Gross had been merely interesting as an object of scientific study for the two analysts. However, as an object (of study), Gross had been "too much" for Jung and Freud. Freud did not want to analyse him and Jung's treatment of him was at times unbelievably farcical. For instance, when Jung was at a loss with the treatment they would change roles and Gross would analyse Jung, who actually said he benefited from this (Letter 95, p. 153). Was Jung in analysis with Gross? This question is not intended to be merely cynical. Jung abandoned his analytical position vis-à-vis Gross by turning the latter into the object of his own demand or desire for analysis. Both Freud and Jung rejected Gross for analysis. He was the waste product of their desire and therefore also the waste product of the psychoanalytic establishment. In relation to Gross's ideas about psychoanalysis, Jung wrote to Freud: "Still, there must always be a few flies in the ointment of the world" (Letter 46, p. 90). Jung knew only too well (as indicated by the next sentence in the letter) that the world turned around the fly in the ointment.[15]

What captures our desire to know is what we do not understand; it is that "thing" that remains an enigma to us. This is precisely the position of the analyst who, in that position of abject object, provokes the unconscious of the patient. Not that this desire to know is always a desire to know the truth. Not at all. It might very well be the desire for a knowledge that doesn't want to know the truth of the unconscious. That is why it is so important to stick with the patient and to carry him or her through that barrier of ignorance. Freud and Jung did not stick with Gross. He was a toxic presence in the eye—or rather ear—of the psychoanalytic establishment with his strange ideas and bizarre behaviour. It is certainly no coincidence that Gross was an addict. As indicated, Gross provoked a desire for scientific knowledge in Freud and Jung, but it was not a desire to know the truth.[16] The desire for truth would have been an analytical desire, namely the desire to carry Gross and themselves through the impasse of their ignorance about addiction.

In relation to Gross and addiction, Freud temporarily left his analytical desire and became ignorant. That is what happens sometimes when one is confronted with a disturbing waste product; a remainder we do not understand. This piece of the real is called the "object a" by Lacan. It is also the provocative position of the analyst. Gross was a waste product of the history of psychoanalysis (Jonckheere, 1987, p. 159). The thesis proposed here is that addiction is the waste product of psychoanalysis in the same way as psychoanalysis is the waste product of a science that does not want to know about the subject. The question is: does psychoanalysis have the courage to carry itself through its impasse of ignorance about addiction? In other words, will psychoanalysis allow addiction (as waste product) to be its analyst and as such provoke a new kind of knowledge about it? Only time and respons-a-bility will tell. Addiction is a toxic presence in culture, but so was hysteria at one time.

The loss of object

In *Psychoanalytic Notes on an Autobiographical Account of a Case of Paranoia*, published in 1911, Freud wrote the following:

> Alcoholic delusions of jealousy. The part played by alcohol in this disorder is intelligible in every way. We know that that source of pleasure removes inhibitions and undoes sublimations. It is not infrequently disappointment over a woman that drives a man to drink—but this means, as a rule, that he resorts to the public-house and to the company of men, who afford him the emotional satisfaction which he has failed to get from his wife at home. If now these men become the objects of a strong libidinal cathexis in his unconscious, he will ward it off with the third kind of contradiction: "It is not I who love the man—she loves him", and

he suspects the woman in relation to all the men whom he himself is tempted to love (Freud, 1911c, p. 64).

In order to understand the full implications of this quote it is necessary to look at its immediate context. Freud was of the opinion that what lies at the heart of cases of paranoia is a homosexual wishful fantasy of loving a man. He stated that the principle forms of paranoia can all be represented as contradictions of the following single proposition: "I (a man) love him (a man)" (Ibid., p. 63). This underlying fantasy can be contradicted in the unconscious in three different ways. The third way of contradicting the original proposition can be detected in delusions of jealousy, and the alcoholic delusion of jealousy is one of them (Ibid., p. 64).[17] The man who thinks he loves a man will contradict this unconscious fantasy by thinking that it is the woman (his wife) who loves the man instead of himself. This man will resort to this kind of contradiction in order to defend himself against a libidinal bond with other men which has become too intense, as a result of seeking compensation in the pub for what he didn't get from his wife at home.[18] This form of drinking refers to a specific kind of alcoholism and it will be studied in some detail later on in this work, where it will be asserted that it is not only disappointment over a woman that can drive a man to the pub, but a fear of her as well. Disappointment suggests the loss of a love object.

Freud took up the relationship between the loss of object and the use of toxic substances once more in his article from 1917 entitled *Mourning and Melancholia*. It is interesting to note that Freud mentioned that it is not only the case that alcohol removes inhibitions, but that alcohol is also capable of undoing sublimations. Here again one encounters the antagonistic relationship between language and alcohol (or drugs), if one considers sublimation to be a transformation of the drive into a cultural production commanded by language. Freud's reference to sublimation in this context suggests that the use of alcohol (and drugs) can result in a more immediate and total satisfaction of the drive than the less direct route of culture and language. This is an indication of the role alcohol and drugs can play in the attempt to overcome the limitations inherent in human pleasure. Freud returned to these limitations and their relationship to alcohol in more detail in 1912.

In *On the Universal Tendency to Debasement in the Sphere of Love* Freud wondered why the relationship to the sexual object is problematic in nature (Freud, 1912d, pp. 188–189). He believed that there was something in the drive that was unfavourable for satisfaction. He provided two reasons for this: firstly, the "disphasic" onset of object-choice and the barrier against incest lead to a situation in which the final object of the drive is only a surrogate for the real object; secondly, the sexual drives are component drives and even in the genital phase of sexual development their unification is not be complete, i.e., some of these component drives will be repressed or else put to other use than the aim of satisfaction. Alcohol is able to create a false harmony in this frustrating chaos. Freud wrote:

> Consider, for example, the relation of a drinker to wine. Is it not true that wine always provides the drinker with the same toxic satisfaction, which in poetry has so often been compared to erotic satisfaction—a comparison acceptable from the scientific point of view as well? Has one ever heard of the drinker being obliged constantly to change his drink because he soon grows tired of keeping to the same one? On the contrary, habit constantly tightens the bond between a man and the kind of wine he drinks. Does one ever hear of a drinker who needs to go to a country where wine is dearer or drinking is prohibited, so that by introducing obstacles he can reinforce the dwindling satisfaction that he obtains? Not at all. If we listen to what our great alcoholics, such as Bocklin, say about their relation to wine, it sounds like the most perfect harmony, a model of a happy marriage. Why is the relation of the lover to his sexual object so very different? (Ibid., p. 188).

Freud's hope for the existence of a perfect pleasure principle seems to have been reduced to the case of the relationship between the alcoholic and his alcohol. It is important, however, to read the above passage with a certain amount of irony. The marriage that comes across as completely harmonious is indeed often explosive and in the case of the alcoholic his or her partner is often destroyed in the end. It seems as if Freud was asking himself why people are constantly duped with regards to pleasure and satisfaction. Restrictions on sexual behaviour lead to frustration of sexual pleasure, but complete sexual freedom leads to a diminution of the psychical value of erotic needs, and in that case people require obstacles to heighten their sexual libido (Ibid., p. 187). A certain amount of suffering cannot be avoided because the encounter between the drives and civilization is always a missed encounter. Freud wrote: "The instincts of love are hard to educate; education of them achieves now too much, now too little. What civilization aims at making out of them seems unattainable except at the price of a sensible loss of pleasure; the persistence of the impulses that could not be made use of can be detected in sexual activity in the form of non-satisfaction" (Ibid., pp. 189–190). This passage is crucial for understanding the essence of Freud's thinking on addiction. The price we pay for living a human life is a loss of object (the total pleasure or satisfaction of the incestuous relationship). This loss is the cause of our desire. The fulfilment of this desire will be too much whilst the lack of fulfilment will achieve too little for the subject. This subject wants more than that imbalance. One way of redressing the balance is via the habitual stability of toxic satisfaction. The only problem is that this will eventually prove again to be too much for the subject, but at a different level than satisfaction. Indeed, this subject will eventually pay a price, but this time with his or her life.

Freud also discussed the question of the loss of object in *A Metapsychological Supplement to the Theory of Dreams*, published in 1917. In this article Freud said that dreams are hallucinated wish-fulfillments. Thus, he proposed a comparison of dreams with the pathological states which are akin to them (Freud, 1917d, pp. 222–223). In certain psychotic conditions the ego has to face a loss which is unbearable, whereupon it will suspend its relationship to reality. This suspension leaves room for the projection of wishful internal fantasies onto the external world in the form of hallucinations. In a footnote to this discussion Freud wrote the following:

> I may venture to suggest in this connection that the toxic hallucinations, too, e.g. alcoholic delirium, are to be understood in an analogous fashion. Here the unbearable loss imposed by reality would be precisely the loss of alcohol. When the latter is supplied, the hallucinations cease (Ibid., pp. 233–234).

It is interesting that Freud did not relate the hallucinations to the chemical effects of toxicity, but to the loss of an object (in this case alcohol) in reality. The hallucinations are a psychic compensation for this loss and are therefore caused by a lack. The question that should be asked here is: what is the nature of the primary relationship between the subject and alcohol which caused the hallucinations in the subject in a secondary movement? Is the nature of that relationship also based on a lack? Perhaps it might be possible to formulate an answer to those questions after a consideration of Freud's paper *Mourning and Melancholia*, which was also published in 1917. However, before doing this it is important to emphasize Freud's reference to hallucinations in the above quote. It becomes clear in reading Freud's work that children and adults hallucinate because of a loss. Hallucinations are a mental compensation for a real loss and they represent a desire for what was lost. Small children hallucinate the breast and, considering that the breast brought them considerable satisfaction, it is possible to say that children hallucinate an object of desire. But why hallucinate? Children hallucinate because it is the only satisfaction available to them at the point when they have lost the original object; and this original object is ultimately nothing else than the body of the mother that was forbidden to them on the basis of the prohibition of incest. This loss, or lost object, is one form of what Lacan calls the "object a".

In *Mourning and Melancholia* Freud wrote:

> Alcoholic intoxication, which belongs to the same class of states, may (in so far as it is a state of elation) be explained in the same way; there is probably a suspension here, produced by toxins, of expenditures of energy in repression. The popular view likes to assume that a person in a manic state of this kind finds such delight in movement and action because he is so "cheerful". This false connection must of course be put right. The fact is that the economic condition in the subject's mind referred to above has been fulfilled, and this is the reason why he is in such high spirits on the one hand and so uninhibited in action in the other (Freud, 1917e, p. 254).

The class of states Freud was referring to in this quote are the states of mania. As he suggested, the high spirits and the uninhibited behaviour are not due to a cheery mood, but are the direct result of the chemical action of alcohol on expenditures of energy in the subject. Freud explained the states of mania by saying that "as a result of some influence, a large expenditure of psychical energy, long maintained or habitually occurring, has at last become unnecessary, so that it is available for numerous applications and possibilities of discharge..." (Ibid., p. 254). But what is this "influence" that was able to free up the psychical energy that can be used to produce a manic state? Freud suggested that the ego must have got over the loss of object (for instance, the death of a loved one) and that the energy that had become available by overcoming this loss, could then be employed elsewhere.[19] Freud indicated that we can see that the subject has been able to liberate him or herself from the object which was the cause of his or her suffering when they embark on the manic chase for new objects (Ibid., p. 255).

There is mourning and melancholia and then there is mania and alcoholic intoxication; and all these could be considered as pathological states, but it is, however, important to contemplate the differences between the two pairs. There is a difference which is immediately obvious; in states of mania and alcoholic intoxication the subject is full of something, full of (a surplus of) energy and therefore (hyper)active and cheerful. In states of mourning and melancholia, the subjects have experienced a loss; they are empty, depressed and have no energy at all. Why, then, should mania and alcoholic intoxication be called pathological states? They are pathological states because they are reaction-formations against— and indeed ultimately based on—what caused mourning and melancholia. It is therefore essential to look at the difference between mourning and melancholia. Mourning is related to the loss of a loved object in the external world and the mourning process consists of having to let go of this loss in the inner world. The external loved object had become part of the ego and now the ego has to give up part of itself. Mourning is a normal reaction of the ego to the loss of an object which is only a substitute for a more fundamental object that had to be given up much earlier on in life. This fundamental loss was the result of the Oedipus Complex, a process in which the child had to lose the person who was closest and dearest to him in order to gain access to the domain of human sexuality and desire. The process of mourning only concerns the loss of daily objects of human reality such as partners, family members, friends, and so on. Melancholia is different in the sense that there is an entirely different kind of loss at stake, a loss that is much more problematic and painful. What happens in melancholia is that, in replacing the lost object, the ego finds itself invested with all the cathexis originally attached to the object. In other words, the ego has to give itself up and that has very painful consequences for the subject.

But there is something even more problematic about melancholia. Freud seems to suggest in his article that the original object was not given up entirely, or rather, that the ego had come to replace this original object with itself, a replacement which led to the foundation of a narcissistic identification. He came to the conclusion that the reaction of the melancholic to a loss is so strong because, from the very beginning, "object-choice has been effected on a narcissistic basis" (Ibid., p. 249). In other words, the loss in melancholia is the loss of the original loss.[20] The melancholic was never able to completely give up the original object because it was retained, to some degree, within his or her own image. This loss of loss causes a lack of desire in the melancholic who, as a consequence, feels that there is nothing more to live for. *Mourning and Melancholia* is an essential article for understanding mental pain from a Freudian point of view. In this point of view, pain is related to forms of loss that are constitutive of the foundations of—and inherent in—human existence.

There can be no doubt about the fact that some aspects of addiction are ways of dealing with this pain. In this sense, alcohol and drugs are substitute objects that can cause immediate relief of pain. But there is more to pain than meets the eye. Pain can be the cause of pleasure. The relief of pain can lead to the sensation of pleasure in the same way as the retrieval of loss can lead to the temporary state of mania. In *Mourning and Melancholia* Freud attributed the cause of mania to an amount of psychical energy that has been freed up and made available to the subject after a loss that had been mourned or was undone. This energy would otherwise be spent on the process of mourning or the work of repression. This surplus energy is also important in relation to addiction, as it is something that can be artificially provided by the chemical effects of drugs and alcohol. This surplus energy is highly sought after by subjects who look for manic pleasure as a compensation for a loss which is inevitable but still unbearable to them. Freud had already come across the value of this surplus energy in his work on cocaine. Chapter 1 on cocaine refers to the fact that in this period Freud had great expectations about the use of this energy in the sense that he hoped it could be employed for the good of mankind. Then his expectations became a great deal more negative. This surplus of energy is a precursor of another aspect of Lacan's concept of "object a".[21] The "object a" as a surplus-of-jouissance.[22]

Toxicity revisited

In lecture 24 from *Introductory Lectures on Psychoanalysis* published in 1917, Freud discussed the actual neuroses and the addictive use of toxic substances. He wrote:

> Clinical medicine has given us a valuable pointer towards an interpretation of these disturbances, and one that has been taken into account by various inquirers. The "actual" neuroses, in the detail of their symptoms and also in their characteristic of influencing every organic system and every function, exhibit an unmistakable resemblance to the pathological states which arise from the chronic influence of external toxic substances and from a sudden withdrawal of them—to intoxications and conditions of abstinence. The two groups of disorders are brought together still more closely by intermediate conditions such as Graves' disease which we have learned to recognize as equally due to the operation of toxic substances, but of toxins which are not introduced into the body from the outside but originate in the subject's own metabolism. In view of these analogies, we cannot, I think, avoid regarding the neuroses as results of disturbances in the sexual metabolism, whether because more of these sexual toxins are produced than the subject can deal with, or whether because internal and even psychical conditions restrict the proper employment of these substances. The popular mind has from time immemorial paid homage to hypotheses of this kind on the nature of sexual desire, speaking of love as an "intoxication" and believing that falling in love is brought about by love-philtres—though here the operative agent is to some extent externalized (Freud, 1916–1917, p. 388).

Freud again linked the actual neuroses and addictions to toxic substances. In 1897 Freud had already written to Fliess about the connection between addiction (to masturbation) and neurasthenia.[23] Freud brought the actual neuroses and the addictions to toxic substances closer together this time by comparing both to diseases which are caused by toxins produced by the metabolism of the body, (such as Graves' disease). The only difference between the actual neuroses and the addictions is that in the former the pathology is caused by something within the body, whilst in the latter the pathological states are caused by something external. But this difference fades when we consider an observation and two questions respectively. Freud attributed the cause of the actual neuroses to actual sexual practices, life styles and circumstances, such as masturbation, coitus interruptus, deliberate abstinence and age.[24] He said that what unites all these causes is the factor of abstinence (Freud, 1894, p. 79). That means that the internal sexual toxins are produced by external behaviours and circumstances, i.e., external to the body that produces these toxins. The difference between inside and outside (of the body), or internal and external causation, is not so clear. It becomes even more problematic when one considers the following questions: do the external toxins of drugs and alcohol produce or affect internal toxins and could it be possible that the habitual intake of external toxins is related to an internal metabolism which creates a harmful "toxicity" in itself? The apparently straightforward question of what is inside and outside (or internal and external) of mind and body has been problematized by Lacan who stated that the subject and his or her body is constituted in the field of the Other or language. This question and the status of the body in Lacan's work will be considered further when the possibility of a psychoanalytic conception of toxicity is explored in Part III of this work. That is an important aspect of a Lacanian theory of addiction.

Two statements made by Freud when he discussed actual neurosis and toxicity strike one as remarkable. He said that psychoanalysis is only a superstructure which one day will be replaced by its organic foundation and that the actual neuroses, because they have been generated by "direct toxic damage", cannot be treated by psychoanalysis and must ultimately be clarified by biologico–medical research (op. cit., p. 389). The implications are that all the neuroses have an organic basis and that the actual neuroses and toxicomanias do not belong to the theoretical and clinical field of psychoanalysis.[25] However, on the basis of Lacan's concept of the real it is possible to argue that the toxicomanias (and the actual neuroses) can (and in fact should) be included in the field of psychoanalysis and that all the neuroses contain a real kernel instead of an organic one.[26] Moreover, it can be demonstrated that the application of biologico–medical science to the field of addiction leads to an inevitable theoretical and clinical impasse.[27]

In a paper from 1919 entitled *Lines of Advance in Psycho-Analytic Therapy*, Freud made a throwaway comment on the treatment of alcoholics which is nevertheless relevant because of its context. In this paper, read out to a congress, Freud had taken it upon himself to review the therapeutic procedure (Freud, 1919a, p. 159). The paper gravitates around one famous statement: "analytic treatment should be carried through, as far as possible, under privation—in a state of abstinence" (Ibid., p. 162). This statement can be interpreted as a reaction against Ferenczi's suggestions that more direct and active involvement of the therapist with the patient could lead to a more efficient and perhaps shorter treatment. The activity on the part of the therapist that Freud proposed should be an energetic opposition to what he calls "premature substitutive satisfactions" (Ibid., p. 164). By the latter he meant all kinds of activities, preferences and habits. In other words, this means anything that might distract the patient from recovery through the work of analysis, including habitual behaviours (or addictions). The word recovery in this sentence is emphasized in order to highlight that analysis itself can be a form of distraction. Freud said: "The patient looks for his substitutive satisfactions above all in the treatment itself, in his transference-relationship with the physician; and he may even strive to compensate himself by this means for all the other privations laid upon him" (Ibid., p. 164). The relationship with the therapist may indeed become a relationship of dependency and that is a danger for people whose pathology is one of dependency (such as addicts and obsessionals). For them the therapeutic relationship has become a toxic relationship. That the therapeutic relationship can compensate for all kinds of privations is best illustrated by the empirical fact that addicted people are more than capable of staying away from alcohol and drugs, providing they have an ideal they can adhere to and look up to. The therapist can function as such an ideal for the addict. The tendency in addicts to idealize the therapist or treatment ideology is not without danger for the treatment. This problem will be investigated in detail, as it is an important indicator for the direction of a treatment of addicts.

Freud made it abundantly clear that patients must be denied those satisfactions which they desire most (Ibid., p. 164). If this does not happen the patients will not assume responsibility for their lives (and suffering). The therapist should not give in to the demand of the patient. This is an ethical imperative in psychoanalytic treatment with special relevance for the treatment of addicts. But it is an imperative that only works on condition that the void left by abstinence and privation is filled with words and language. Towards the end of his paper, Freud expressed the hope that society might one day provide assistance for the mind, as it does for the body, because the neuroses threaten public health as much as physical illness does. He wrote:

> When this happens, institutions or out-patient clinics will be started, to which analytically-trained physicians will be appointed, so that men who would otherwise give way to drink, women who have nearly succumbed under their burden of privations, children for whom there is no choice but between running wild or neurosis, may be made capable, by analysis, of resistance and of efficient work (Ibid., p. 167).

This remark about drink states that analysis might prevent the onset of an addiction and implies that the cause of addiction is a mental one. Good care, good advice, legal and social assistance are not sufficient for the treatment of addictions. But Freud recognized that the technique of analysis might not be sufficient either and he suggested that the technique might have to be adapted (Ibid., p. 167). Despite Freud's hope for more support from society for mental suffering in the future, one is left with a strong feeling that Freud was sinking ever so slightly deeper into a pessimism concerning the human condition and what could be done about it clinically. He was coming to the period when he goes to war on those who promise happiness. Why was that? He had discovered the death-drive.

Notes

1. Freud recognizes a number of phases of sexual (masturbatory) activity in children (Freud, 1905d, pp. 188–189). Infants can have their genitals stimulated by parents or carers through cleaning, dressing and toilet activities. The rubbing movements involved in these activities can produce satisfaction. In a second phase the masturbatory activity seems to disappear and in a third phase there is a return. In this last phase the children want to actively produce the sexual pleasure that can be derived from the manipulation of their own genitals and parts of the body. External contingencies (such as seductions) may play an important role at this stage in the choice of form and object for masturbatory activity. Under these external influences children can

become polymorphously perverse (p. 191). That means that almost any part of the body can become a means to sexual pleasure and indeed why not the body as a whole? This last point is important as it can be argued that some addictions are a pleasure seeking activity of the body.
2. In his postscript to the "Dora Case Study" Freud refers to an organic factor at work in the sexual function which contributes to the cause of the psychoneuroses and he likens the effects of chronic drug use to the psychoneuroses instead of the actual neuroses (Freud, 1905e, p. 113). In order to avoid confusion it might be helpful to consider the following point: Freud suggests in his article *My Views on the Part Played by Sexuality in the Aetiology of the Neuroses* that the actual neuroses are directly determined by a somatic factor and the psychoneuroses are a psychic response to somatic changes caused by disturbances of the sexual metabolism (Freud, 1906a, pp. 278–279). This suggestion by Freud has an important implication: it implies that the psychoneuroses are ultimately based on an actual neurosis and that the former are a way of processing the latter. The minutes from the meeting of the Vienna Psychoanalytic Society which was held on 24 April 1912 state the following: "The essential factor in the relationship between neurasthenia and psychoneurosis is this: neurasthenic symptoms are not structured like psychoneurotic phrenomena. The symptoms do not come about psychogenically; rather they underlie the psychogenic symptom" (Nunberg and Federn, 1975, p. 93).
3. Despite his numerous assertions about toxic substances in the body Freud was doubtful about the connection between toxic sexual substances and toxic chemical substances. In a footnote to the above mentioned passage he writes: "The question of what interplay arises in the course of the sexual processes between the effects of purely toxic stimuli and of physiological ones cannot be treated, even hypothetically, in the present state of our knowledge. I may add that I attach no importance to this particular hypothesis and should be ready to abandon it at once in favour of another, provided that its fundamental nature remained unchanged—that is, the emphasis which it lays upon sexual chemistry" (Freud, 1905d, p. 216). It is perhaps worth mentioning that Freud never abandoned this hypothesis, although he never explored it any further.
4. A hilarious speech at a drinks party.
5. A funny and ironically written commentary on the proceedings of a meeting.
6. With little wit and much pleasure.
7. Freud was already interested in this question of high spirits in his work on cocaine.

8. From letter 46 from the Freud–Jung correspondence, it can be learned that the analyst Otto Gross had rather strange and rebellious ideas about the transference and about sexuality. Jung writes to Freud that Gross thinks that the transference is a symbol of monogamy and sexual repression. The transference has to be stopped by turning patients into sexual immoralists; a process which restores them back to health (McGuire, 1974, p. 90).
9. Lieven Jonckheere in his fascinating short study on Gross, points out that it is peculiar that knowledge about the time and cause of death had to come from research material concerning the writer Kafka who knew Gross; it did not come from the historical accounts of psychoanalysis (Jonckheere, 1987, p. 160).
10. In Chapter 1 it was mentioned that Freud's relationship to cocaine had brought him certain difficulties.
11. In other words, you can't physically force someone to accept help.
12. The solution that was once provided by the drug of alcohol is now demanded from the analyst or therapist.
13. In this letter Jung wrote to Freud. "One thing alone bothers me and that is the affair with Gross. His father has written urging me to take him back with me to Zurich. As ill luck would have it, I have some urgent business on the 28th with my architect in Munich. In the meantime of course Gross will give me the slip" (letter 85, p. 142).
14. Jung writes to Freud in this letter: "His exit from the stage is in keeping with the diagnosis: the day before yesterday Gross, unguarded for a moment, jumped over the garden wall and will doubtless turn up again in Munich here, to go towards the evening of his fate. Gross left because he thought he was cured" (Letter 98, p. 156).
15. This next sentence is: "What else is civilization but the fruit of adversity?" (p. 90).
16. It is a somewhat ironical twist of fate that Jung was instrumental in the setting up of A.A. One of the American founding members of A.A. went to Jung for advice about how to be cured from alcoholism. Jung didn't know how to help this man, but gave him the idea that a religious conversion would probably be the only thing that could do the job. The rest is history.
17. The first way Freud mentions is by the reverse of the original proposition which says "I do not love him—I hate him." In paranoia this position will lead to a projection of the opposite onto external reality. The subsequent perception of this reality reads as if "he hates (persecutes) me". The paranoiac will feel prosecuted by the man whom he thinks hates him. The second form of contradicting the original proposition happens in erotomania where the "I (a man) love him"

becomes "I do not love him—I love her." Following the logic of projection this proposition is transformed into "I observe that she loves me." Freud adds that indeed infatuations invariably begin not with an internal perception of being infatuated but with an external perception of being loved (Freud, 1911c, p. 63).

18. It is rather seductive to conclude on the basis of this that there is a clear connection between alcoholism and homosexuality. This connection is not clear at all and it is important to keep in mind that Freud referred to the fantasy of loving a man and not to a homosexual object choice.

19. In this paper Freud explains melancholia as follows: There was once a very strong libidinal attachment to a loved person or object. Then, through circumstance or disappointments, this object-relationship is shattered and the libido is withdrawn from this object. The freed libido is not attached to another object or objects but was withdrawn into the ego. In other words, the ego identified with the object and took its place. The ego sinks into a deep melancholia, because it is judged critically and negatively as though it was the lost object itself and therefore the cause of all the suffering by what Freud calls a special agency. This special agency will later become the superego.

20. In a recent talk in Dublin on addiction Charles Melman said something similar: "But the clinical experience shows that I can also lose the initial loss, the fundamental loss, namely what allowed desire to exist and be organized. In that case I enter into a state of melancholia. This is what Freud says in his article Mourning and Melancholia. This is just to tell you that we are all dependent. Because we all depend on that original loss and if this original loss is lacking you find depersonalization and melancholia. And if you reflect a little you can easily see that each one of us is in a state of addiction to the agency that is represented by this original loss. This original loss therefore which organizes desire, which Freud called libido and which Lacan gave a more precise name, the Phallus" (Melman, 1999, p. 2).

21. Another is the aforementioned aspect of the loss or lost object.

22. The difficult but important concept of jouissance will be explored in greater detail in Part II and especially Part III (Chapter 7). Just to say here that there are different modes of jouissance and that it relates to Freud's concept of psychical energy in the sense that it is something that can be painfully accumulated and pleasurably discharged.

23. See page 30.

24. In Draft E. Freud provides a full list of the sexual causes of anxiety neurosis (Freud, 1894, p. 79).

25. As indicated before the issue of the organic basis for all the neuroses has been a long-time preoccupation of Freud. It also came up in a

discussion 7 years earlier in a meeting of the Vienna Psychoanalytic Society which was held on 1 June 1910. In the minutes of that meeting the following remarkable sentence can be read: "Besides, the theory of the neuroses never was a purely psychological one, for sexuality is indeed, also an organic factor" (Nunberg & Federn, 1967, pp. 564–565).
26. Like jouissance the concept of the real is complex and will be explored in detail in this work. For the time being it will suffice to say that the real refers to those aspects of human existence that resist understanding or symbolization and are therefore unbearable and traumatic. The real is the limit to any human activity.
27. For this the reader is referred to Chapter 8.

CHAPTER FOUR

Freud's war during the "inter-bellum": the death-drive and the extermination of happiness

> "But I took it:—and in an hour, oh heavens! What a revulsion! What an upheaving, from its lowest depths, of the inner spirit! What an apocalypse of the world within me! That my pains had vanished, was now a trifle in my eyes:—this negative effect was swallowed up in the immensity of those positive effects which had opened before me in the abyss of divine enjoyment thus suddenly revealed. Here was a panacea for all human woes: here was the secret of happiness, about which philosophers had disputed for so many years, at once discovered: a happiness might now be bought for a penny, and carried in the waistcoat pocket: portable ecstasies might be had corked up in a pint bottle: and peace of mind could be sent down in gallons by the mail coach"
>
> T. De Quincey, *Confessions of an English Opium Eater*, p. 71

Beyond the limit and back to masturbation

In 1920 Freud published *Beyond the Pleasure Principle*. In this article he made it clear that there was something disturbing the pleasure principle, which simply states that accumulation of tension is unpleasant or painful and the reduction of tension or relaxation is agreeable or pleasurable. He discovered that sometimes people pursue something more and beyond the limits of pleasure and the name he gave to the pursuit of this something more was the death-drive. He named it thus because, as a pursuit, it is neither in the service of human life nor in the service of the common good. The pleasure principle is a failure for both the individual subject as well as for society at large. The problem of pleasure and the question of the death-drive will be explored further, as both concepts are crucial for an understanding of the use of drugs and alcohol from a psychoanalytic perspective. It is most peculiar that Freud did not refer to drugs, alcohol, toxic substances and addiction at all in this article. It was only in 1930, when he published *Civilization and its Discontents*, that he openly addressed the questions of pleasure and happiness in relation to the use of drugs (1930a).

In two studies published in 1925, *An Autobiographical Study* and *The Resistances to Psychoanalysis*, Freud made some statements about intoxication that were similar in content and add little to what he had said so far about addiction and intoxication. In the first article he wrote:

> There must also have been good reason why the true spontaneous neuroses resembled no group of diseases more closely than the phenomena of intoxication and abstinence, which are produced by the administration or privation of certain toxic substances, or than exopthalmic goitre, which is known to depend upon the product of the thyroid gland (Freud, 1925d, p. 25).

This was followed in the second article by:

> From a clinical stand point the neuroses must necessarily be put alongside the intoxications and such disorders as Graves' disease. There are conditions arising from an excess or a relative lack of certain highly active substances, whether produced inside the body or introduced into it from outside—in short, they are disturbances of the chemistry of the body, toxic conditions (Freud, 1925e, pp. 214–215).

These remarks confirm Freud's belief in the existence of toxic substances in the body that cause suffering; they also confirm his hope that some day we will find the true nature of these substances. The point to be emphasized here is that these toxic substances can be administered (or distributed) and that they can undergo quantitative changes which may cause an excess or a lack of something. In that sense, as Freud seemed to suggest, the neuroses and addictions differ very little; indeed perhaps they do not differ at all. Despite the fact that Freud added little to what he had said with these remarks, they are nevertheless interesting in so far as Freud stressed the factors of administration, excess and lack. It is obvious that these factors play a dominant role in the clinical picture of addiction. We will also demonstrate that they are building-bricks for a psychoanalytic theory of addiction.

In *The Future of an Illusion* from 1927, Freud was interested in the theme of the antagonism between man and civilization, the problem being that because man finds it difficult to reconcile himself with his fate, contentment eludes him. Freud wondered why it was that man tries to find a solution in religion rather than in reason and science. To an imaginary adversary, who argued against Freud's position, he attributed the following questions: "Since men are so little accessible to reasonable arguments and are so entirely governed by their instinctual wishes, why should one set out to deprive them of an instinctual satisfaction and replace it by reasonable arguments? It is true that men are like this; but have you asked yourself whether they must be like this, whether their innermost nature necessitates it?" (Freud, 1927c, p. 47). Freud's objection to these tendentious questions was simply that one should at least try to find an alternative to the "religious prohibition of thought" (Ibid., p. 48). He did agree, however, on the one point that it would not make sense to take religion away from people by force. He said:

> And even if this did succeed with some, it would still be cruel. A man who has been taking sleeping draughts for ten years is naturally unable to sleep if his sleeping draught is taken away from him. That the effect of religious consolations may be likened to that of a narcotic is well illustrated by what is happening in America. There they are now trying—obviously under the influence of petticoat government—to deprive people of all stimulants, intoxicants, and other pleasure-producing substances, and instead, by way of compensation, are surfeiting them with piety. This is another experiment as to whose outcome we need not feel curious. Thus I must contradict you when you go on to argue that men are completely unable to do without the consolation of the religious

illusion, that without it they could not bear the troubles of life and the cruelties of reality. That is true, certainly, of the men into whom you have instilled the sweet—or bittersweet—poison from childhood onwards. But what of the other men, who have been sensibly brought up? Perhaps those who do not suffer from the neurosis will need no intoxicant to deaden it. They will, it is true, find themselves in a difficult situation. They will have to admit to themselves the full extent of their helplessness and their insignificance in the machinery of the universe; they can no longer be the centre of creation, no longer the object of tender care on the part of a beneficent Providence. They will be in the same position as a child who has left the parental house where he was so warm and comfortable. Men cannot remain children forever; they must in the end go out into "hostile life". We may call this "education to reality". Need I confess to you that the sole purpose of my book is to point out the necessity for this forward step? (Ibid., p. 49).

It only becomes clear what this "education to reality" actually means towards the very end of this book where he reveals the real purpose of this work. He finishes the book by saying: "No, our science is no illusion. But an illusion it would be to suppose that what science cannot give us we can get elsewhere" (Ibid., p. 56). By that he means that the only way of making progress is through science, but—and this is crucial—progress can only be made based on a conception of science that includes psychoanalysis or the unconscious. Freud's conception of the unconscious is an ethical one. That means that man has to work hard at making unconscious knowledge conscious by assuming subjective responsibility for the experiences that have marked him or her. Moreover, man has to accept the hostility and futility of human reality and life. Man has to let go of motherly care and homely protection. In the above quote Freud indicates that anything that allows man to keep up the illusion that this can be avoided is welcome. To put this differently: anything that allows man to avoid castration or to avoid the prohibition of incest is pursued with a great passion. This is where drugs and religion (as the opiate of the people) find a place. That is why Freud is confident that the "American Prohibition" is doomed to failure. But he is equally aware of the danger of taking these "consolations" away from people. They serve a purpose in that they resolve an unconscious conflict. In that sense they are a symptom and must be "worked through" rather than "cut out". In a very short but extremely interesting article called *Humour*, from 1927, Freud wrote:

> These last two features—the rejection of the claims of reality and the putting through of the pleasure principle—bring humour near to the regressive or reactionary processes which engage our attention so extensively in psychopathology. Its fending off of the possibility of suffering places it among the great series of methods which the human mind has constructed in order to evade the compulsion to suffer—a series which begins with neurosis and culminates in madness and which includes intoxication, self-absorption and ecstasy (Freud, 1927d, p. 163).

Since writing *Remembering, Repeating and Working Through* in 1914(g), Freud had known that people are sometimes compelled to repeat aspects of their unconscious despite the fact that this brings them suffering. And since *Beyond the Pleasure Principle*, he had understood that pleasure is not the only aim in human life and that the compulsion to repeat can be a compulsion to suffer. In *The Economic Problem of Masochism*, he wrote: "If pain and unpleasure can be not simply warnings but actually aims, the pleasure principle is paralysed—it is as though the watchman over our mental life were put out of action by a drug" (Freud, 1924c, p. 159). The watchman is not very good at his work and is easily distracted by the promise of a drug. Humans are in conflict because they are compelled to go beyond the limit of pleasure into a realm that causes them suffering. This conflict can lead to the psychopathology of using drugs or alcohol. The use of drugs here does not aim at paralysing the pleasure principle, but aim instead at paralysing the compulsion to suffer in the realm beyond pleasure. In this case the use of drugs aims at the death-drive. In other words, it aims at reactivating the pleasure principle or, as Freud said of the function of humour, it aims at "the putting through of the pleasure principle". And with that aim comes "the rejection of the claims of reality". To favour the pleasure principle is to disfavour the reality principle (at least in this context). There is no drug available (yet) that can favour the reality principle, but it is without a doubt the case that the effect of drugs or alcohol can paralyse the reality principle.

It is important to mention this, as this form of drug or alcohol use has more to do with the escape from the hardships of social reality than with the conflicts in the subject caused by the compulsion to suffer. In what way does humour differ from all these pathological solutions? Humour also rejects reality to some degree and favours the pleasure principle. Freud explains humour by saying that the humorist changes the psychical accent from the ego to the superego and in this movement the reactions of the ego are diminished (Freud, 1927d, p. 164). The ego is at the mercy of the superego and the latter will be able to dictate how the former will behave and feel. Normally that would lead to intense moral conflict for the subject as the ego has difficulty living up to the ideal set by the superego.[1] What happens in humour is that the superego says: "Look! Here is the world! It seems so dangerous, but it is actually nothing but a game for children—its only worth is that one can make a jest about it!" (Ibid., p. 166). Humour is a way of protecting the ego from suffering, but it is a way of consoling that not everyone is capable of. Freud stated that this does not contradict the fact that the superego originated from the parental agency (Ibid.). Our capacity for humour, as well as our propensity for the pathology of addiction, is embedded in the family story. The story of the latter needs a desire to be told, the former tell their own story.[2] Freud made it clear that humour produces a relatively small amount of pleasure, and that it is something that takes place between people. These two aspects stand in complete opposition to the "self-absorption" and search for "ecstasy" that we encounter so often in addicts.

The following year Freud returned to the relationship between addiction and masturbation in his study of the Russian writer Dostoevsky. This study consists of two parts. The first part deals with Dostoevsky's ambivalent relationship to his father, his deep sense of guilt, his epileptic attacks, his need for self-punishment and his masochism. The second part deals with Dostoevsky's passion for gambling as a reaction against a compulsion to masturbate. Freud wondered what aspect of the childhood of a gambler is repeated in the game (Freud, 1928b, p. 191). He found an answer in a story called *Vierundzwanzig Stunden aus dem Leben einer Frau* (Twenty Four Hours in a Woman's Life) written by the novelist Stefan Zweig.[3] The answer is something of a surprise.

Masturbation never lets go

Briefly summarized, the story by Zweig goes as follows: A woman in her forties, widowed at a young age and with two sons, visits the gaming rooms in Monte Carlo. There she is struck by a pair of hands that seem to reveal an unlucky gambler; a handsome man of the same age as her eldest son. The gambler leaves the room in despair after having lost everything. The woman follows the young man and in an effort to save him she approaches him. He tries to shake her off thinking she is a prostitute. However, she persists and eventually they go to his apartment where they go to bed. The next day she gets him to promise her that he will never gamble again. She gives him money for the train to go home and arranges to meet him at the train station before he leaves. Suddenly she realizes that she really loves him and she changes her mind. Instead of saying goodbye she decides to join him. A number of things go wrong and she misses the train. In her longing for the lost young man she returns once more to the gaming rooms and there she is confronted with the horror of seeing the hands that had gone back to play. She reminded him of his promise, but consumed by his passion to play he throws the money that she had given him at her. Later she hears that he had committed suicide. End of story!

In his analysis of the story, Freud revealed that it was based on the fantasy of young boys who hope that their mother will initiate them into sexual life in order to save them from the harm of masturbation (Ibid., p. 193). He wrote:

> The "vice" of masturbation is replaced by the addiction to gambling; and the emphasis laid upon the passionate activity of the hands betrays this derivation. Indeed, the passion for play is an equivalent of the old compulsion to masturbate; "playing" is the actual word used in the nursery to describe the activity of the hands upon the genitals. The irresistible nature of the temptation, the solemn resolutions, which are nevertheless invariably broken, never to do it again, the stupefying pleasure and the bad conscience which tells the subject that he is ruining himself (committing suicide)—all these elements remain unaltered in the process of substitution (Ibid.).

Freud concluded that the narrative hides the analytical truth that the fantasy of the boy can sometimes coincide with an unconscious desire in the mother. This unconscious desire is the love for her son and, in this story, "Fate" led to the realization of this desire and the lethal consequences for the son (Ibid., p. 194). The fantasy of the boy is a most peculiar rescue fantasy. It is the fantasy to be rescued from masturbation through incest. As implied out earlier, there is a connection between masturbation and incest in Freud's thinking. Dostoevsky experienced conflict between early infantile desires (masturbatory ones and incestuous ones) and the wish to suppress these. The guilt of giving in to the temptation (for masturbation and incest) and the fear (of castration) that would suppress the temptation, expressed itself in the ambivalent feelings towards his father as the agent of prohibition. The addiction to gambling and the struggle to give it up is a repetition of this ambivalence and conflict. Dostoevsky was a compulsive gambler because he needed the dynamic between fear and guilt in order to be able to live through and live with his conflict. Chapter 6 will demonstrate that the oscillation between fear and guilt forms an essential part of the clinical picture of compulsive gambling. Let's return to Freud's thinking on the question of masturbation (and its relationship to addiction and incest) in order to further substantiate earlier remarks about the subject and in order to clarify the connection between masturbation, gambling, and addiction in general.

The question of masturbation is a very complex one. Masturbation is neither a conceptual nor a clinical unit. Freud said that if we treat masturbation as a clinical unit (and not as something that relates to the various and component aspects of the sexual life of the subject) the problem of masturbation becomes insoluble (Freud, 1909d, p. 202). In other words, it is only possible to diagnose masturbation as harmful on condition that it is analysed in relation to other aspects of the subject's (sexual) life and history. Masturbation is not just the frantic activity that some boys and girls are capable of during puberty (and perhaps long after). It goes back to infantile sexuality and includes all kinds of auto-erotic activities.[4] Freud thought that the relationship between (pubertal) masturbation and infantile sexuality was of enormous importance. He wrote in lecture 33 from *New Introductory Lectures on Psycho-Analysis* that "masturbation is the executive agent of infantile sexuality" and he indicated that the facts surrounding infantile masturbation greatly influence the development of the neurosis of the subject (Freud, 1933a, p. 127).[5]

Thus, it is no wonder that he concluded a discussion on masturbation by saying that the subject of masturbation is quite inexhaustible (Freud, 1912f, p. 254).

In *Contributions to a Discussion on Masturbation* Freud stated that damage due to masturbation can occur in three different ways: (1) organic injury may take place; (2) a damaging psychical pattern might develop; and (3) a fixation of infantile sexual aims may occur (Ibid., pp. 251–252). As an "inadequate" form of sexual activity, masturbation can cause a deficiency in the processing of somatic sexual stimuli or physical sexual energies. These "unprocessed" somatic stimuli or energies become toxic and may cause harm in the subject or else the masturbatory activity may use up energy that could have been employed elsewhere.[6] One way or another, because of the interplay between certain behaviour and organic or bodily processes, the subject becomes neurasthenic. The second and third ways in which damage might be done due to masturbation are purely psychological.

The damaging psychological pattern that might develop is a pattern, as Freud wrote, "according to which there is no necessity to alter the external world in order to satisfy a great need" (Ibid., p. 252). In the minutes of a meeting of the Vienna Psychoanalytic Society which was held on 13 November 1907, the same damage is described in different words: "The damaging effect of masturbation is due mainly to a short-circuit: the shortcut between desire and fulfillment. As a consequence the individual stops exerting himself and the external world loses its importance for him" (Nunberg & Federn, 1962, pp. 239–240). Freud mentioned the idea of masturbation as a short cut between desire and satisfaction, allowing the subject to bypass the external world, again in a meeting of 18 November 1908 (Nunberg & Federn, 1967, p. 61). This idea is absolutely crucial for understanding certain aspects of addiction. It has been pointed out before that both masturbation and addiction can produce pleasures for the subject in a manner that is independent of the Other and that they can provide the illusion that there is pleasure to be obtained that is not curtailed or limited by the social bond. This allows one to understand that some addictions function as a social "short-circuit" symptom and contains the desire to pursue a pleasure beyond normal pleasure. This is a form of addiction that tries to break away from the "cut" of castration, that is to say, it tries to regain what had to be given up, or was lost, as the result of castration.

When masturbation leads to a fixation of infantile sexual aims, a neurosis might eventually be the result. For Freud this result of masturbation was extremely important (Freud, 1912f, p. 252). This is the kind of masturbation that occurs in puberty and is accompanied by fantasy. Here, the act of masturbation is attached to a *vorstellung* (a representation) and it is therefore, strictly speaking, not of an auto-erotic nature like infantile masturbation. Freud suggested that this kind of masturbation is important because it leads to fantasy as a compromise mechanism which attempts to reconcile the pleasure principle with the reality principle (Ibid., p. 252). Freud did not give a very clear explanation as to why this connection between masturbation and fantasy could be so injurious for the subject. Nevertheless, it is important to understand what Freud was aiming at in order to make sense of his remarks concerning the relationship between masturbation and the addiction to gambling in the context of his analysis of the "Dostoevsky Case". In the actual minutes of the meeting of the Vienna Psychoanalytic Society in which the damage of masturbation was discussed extensively, one reads that Freud spoke in greater detail about the relationship between fantasy and masturbation. He claimed that injuries come about for a number of reasons, and although he provided a list, there was only one reason that was crucial,[7] and that was because it clarified what was at stake in the game of the relationship between masturbation and addiction: Freud said that injuries came about "as a result of the fact that masturbatory activity is to be regarded as identical with the preservation of the infantile condition in every respect." He continued: "Therein lies the main psychic harmfulness of masturbation, because with it there has been created the basis for a psychoneurosis, which sets in when conflict and rejection are added" (Nunberg & Federn, 1967, p. 562). In an earlier discussion on *Sexual Enlightenment*, Freud had said the following concerning masturbation: "Neurotics are persons who in fantasy have not arrived at a detachment from their first objects; and it is from this content of primitive fantasies that all their feelings of repression follow. For persons who can detach these fantasies from father, mother etc., masturbation has no psychological consequences. They also make an early transition to real objects. Thus the harmfulness of masturbation goes back to the incompatibility of the first object choice" (Ibid., p. 229).

It is clear that it is not masturbation itself that causes all the problems. The real cause is the position of the subject, a position in which masturbation can come to function as a detrimental, injurious symptom; a symptom that is not unlike addiction. The regular attempts to stop only demonstrate the inability to do so. This is the tragic dilemma that the young man had to face in the story by Stefan Zweig. He wanted to stop gambling but couldn't. Freud's interpretation was that he was caught in a conflict between an incestuous sexual desire and the wish to find another sexual object. This young man had not been able to detach himself enough from his first object choice and so his mother became his unconscious object of fantasy. However, this "too much" of the incestuous relationship had to be "cut short" with the game of chance which he was unconsciously predestined to lose in order to create an artificial lack (i.e., the loss of money) in this overwhelming sexual bind. In this kind of (incestuous) bind, an artificial lack has to be created because the loss of loss (as in the case of melancholia), or the lack of distance from the incestuous object, is unbearable for the subject. The game of chance is, in this sense, perfectly consistent with the act of masturbation. If the game of chance creates an artificial limit to the incestuous bind with "Lady Luck", so does the act of masturbation when the unconscious position of the subject is still dependent on the original object choice. The masturbator unconsciously "knows" the human limit to pleasure as he or she produces it all the time rhythmically. Masturbation is a compromise solution between an incestuous desire and the fear produced by the possibility of the realization of this desire.[8] Addiction and masturbation can be ways of avoiding depression (melancholia), pain, and anxiety. The hypothesis is this: when Freud connected masturbation to addiction, he did so to demonstrate the existence of a fundamental and internal impotence in humans for experiencing pleasure.

The thesis proposed here, that the masturbation issue played a very important, even central role, in Freud's thinking, is illustrated by the fact that he returned to it towards the very end of his life. On 3 August, 1938, Freud made some notes on masturbation. These notes were part of a series of notes that he wrote not long before he died and which were posthumously published in 1941 under the heading: *Findings, Ideas, Problems*. He wrote:

> The ultimate ground of all intellectual inhibition and all inhibitions

of work seems to be the inhibition of masturbation in childhood. But perhaps it goes deeper; perhaps it is not its inhibition by external influences but its unsatisfying nature in itself. There is always something lacking for complete discharge and satisfaction—*en attendant toujours quelquechose qui ne venait point* (always waiting for something which never came)—and this missing part, the reaction of orgasm, manifests itself in equivalents in other spheres, in absences, outbreaks of laughing, weeping, and perhaps other ways. Once again infantile sexuality has fixed a model in this (Freud, 1941f, p. 300).

The first sentence of this quote indicates that (intellectual) work is a sublimation of infantile sexual activity and it implies that if children were given the unrestricted freedom to indulge in these activities they would work in a much more productive way as adults.[9] The prohibition of sexual activity and masturbation would lead to repression, and maintaining repression causes an expenditure of energy that could be detrimental to work and intellectual activity later in life. Unlimited sexual freedom for children would save energy and this could be put to work. If only this was possible. Freud stated that there was something in the very nature of masturbation itself (and therefore in infantile sexuality) that is problematic or unsatisfactory. There is something lacking that cannot be discharged, there is something missing in the orgasm itself that falls short of complete satisfaction. And this surplus-energy, this more-to-be-enjoyed, this something that lies waiting to be used usefully and pleasantly, finds itself manifested or perhaps wasted away in laughter, crying and other "psychopathologies of everyday life".

Again, a forerunner of Lacan's "object a" can be detected. It is the cause in the subject of his or her impotence for pleasure, that is to say, for a pleasure that would not be "missing any part", that would not look for anything more and that would ultimately be based on a complete discharge of energy. This fundamental impotence hides the impossibility for complete freedom in work and indeed perhaps all other aspects of human existence. What is this impotence? It can only be the constitution of the subject in the realm of language and culture. This constitution is a process of having to let go of an incestuous oneness with the mother compensated by an orientation towards the law as a symbolic representative of the (name) of the father. The price we pay for this loss and orientation is our disease in culture. This is our fundamental incapacity to be totally happy.

Dis-ease in culture and an ideal as remedy

Freud's text *Civilization and its Discontents* from 1930, is a text that deals with the human inability for happiness. In relation to this inability, and our ways of trying to cope with it, Freud wrote:

> The programme of becoming happy, which the pleasure principle imposes on us, cannot be fulfilled; yet we must not—indeed, we cannot—give up our efforts to bring it nearer to fulfilment by some means or other. Very different paths may be taken in that direction and we may give priority either to the positive aspect of the aim, that of gaining pleasure, or to its negative one, that of avoiding unpleasure. By none of these paths can we attain all that we desire. Happiness, in the reduced sense in which we recognize it as possible, is a problem of the economics of the individual's libido. There is no golden rule that is applicable to everyone: every man must find out for himself in what particular fashion he can be saved (Freud, 1930a, p. 83).

If nothing works for man in his search for happiness, he can in the end always depend on, what Freud called, "the pleasure of chronic intoxication" (Ibid., p. 84). In *Civilization and its Discontents* Freud referred to addiction and intoxication more frequently than in any other of his texts. These remarks will not be analysed here. The implications of these remarks are so substantial and crucial for a (Lacanian) theory of addiction that it is justified to withhold analysis until Part III, where elements are brought together for such a theory. Instead, we will analyse other aspects of this text which form, after all, the basis for Freud's remarks on addiction in this text, and are also relevant for a psychoanalytic understanding of addiction. Moreover, as Lacan says in his Seminar on Ethics, "*Civilization and its Discontents* is an indispensable work, unsurpassed for an understanding of Freud's thought and the summation of his experience. It illuminates, emphasizes, dissipates the ambiguities of wholly distinct points of the analytical experience and of what our view of man should be..." (Lacan, 1992, p. 7). Addiction, as a fundamental human experience, has to be included in this view of man.

The text can be divided into three parts. The first part, in which all of Freud's references to addiction and intoxication occur, deals with the question of happiness and the difficulties people have in experiencing pleasure. Freud indicated that we are destined to suffer from our ageing and ailing bodies, from the natural world, which can be dangerous, and from the always-problematic social aspect of our existence (Freud, op. cit., p. 77). All three sources of suffering are limitations to the aim of the pleasure principle. Unrestricted and immediate satisfaction of the drives would yield the greatest form of pleasure, but that is not realistic and therefore suffering cannot be avoided. So what can we do to avoid, or rather lessen, our suffering? Freud gave nine possibilities to alleviate suffering (pp. 77–85). One way of "managing" suffering is by influencing the drives through the use of drugs.[10]

The second part of the text deals with the question of civilization. For Freud civilization is a way of regulating the relationships between people. In other words, it is a way of regulating the pleasures that we can have and the ones, indeed, that we can not have. A large part of civilization has to do with the management of an economy of libido and drives. An important aspect of civilization is that one has to renounce some of the satisfaction of these drives. The regulations of our relationships with others severely restrict possibilities for happiness. It is a most peculiar paradox that one should suffer from something that attempts to make things possible between people. Even science and religion have not been able to help very much in this respect. We have made extraordinary progress through scientific endeavours and we have gained much greater control over nature, but none of these achievements have made man much happier. The threat from the external world is clearly not the greatest cause of our suffering. Man is now closer to being in the position of God, because scientific progress has made possible the achievement of what was hitherto thought possible only on the basis of divine intervention. But, as Freud claimed, man does not feel happy in his Godlike character (Ibid., p. 92). Thus, religion doesn't do it for man either. The renunciation of libidinal satisfaction that is demanded by religion, has to be compensated by a blind faith in a (cultural) ideal. It is relevant to mention science and religion in this discussion, because it will be demonstrated later that the thirst for scientific explanations and the identification of, and indeed with, an ideal, are important characteristics of the clinical picture of addiction. What all civilizations have in common is the fact that the individual demand for happiness has to negotiate with the cultural demands for regulation and distribution of pleasure. In what way does civilization demand this regulation and distribution? Freud's answer was: "Thou shalt love thy neighbour as thyself". It is not difficult to recognize that, behind this cultural ideal, one finds the existence of its very opposite, namely, human aggression. People are not very nice and, in fact, they are ultimately quite happy to use others, inflict pain and kill for their own pleasure. But let's thank the "Heavens Above" that this is not the only tendency in people. There is the other tendency in people (and civilization) that looks to combine individuals, that wants to create unity and ultimately aims at a total oneness of mankind. This human tendency is in the service of Eros, whilst the previous tendency serves Thanatos. Freud stated that the meaning of the evolution of civilization is the struggle between Eros and destruction, that is to say, between the life or sex drive and the death-drive (Ibid., p. 122). Thus far Freud had not said anything startling. The tone and direction of the text change after he wondered why it was that only humans experience that peculiar cultural struggle and not animals (p. 123). This question introduces the third part of the text which is complicated and theoretical. It deals with his concepts of a "sense of guilt" and the "superego".

In the third part of the text, Freud questions how it is possible that civilization is able to curtail the death-drive and aggression. He claims that aggression is turned inwards and introjected. Aggression is now aiming at the ego of the subject and in that way it fights against the desire for aggression. In other words, the struggle has been internalized. The battle rages on within the subject where the ego defends itself against the attacks on it by the superego. But how did this superego come about? It is clear that there is an extraneous factor at work, a factor that does not exist for animals. This factor is other people (the Other). In their state of "organic insufficiency" and helplessness, infants are totally dependent on this Other and they remain dependent on him or her for an unusually long time (at least when we compare this situation to animals).[11] There is initially a fear of the Other. This fear is of a twofold nature. There is fear of the loss of protection by this Other; this is ultimately a fear of loss of love, and it relates to the fact that this love or protection can be withdrawn or given up by the Other in an aggressive movement. The result is that the infant is exposed to all kinds of dangers. The relationships to the (parental) Other are always of an ambivalent nature. That is one of the reasons why the avoidance of the encounter with the Other—even later in life—is to some degree welcomed by certain subjects. It is an avoidance that is highly desired by addicts. When the fear of the Other is internalized into a fear of the superego, a most peculiar phenomenon occurs: the more the subject tries to comply with the demands of this internal Other, i.e., the more virtuous he or she tries to be, the more guilty, sinful or anxious he or she will feel. There is a paradox in that the seeming renunciation of the satisfaction of sexual or aggressive drives leads to an even greater sense of guilt or anxiety. This is a guilt and an anxiety that is much greater than the anxiety or guilt that originally caused the renunciation.

Freud's explanation of this paradox sets psychoanalysis apart from the other (human) sciences in two ways. Firstly, the fact that people experience more guilt and anxiety after giving up on their desire for satisfaction is a clinical fact that can only be discovered (*züfallig*, or, as if by accident) by one's being open to hearing it, that is, by being receptive to being surprised. This is something that goes so much against common sense logic, or the scientific desire for predictability, that one tends to miss the significance of what is unconsciously conveyed through what people actually say concerning the issues around this fact or, indeed, what they reveal about it in their behaviour. Secondly, the implication behind Freud's explanation, as mentioned before, is that the relationship between inside and outside is not straightforward in psychoanalysis. What is outside can be incorporated and what is inside can be projected outwards. How does Freud explain the aforementioned paradox? He looks at the development of the superego and the sense of guilt in the child. Because this Other wants to curtail the sexual satisfaction that the child derives from its drives,[12] the child has aggressive feelings towards the Other; but, the child must now also renounce the aggression that is directed against this Other. How does the child resolve this problem? The child takes the authority into itself; it incorporates the element of prohibition from the Other, that is to say, the law that was the original object of aggression. This law—or rather—the representative of this law becomes the superego of the child after having been incorporated. This superego takes over all the aggression that the child originally had expressed against the external object, namely the Other that was the law before it was incorporated.

All this still does not explain why every renunciation of satisfaction leads to further guilt and anxiety. It is, however, explained when one realizes that every renunciation will only lead to more desire and this desire cannot be hidden anymore from the authority. The reason for this is obvious: the authority has been internalized and is now part of the subject. The superego keeps a close watch over this economy of desire. The price we pay for partaking in civilization is a sense of guilt and anxiety, and the loss of happiness. It is the internalized law that regulates our pleasures, desires, and aggressions. This law regulates civilization, but it tears the subject apart at the same time in a way that is fundamental and beyond repair. The struggle between the dependency on authority for its love and the aggressive desire for instinctual satisfaction is reflected in the battle between the desire for unification and the desire for personal happiness. This struggle is about the economics of libido and, more specifically, this struggle concerns the distribution of libido between ego and objects (Ibid., p. 141). There is absolutely no doubt about the fact that drugs, and addictions in general, play a huge role on this battlefield.

In the last paragraph of *Civilization and its Discontents*, Freud introduced the idea that a civilization might develop a "cultural superego" (Ibid., pp. 141–144). As it is no doubt the case that a community of people can set up ideals and demands for the individual subjects, this concept needs little justification. One of those cultural demands of the subject is to keep pleasure, or the satisfaction of the drives, within the limits of what is socially permissible. This renunciation of the satisfaction of aggressive and sexual impulses is at the service of the regulation of the relationships between people. This commanding aspect of the cultural superego is antagonistic to the happiness of the individual subject and, in that sense, it ignores, as Freud said, "the facts of the mental constitution of human beings" (p. 143). Man has to make enormous sacrifices in order to be part of the human community. Beyond certain limits it becomes difficult to control the drive for libidinal satisfaction. The thesis proposed here is the following: this sacrifice can be made providing there is compensation available. This compensation is available in the form of a second aspect of the cultural superego. As just indicated, the first aspect concerns the cultural demands for restraint and renunciation by the subject.

The second aspect concerns the identification with cultural ideals.[13] This process of identification leads to an aspect of the superego of the subject that is called the ego-ideal. The setting up of an ego-ideal is the necessary compensation for the sacrifices that are demanded of the subject. In other words, these ideals compensate for the loss (of object of satisfaction) that is demanded by the Other. The demand of the Other is difficult to negotiate for the subject. Freud wrote: "If more is demanded of a man, a revolt will be produced in him or a neurosis, or he will be made unhappy" (Ibid.). In that case the identification with—or the dependence on—an ideal, an ideology or a masterful figure can function as a remedy for the deficiency in happiness and loss of pleasure.

Bearing in mind that the demand of the Other results in lost satisfaction, which itself becomes an object of desire for the subject, what happens when the ideal of the subject and the result of the demand of the Other appear in the same place? An answer to this question depends on what the representative or incarnation of the ideal is. There are many possibilities as to what can represent or incarnate the ideal for the subject. There are four possibilities that are of interest here: if the representative is another person we have a hypnotic relationship; if the representative is an idea, or system of ideas, we have a (scientific) ideology; if the representative is the incarnation of the final truth we have religion; and finally, if the incarnation is a consumable object we have addiction or dependency. Addiction, in this sense, is a dissolution of the superego or an eclipse of the ego-ideal. It will be demonstrated in Chapter 9 that the attempt by the subject to merge the ego-ideal with the object creates a specific social bond of addiction. In the present context it is relevant to refer to the fact that the recovery process of addicts is often tinged with ideological or religious overtones and that treatments often base themselves on a (moral) ideal. Let's conclude this analysis of *Civilization and its Discontents* with a question. If Freud's superego represents the command for prohibition and renunciation, what does the superego represent around the turn of our millennium? In order to provide a satisfactory answer to this question, it will be necessary to leave it until we have processed some of Lacan's ideas. First, however, a brief encounter with a world leader from the not too distant past.

Woodrow Wilson lacked neither a severe superego nor a strong ego-ideal. Consequently, he was a driven, but profoundly unhappy man, who collapsed mentally and physically on a number of occasions, but these were not his only achievements. He was the president of the United States of America and he signed the Versaille Peace Treaty. In his role as president of the most powerful state in the world, and in his role as "peacekeeper", Wilson's influence was enormous and it was immediately felt as such in Europe. The curious relationship between his achievements and his profound neurosis is probably what prompted Freud to collaborate with Wilson's "friend", the American ambassador Bullitt, on this study of Wilson.[14]

This collaboration eventually produced a dreadful book that seems devoid of ideas and inspiration. The book is nothing but the "wild", rigid, and repetitive application of (only a few) Freudian notions to the personal and political life of Wilson. It was written over a period of a number of years in the 1930s and a final draft was produced in 1938.[15] The book is interesting in that it shows that an ego-ideal is not only able to disarm a crushing demand of the super-ego, but it can even lead to major achievements when channelled properly. However, Wilson's unhappiness and near loss of sanity illustrate that this does not usually happen without paying a price. Throughout the book Freud and Bullitt describe how Wilson looked up to his father, how he identified with him as an ideal and how, at the same time, he aggressively tried to fight his dependency on him. Wilson's father was a Presbyterian minister and so, on the basis of the process of identification with his father, the influence of religious ideals remained with him for the rest of his life. Wilson was so deeply caught up in the ambivalent and passive feelings towards his father that it consumed nearly all his libido. The result was that he had very little time (or sexual drive) left for women. His libido became exclusively concentrated on the relationships with men, who eventually replaced his father as the libidinal object of his attentions.[16] Wilson, as an obsessional neurotic, did not become an addict. His religious and political ideals not only pacified the drive produced by the demand of the (parental) Other, but combined themselves with this drive and turned it into a tornado of motivation and aspiration. For a study that concerns itself with a character who was completely ruled by habit formation, it is, to say the least, interesting to note that there are only two references to addiction in the entire book. The first reference is related to speech-making:

But after his father's death his addiction to speech-making, which was already excessive, grew to fantastic proportions; his desire for a friend to love became an imperative need; and his interest in all forms of religious activity increased. It is obvious that the loss of major outlets for his passivity to his father had put severe pressure on its minor outlets and increased the evacuation of libido through speech-making, passionate friendship, submission to God and identification with Christ (Freud & Bullitt, 1966, p. 112).

This quote underlines the fact that Wilson's addiction (to speech-making) was related to the ambivalent nature of the relationship to his father and that his addiction was an identification with an ideal (or unary) trait in the father. Wilson's father, being a Presbyterian minister, had to make speeches and sermons all the time. Freud's reference to Wilson's addiction implies that some addictions can be based on an identification with someone. This kind of addiction is a symptom that is symbolically structured. Speech-making is of course a very symbolic activity. Addiction to speech-making is a perfect example of a symptom as an appeal to the Other.[17] This is different from most other forms of addiction, because most other forms of addiction (the toxicomanias) attempt to avoid the encounter with the Other by taking the toxic shortcut via the body. The second reference to addiction in this study is related to alcoholism:

Determination which springs from the superego is often as powerless as the determination of the habitual drunkard to abandon drink (Freud & Bullitt, 1966, p. 235).

It is often proclaimed by supporters of the "disease concept" of addiction, and the adherents of the anonymous self-help groups, that the addict is helpless in the confrontation with alcohol and drugs, and that the only way to recover is to admit that the power of drugs or alcohol is overwhelming and to accept defeat. Accepting powerlessness allows the addicts to abstain from drugs or alcohol, but in order for this to work one has to adhere to what is called a "Higher Power".[18] The external or internal command to abstain is not enough for the addict and this renunciation has to be compensated by the identification with—or adherence to—an internal or external ideal. Willpower and self-determination are not sufficient when abstinence and renunciation are the objects of recovery. Equally, as mentioned before, the renunciations and lack, caused by the demand of the superego, often require an (ego) ideal or idealization. Determination that springs from the superego does not work because that determination is related to an irretrievable loss (the demand of the Other as the cause of one's desire). Determination implies a terminus, a final solution, a total satisfaction of desire. Total satisfaction of desire would imply the annihilation of what is typically human in the subject. That is why it is possible to say that the determination springing from the superego is the death-drive. This determination is powerless because it wants to find total satisfaction and eliminate desire. It fails because this determination implies a move beyond the pleasure principle into the realm of death.

Let's finish this exploration of Freud by briefly (re)turning to the question as to why it is the case that not all humans are addicted. This is certainly a legitimate question, especially when considering that our lot in life is one of unease and lack of satisfaction and, to be frank, it can easily be accepted that drugs and alcohol are immediate and very effective ways of alleviating suffering. Related to this question is another question: what kind of science can take as its object the unease-causing-remainder that is produced in the encounter between the subject and culture? It certainly cannot be a science that forecloses the investigation of a subject who has to come to terms with this remainder. Neither can it be the kind of science that produces objects which, on incorporation, wipe away the unease-causing-remainder.

At the very beginning of his career Freud thought he had found such an object, but, for very good reasons, he lost it. It was the loss of faith in the existence of such an object that allowed Freud to discover psychoanalysis as a theory and a treatment that includes the subject and his or her responsibility. In Part II the post-Freudian field will be explored in terms of addiction. An analysis of this field will, curiously enough, demonstrate the necessity for an inclusion of the subject in the theory and treatment of addiction.

Notes

1. The superego is an identification with an ideal.
2. The desire referred to here is the desire of the addict, but it is also the desire of the analyst or therapist to make the addict speak.
3. This story appeared in a collection of stories called *Die Verwirrung der Gefühle* (Confusion of feelings).

4. For a detailed exploration of infantile sexual behaviour as a masturbatory activity the reader is directed to Freud's paragraph called "Masturbatory sexual manifestations" from his *Three Essays on the Theory of Sexuality* (Freud, 1905d, pp. 185–193).
5. In the so-called "Ratman Case Study" Freud wrote: "The masturbation of puberty is in fact no more than a revival of the masturbation of infancy, a subject which has hitherto invariably been neglected. Infantile masturbation reaches a climax, as a rule, between the ages of three and four or five; and it is the clearest expression of a child's constitution, in which the aetiology of subsequent neuroses must be sought" (Freud, 1909d, p. 202).
6. The second possibility has been argued in a meeting of the Vienna Psychoanalytic Society and was worded as follows: "Another damaging result of masturbation lies in the consumption of energy used up in the internal struggle" (Nunberg & Federn, 1962, p. 240).
7. Injuries might come about for the following (less crucial) reasons: "through the preponderance of fantasy life over reality, a situation that forms a pattern for a number of other functions; through the excessive demands that the individual concerned, as the result of being spoiled by his fantasy, makes upon reality, which can never satisfy him; through the individual's inability to tolerate sexual restrictions, which life—especially married life—makes unavoidable; through the general debasement of sexual life, which results from the cheapness and easy availability of the sexual act and the social disdain attached to it. Masturbators of this type are thereafter unable to have intercourse with persons whom they love and esteem, but only with those whom they disdain" (Nunberg & Federn, 1967, p. 562).
8. A solution like this is illustrated by the example of an addict who in the depths of his despair sometimes used to masturbate non-stop in front of the sea in order (perhaps) to mark the impossibility of an oceanic feeling of oneness with his orgasms.
9. It is presumed that Freud here refers to masturbation as infantile sexual activity and not to the later forms of masturbation. A distinction he was keen on making several times.
10. The other eight possibilities are as follows: we can kill off the drives or master our internal needs through rigorous meditative practices or Eastern wisdom; we can control the drives with the help of a strong ego function; we can displace libido through sublimation and find satisfaction in art and science; we can find satisfaction by moving away from reality into the realms of illusion, imagination and fantasy; we can find happiness in isolation when others bring us trouble; we can change our reality in our mind through delusion of which religion is

one (a delusion) that is shared between people; we can displace our libido onto other people and find happiness in love and, lastly, we can find satisfaction in beauty and aesthetics.
11. Man is born prematurely, more prematurely than any other living being. It is on the basis of this fact that Lacan explains the existence of a mirror stage in the development of the human being as the basis for the formation and functioning of the ego (Lacan, 1977[1948], p. 4).
12. As indicated before, the prohibition of incestuous and masturbatory activities is a cultural necessity.
13. Freud does not make a strict distinction between the cultural ideals and the individual's ideals. He likens these ideals to the personalities of great leaders, Jesus Christ and the primal father (Freud, 1930a, pp. 141–142). From Freud's reference to the primal father we can infer that the ideal also, or perhaps especially, refers to the symbolic father as the representative of the law of culture or the prohibition of incest. The primal father was killed by the sons in order to gain access to all his possessions. But the criminal act resulted in the necessity of the law which could distribute the spoils and ultimately create a sense of community amongst them. For a detailed analysis of this story we refer the reader to Freud's Totem and Taboo (1912–1913).
14. In the foreword to their book Bullitt indicates that himself and Freud had been friends for a while and that the idea of a collaboration on a study of Wilson might have lifted Freud out of a state of depression and revived his spirits (Freud & Bullitt, 1966, p. v).
15. The book itself wasn't published until 1966.
16. This begs the question whether the additions that Freud wanted to make to the text and that Bullitt refused to accept point blank, alluded to the possibility that Wilson might have been fighting to keep a homosexuality latent for most of his life. Bullitt writes: "I carried the manuscript to Freud, and was delighted when he agreed to eliminate the additions he had written at the last minute, and we were both happy that we found no difficulty in agreeing on certain changes in the text" (Freud & Bullitt, 1966, p. viii).
17. Symptoms, speech and speech-making have in common the fact that the subject who carries these wants to be heard. A symptom, in the psycho-analytic sense of the word, is a resolution to an underlying conflict, but it is a resolution that is demanded from and has to come from the field of the Other. In this sense a symptom solicits interpretation.
18. Step one of A.A. says: "We admitted we were powerless over alcohol—that our lives had become unmanageable" (A.A., 1952, p. 5). Step two says: "Came to believe that a Power greater than ourselves could restore us to sanity" (Ibid.).

Conclusion

A close reading of Freud's texts is always a rewarding experience, especially when this reading is done on the basis of the development of his work. This reading of Freud's work on addiction has indeed revealed material that is complex, rich, and diverse in nature. It has to be said that this result was somewhat unexpected, as the task of reading was begun thinking that Freud had no real interest in addiction. However, when the task was completed, this thought was immediately dispelled. Anna Freud made a very interesting observation when she said "analysts were baffled at all times by addictive states and therefore sought to explain them in terms of the prevailing interest of the period" (Yorke, 1970, p. 156). This observation is interesting for a number of reasons. It suggests that there is something about addiction that makes knowledge about it very difficult. It also suggests that when one is confronted with such a lack of knowledge, one begins to depend on the established forms of understanding (the forms currently available as explanations for the phenomena in question). Indeed, people have a great need to explain things. Not knowing leads to anxiety. Knowledge in the form of explanations is a way of calming anxiety. This is an interesting phenomenon in relation to addiction, especially when considered from the point of view of the addict. The relationship between knowledge and addiction will be discussed in Chapter 9.

Freud was reluctant to treat addicts or to study addiction but, from a theoretical point of view at least, he seemed far more open to new approaches to the problem of addiction than most of his contemporaries; indeed, he was more open than the people who came after him. Freud's work always contains a tension between established forms of knowledge and something not understood. This tension would often produce a shift in his thinking and a new way of working with his patients. His *Cocaine Papers* are a good example of that tension. Freud very much wanted to hold on to the scientific framework of physics, energetics and thermodynamics, whilst his research on the effect of cocaine on people forced him to shake and pull at that framework. Something in his research efforts on cocaine brought him problems in terms of finding a formal cause for the effects of a drug on people. He would have to wait a while to formulate a material cause,[1] i.e., a cause that relates to language and that is particular to the subject. However, in his work on cocaine, Freud was already giving clear indications that addiction was a problem that was situated at the level of the subject, (the subject being the variable factor in the *Cocaine Papers*, not the object-drug). This idea runs through the whole gamut of his work.

Freud would never find a formal cause or a general explanation for the effect of drugs; neither would he find a cause or explanation for the different effects that the same drug has on different people. This has an important implication: it does not make sense to develop a diagnosis of addiction that is based on the effects of drugs, at least not from a psychoanalytic perspective. Knowing that an excess of alcohol and drugs is bad for you does not provide a sufficient basis or guarantee for a proper diagnosis. This is also the reason why, in the present work, a distinction between the different drugs and their effects is not considered to be crucial for a clinical approach to addiction. A psychoanalytic approach to addiction cannot and should not, start with the object-drug but with the subject who takes the drugs. Drugs do not produce knowledge. Knowledge is produced by the subject (as addict) for the subject (of the scientist). There is no way around the fact that knowledge about the drug, including its effects and their causes, can only be a knowledge that comes from the subject. However, having said that, it must be added immediately that a distinction was made at the level of the object, for reasons that were indicated in the preface, between the toxicomanias (the addictions to chemical substances) and other forms of addiction. The real act of chemical intoxication is not the same as the symbolic act of gambling, nor is it the same as the real act of sex for those who consider themselves sex addicts.

Nevertheless, Freud established a connection between addiction and sexuality. This kind of connection does not proclaim that wanting a lot of sex does not necessarily warrant a diagnosis of addict. In fact, Freud's position was precisely the opposite of this. The first time he wrote about the relationship between sexuality and addiction he announced that addiction was a substitute for sexual activity. His subsequent introduction of masturbation was crucial for three reasons. Firstly, he claimed that masturbation was one of the causes for actual neurosis. This implied that there was a connection between the "prototype of an addiction" and a lack, or a symbolic insufficiency underlying the kind of pain and suffering that cannot be assuaged through fantasy or symptoms. Secondly, the link between masturbation and actual neurosis introduced the question of a differential diagnosis into the pathology of addiction, because the distinction between the actual neuroses and the psychoneuroses was Freud's first contribution to the establishment of a differential diagnosis for psychopathology. Thirdly, the issue of masturbation introduced the crucial, but very problematic, question of pleasure into the pathology of addiction. As an artificial means of obtaining pleasure, masturbation provides the prototype for all other forms of addiction.

An artificial way of producing pleasure is a peculiar description to give masturbation really; because it so obviously produces pleasure, one is inclined to forget that sexual pleasure is profoundly related to the Other. From the very beginning of his work Freud considered the fact that sexuality caused problems for people. Masturbation creates the illusion that through avoiding the encounter with the Other, (which masturbation obviously allows you to do), these sexual difficulties can be avoided. What is more, masturbation even facilitates the notion that the pleasure "at hand" promises something more; but this can only be a fleeting notion because the climax of masturbation is, inevitably, its biggest disappointment.

Masturbation demonstrates the human incapacity for pleasure and the inability to accept this. Addiction and masturbation seek to resolve this problem of pleasure independently of other people by chasing a more total kind of pleasure. The difference between the masturbator and the addict is that the former experiences the lack after the point of orgasm, whilst the latter is able to live that little bit longer with the illusion that the "something more" is a possibility. That is the real danger of addiction from a Freudian point of view.

The activities of addiction and masturbation are related to a lack that causes mental pain, which in turn is the cause of these activities. Hence, Freud located the cause of addiction in the subject. He had already made this claim in his work on cocaine, and he would hold on to it for the rest of his life. The problem was, however, that he proposed a solution that had a general application, namely a good dose of "normal" sexuality, which would, of course, promise a decent level of pleasure. This is surprising, in some ways, as it was Freud's own idea that human sexuality is inherently problematic. It is clear that, for Freud, the issue of pleasure was a problem that he would never manage to rid himself of.

In his work on humour and jokes Freud established a clear connection between language, pleasure, and the distribution of pleasure. He claimed that the demands of rationality and language repress the pleasure implied in the freedom of being non-sensical. Both humour and alcohol can produce pleasure by disinhibiting repression and thereby saving us some energy that would otherwise be spent on keeping things repressed. The saving of energy produces the feeling of pleasure. Naive as this may sound, it is important not to lose sight of the fact that for the first time here, an explicit connection was made between language and pleasure; a connection that would later lead to Lacan's theory of pleasure—a theory that overcomes the pitfalls of Freud's theory of pleasure. Moreover, this later theory of pleasure has so far not been surpassed by any other science that has bothered to concern itself with the question of pleasure.

Despite all these contributions, Freud was extremely reluctant to deal with addicts, as exemplified in the Gross affair. An exploration of the Gross affair led to a number of questions that are still valid today. Is a dual treatment needed? Can therapy help those people who are under the influence? What pathology underlies addiction? How can a demand for help be created in the addict? Why is the transference such a problem in addiction? Above all, the Gross affair made it abundantly clear that addiction was excluded from psychoanalysis because it disturbed its theory and treatment method. This puts addiction in an ideal position to question the Freudian endeavour.

Freud kept hoping for the existence of a more perfect pleasure principle. Maybe that is one of the reasons why he was unable to deal with addiction. If addiction has only taught us one thing, it is that one can be sure of the fact that a perfect pleasure does not exist. Curiously enough, it is still necessary to have a theory to ground that fact. Fortunately, that theory exists in the work of Lacan. Whilst Freud hoped for a better pleasure principle, at the same time he wondered why people are constantly duped with regards to pleasure, drugs and alcohol. He had no real answer, but he could conclude that alcohol and drugs lead to a more total satisfaction than language and reality. He also concluded that loss is not only fundamental, but that it is at the heart of the human experience. Before he applied this conclusion to his thoughts on civilization at large, Freud located a problem in the form of a toxicity within the subject, or rather, within the body of the subject. This introduced a new kind of toxicity which Freud called sexual toxins. Again, these toxins were related to an insufficiency in sexual activity. However, instead of prescribing healthy sexual relations, he suggested now that patients should actuallly be denied something. He recognized the dangers of a therapeutic relationship which does not deny the patient anything, or which gives in to the demands of the patient. This can result in a destructive kind of idealization which can, in turn, lead to the problem of dependency in the relationship with the therapist. There is no need to emphasize the implications of that for addicts.

Still, Freud's hope for a pleasure principle that would do its work properly continued, even after he introduced the death-drive into his theory. What disturbs the pleasure principle is, in fact, the death-drive. Masturbation continued to be important for Freud's thinking on pleasure; at this stage in his work it highlighted the problem of a short cut between desire and fulfilment. In other words, although masturbation is one way of avoiding castration, it continually demonstrates how impotent people are in reaching a level of pleasure they can be happy with. Freud came to the conclusion that people are not a happy lot. Being part of culture seems to imply guilt and anxiety. This means that once you participate in culture, once you subject yourself to its rules and regulations, there is a demand on you, and this demand is to renounce or sacrifice a certain amount of pleasure and satisfaction. But the question is: for whose enjoyment or employment is this sacrifice made? Freud's answer is that it is for the good of culture. Namely, what is given up in terms of satisfaction can be put to good use elsewhere. This is not Lacan's answer. But then, our demanding cultural superego has changed and the death-drive has become more obvious, at least in some ways.

There is an important and complicated connection between the death-drive and addiction. The death-drive is a concept that separates Freud from most of the post-Freudian writers. With the exception of people such as Jacques Lacan and Melanie Klein, most of the post-Freudians rejected the idea of a death-drive. The death-drive was an extremely important concept for Freud in order to make sense of certain experiences and aspects of human life. He defended his concept vigorously. Lacan considered the concept of the death-drive to be central to the theory of the unconscious and therefore central to the psychoanalytic experience. In Seminar II, he wrote:

> In man there's already a crack, a profound perturbation of the regulation of life. That's the importance of the notion introduced by Freud of the death instinct. Not that the death instinct is such an enlightening notion in itself. What has to be comprehended is that he was forced to introduce it so as to remind us of a salient fact of his experience, just when it was beginning to get lost. As I observed a little while ago, when an apperception of the structure is ahead of its time, there is always a moment of weakness when one is inclined to abandon it. That is what happened in the circle around Freud when the meaning of the discovery of the unconscious was pushed into the background (Lacan, 1988a, p. 37).

It is with some of these analytical thinkers from the "circle around Freud" and with some of the post- Freudian thinkers that Part II is concerned.

Note

1. In *Science and Truth* Lacan refers to four different (Aristotelian) causes that belong to four different discourses or ways of knowing. These

CONCLUSION 91

causes are: efficient cause, final cause, formal cause, and material cause. Magic is characterized by the efficient cause, because knowledge "dissimulates itself as such, as much in the operative tradition as in its act" (1989[1966], p. 19). In religion truth is a kind of negation of itself and it "appears only as a final cause, in the sense that it is deferred to (reporte a) an end-of-the-world judgement" (Ibid., p. 20). Science is not really interested in truth and "the effect (incidence) of the truth as cause in science needs to be recognized in its guise as formal cause" (p. 22). Psychoanalysis attempts to relate the truth on the basis of a material cause and "this material cause is truly the form of impact (incidence) of the signifier that I define therein" (Ibid.).

PART II:
THE POST-FREUDIAN REDUCTION OF A FIELD AND THE FRUITS OF A CONFRONTATION

Introduction

Despite the lack of a substantial psychoanalytic theory on addiction, an enormous amount of articles and books have been written about addiction from a psychoanalytic perspective. So many in fact that an exhaustive review of them would exceed the capacity of this work. The aim is not to give an exhaustive account of everything that has been written in the area of psychoanalysis and addiction, but to analyse in detail a number of articles which have been selected on the basis of two criteria: (a) their importance in terms of an historical, theoretical and clinical understanding of this area and; (b) their relevance to the ideas developed in this work. Surveys and reviews of the literature have been written by Crowley (1939), Rosenfeld (1964), Yorke (1970), de Mijolla and Shentoub (1973), Limentani (1986) and Magoudi (1986).

A compilation and review of the (post-Freudian) psychoanalytic material on addiction is rather problematic. Yorke gives the following three reasons for this, reasons that seem to be inherent to the problem area of addiction:

> In the first place, there is the problem of defining addiction: this is barely attempted by most writers, with the unhappy consequence

that, when they speak of addiction, they are not talking about the same thing, This appears to be a major source of confusion and contradiction in the literature. Secondly, there is the problem of distinguishing clinically between those psychological features which link with the pharmacological effects of the drug concerned and those which appear to be independent of it. Lastly, there is the problem that the majority of writers do not distinguish between addiction to different kinds of drugs; they tend not only to treat the various drugs as identical, but they also include alcoholism as part of the same pathology—which may or may not be the case (Yorke, 1970, p. 142).

Yorke's points are to some degree related to each other. All three are connected in various ways to questions of diagnosis. What is addiction? What are the differences between the normal and abnormal use of drugs? Are there different kinds of addictions and on what are these differences based? Should a diagnosis be based on different drugs and their effects? It is very difficult to define what, precisely, a drug is. There is a common definition of a drug as a substance which is capable of producing alterations of the mind and the body when incorporated. This definition seems to make sense at first, but on reflection it can be seen to have no theoretical or even explanatory value. A lot of things that can be incorporated can be a drug or act like a drug. It is sometimes difficult to distinguish between what is a drug, a poison or a food. Drugs (including alcohol) taken in large amounts can become poisons, but in limited amounts they can function as remedies. If it is difficult to define what a drug is, then it is even more difficult to define what constitutes an addiction to drugs. A definition of addiction should be able to distinguish between normal and abnormal use; between use and abuse.

These difficulties are compounded by the fact that a similar quantity of the same drug will not affect different people in the same way. These different effects of drugs are more than likely related to the psychological features of the people taking them and it cannot be doubted that there must be an extremely complex cause-and-effect dynamic between the former and the latter. If drugs affect different people in different ways, then it will not be valid to distinguish between addictions on the basis of the kind of drug used, unless there exists a clear and unambiguous relationship between certain psychological features and the particular effects of the drug being sought after. Demonstrating the existence of such a relationship has proved extremely difficult. These problems and questions related to diagnosis will be revisited in detail in Chapters 8 and 9.

The task undertaken in Part I required a detailed and close reading of certain psychoanalytic texts in order to yield the necessary results. The Freudian literature was explored in order to produce elements or foundation stones for a classic psychoanalytic theory on addiction by analysing the excavated material. Texts by Abrahams, Radó, Glover and Gross are particularly relevant to the task of investigating post-Freudian literature in Part II. In this part (Chapter 5) the reduction of the Freudian field is analysed in order to produce new foundation stones for a theory on addiction by confronting the (post-Freudian) reduced elements with each other. This point demands some explanation. A reading of the post-Freudian literature shows that it is possible to distinguish between different periods in psychoanalytic thinking about addiction. These are periods in which certain aspects and concepts of Freud's theory dominate over others in order to explain addiction in relatively simple terms. For instance, it is possible to detect a drive-theory of addiction, which mainly covers the period of the first quarter of the 20th century. After that one sees an increase in emphasis on the ego and defence mechanisms. This is the "ego-psychology" period, and its later derivative is called the "self-psychology" period. These periods represent, in their own style, a reduction of Freud's work. Hopefully Part I has demonstrated that Freud's references to—and remarks on—addiction (from the very beginning until the very end) possess a quality of fecundity that appears to have vanished to a large degree with the post-Freudian period (with a few exceptions). The confrontation between the earlier drive-theory and the later ego(self)psychology theory did not, interestingly enough, lead to a synthesis of the two into a higher order of thinking on addiction. In other words, it did not lead to one theory complementing and supporting the other into a higher order of understanding the problem. Surprisingly, it resulted in the production of new theoretical elements and a shift in thinking about addiction. Thus, despite the lack of fecundity in most post-Freudian thinking on addiction, the possibility nevertheless exists to produce some material on addiction, providing one analyses or interprets, not just the relevant texts, but precisely what is lacking in these texts. This is the task set for Part II.

CHAPTER FIVE

Between drive and ego: the ascent of the subject

"It is clear that the promotion of the ego today culminates, in conformity with the utilitarian conception of man that reinforces it, in an ever more advanced realization of man as individual, that is to say, in an isolation of the soul ever more akin to its original dereliction"

J. Lacan, *Aggressivity in Psychoanalysis*, 1977[1948], p. 27

Addicts adrift in contaminated waters

How Abraham got his "kicks"

In a landmark article on addiction from 1933 entitled "The psychoanalysis of pharmacothymia (drug addiction)" Sandor Radö wrote: "The older psychoanalytic literature contains many valuable contributions and references, particularly on alcoholism and morphinism, which attempts essentially to explain the relationship of these states to disturbances in the development of the libido function" (Radö, 1984[1933], p. 61). The "older" psychoanalytic literature considers addiction to be related to a problematic development of the psychosexual stages which would lead to an inhibition or perversion of the sexual drives.

The first article by an analyst that was entirely devoted to addiction by an analyst was written in 1908 by Abraham. He stated that alcohol increases the sexual drives, and therefore sexual activity, by removing resistance (Abraham, 1908, p. 82). The article is interesting in the sense that it sets the scene for a psychoanalytic understanding of addiction for a good few years. Abraham argued that external factors (such as social influences and hereditary make-up) are not sufficient for an explanation of drunkenness (Ibid., p. 89); there must be an individual factor present which causes alcoholism and addiction and this factor, he claims, is of a sexual nature. Alcoholism, sexuality, and neurosis are connected in a variety of ways, and he provided a list of the possible connections between alcoholism and sexuality in the article. He started off by saying that men are more prone to drinking than women as they are culturally encouraged to drink more, but then he wondered whether sexual difference was a factor. He claimed that sublimations and repressions come undone under the influence of alcohol, bringing out the component aspects of the infantile sexual drives.

One of these, that is present in everyone, is the homosexual component, which has been successfully sublimated in most people, until it is undone through drinking. This theme of homosexuality was taken up in a whole series of articles on addiction over the next 15 years.[1] It is important to keep in mind that Abraham did not argue that alcoholics have a homosexual identity. What he did argue was that homosexuality is a repressed, but normal, aspect of the human bond. Alcohol suspends the repression, and the male bonding that ensues indicates a wish for unification with the brotherhood of man. This is interesting because it implies that sexual difference is only one of the differences between people that alcohol undoes, i.e. a desexualization process takes place. Abraham further stated that exhibitionism and sadomasochism are displayed in drinking because these are component infantile drives which become disinhibited and therefore find open expression. He noted that violence and crime are often committed under the influence of alcohol (Ibid., p. 83). Abraham wrote: "The re-emergence of repressed sexual impulses increases the individual's normal sexual activity so that he gets a feeling of increased sexual capacity" (p. 84). There is a close connection between intoxication and sexual excitement. Before getting carried away, let's immediately add that Abraham was not in the business of promoting drink to heighten sexual activity and pleasure. In fact he was totally opposed to de-sublimation. But sublimation isn't the only thing destroyed by drink, the other victim is the sexual potency of the man. Drink becomes a kind of substitute for normal genital sexual activity, creating a link between alcoholism and perversion; a link that is also expressed in the sexual fantasies of alcoholic patients, something that was "picked up" by only a very few writers in the years to come.[2] One remark towards the very end of the article strikes us as particularly important. It highlights a crucial aspect of the phenomenology of addiction and cuts immediately to the core of the problem of addiction: "The drinker makes use of alcohol as a means of obtaining pleasure without trouble" (p. 88). That means the drinker avoids the encounter with the (sexual) Other.

Addiction a perversion?

The first period in thinking about psychoanalysis and addiction is dominated by ideas as outlined in the article by Abraham. This period is called the drive theory period, because it is Freud's libido and psychosexual stages theory that provided the impetus for this kind of thinking. The drive theory period can be summarized as follows: the avoidance of the so-called normal sexual encounter with the Other indicates the search for a sexual satisfaction that belongs to an earlier stage of infantile sexual development. Addicts are fixated to a form of satisfaction that belongs to the oral stage of sexual development, with addiction being a kind of oral perversion that provides the direct satisfaction of an unconscious infantile drive that, for some reason, was never properly overcome or sublimated; so drugs and alcohol can function as substitutes for the gratification of infantile sexual wishes. What characterizes addicts, according to the drive theory, is their inability to be able to deal with frustration and their demand for immediate satisfaction. That means that addicts prefer the immediate pleasure attached to the satisfaction of the drives, to the less immediate satisfaction inherent in human relationships. A couple of writers on this drive theory period referred to connections with narcissism, depression, mania, and paranoia.[3]

A serious problem with the drive theory of addiction is that it is based on the ideal that there is a proper way of repressing or sublimating infantile drives, which will result in a unified drive that has an unproblematic relationship with a sexual object that can be precisely targeted and clearly attained. An unproblematic and unified drive theory was never part of Freud's thinking. From the very beginning to the very end of his work Freud indicated that there was always something problematic involved in the drive. Adhering to an unproblematic drive theory and avoiding the complexities inherent in this aspect of Freud's work will lead to an equally unproblematic and straightforward explanation of addiction: the object drug or alcohol replaces the sexual object. This has no explanatory value at all, because it cannot explain, for instance, why some people become addicted and others do not, unless one truly believes that any person who is not addicted has an extraordinarily satisfying sex-life of the heterosexual and genital kind. That would have to be a sex life without variation and fantasy, because variation and fantasy already form a diversion away from the aim and object of the drive. There is no need to indicate what kind of impasse this idea of normality in sexuality would lead to. What does need to be indicated, however, is the problematic nature and status of the object, and to whom the relation to this object really matters, namely, the subject.

What is peculiar about the drive theory (of addiction) is that it seems that the drives exist as if they lead an independent life. Freud made it very clear from the beginning that the drives do indeed exist, but not with a life of their own. They bother the subject and drive him or her crazy, especially when they cannot find psychic representation. It was stated before that Freud insisted on the idea that when the drives cannot find psychic representation they become toxic and can lead to actual neurosis. It is curious, therefore, that a theory of addiction, which bases itself on the concept of the drives, manages to avoid, despite Freud's clear indications, making the connection between addiction and the actual neuroses. This theory ignores the subject for whom the vicissitudes of the drives have enormous implications.

The direction of the theory changes with Sandor Radö's aforementioned article. This article will be discussed along with two others published around the same time. In 1932 Glover published

"On the aetiology of drug addiction" and in 1935 Alfred Gross published "The psychic effects of toxic and toxoid substances". The articles by Radö and Glover are important because they anticipated the first elements of ego-psychology in the psychoanalytic approach to addiction and they contain information about addiction that is often ignored in non-psychoanalytic literature. Radö and Glover have dominated psychoanalytic thinking on addiction for a very long time. Gross's article was not of great influence and is given a only a minor role in some of the surveys on psychoanalysis and addiction. But Gross's article is important for two reasons: (1) it contains some interesting and original information; and (2) Gross makes a fundamental mistake in his thinking which is very instructive.

*Radö or the failure of an egological lifeline:
addiction as symptom*

Addiction as an ego-boost

Before discussing Radö's article from 1933, it is interesting to look briefly at an article from 1926 entitled "The psychic effects of intoxicants: an attempt to evolve a psycho-analytical theory of morbid cravings". Most of what Radö said in this article he returns to in his article from 1933. There are, however, a couple of interesting aspects to this earlier article that he does not return to. Radö says that the effect of drugs is immediate and central. At that stage of his thinking he considers addiction to be a substitute for sexual activity. Drugs provide a kind of satisfaction that by-passes the erotogenic zones. In that passing movement it avoids the complications inherent in the sexual usages of these zones. Addiction, so to speak, sexualizes the whole body, providing it with, what Radö called, an "alimentary orgasm". What turns people into addicts is the predominance of an oral satisfaction that can be produced at will and has all the hallmarks of an orgasm invading the body. It is clear that Radö's thinking on addiction in 1926 was still steeped in drive theory. Some elements of the drive theory were retained in his article from 1933, but he also introduced other elements that belong to, what will later be called, ego-psychology. He stated that what makes an addict is not the drug, but the impulse to use drugs (Radö,

1984[1933], p. 60). Addiction is one single disease because drugs can easily be exchanged for one another. So, the underlying unifying factor causing the disease is a singular general craving. There are two types of drugs: (1) sedatives, hypnotics and narcotics; all the ones that lessen pain; and (2) stimulants and euphorants; all the ones that provide pleasure. Radö called this pleasure: "the pharmacogenic pleasure-effect" (Ibid., p. 61). A psychological factor is also present which co-determines (with the properties of the drugs themselves) the effects of drugs. The patient, of course, will have to pay a heavy price in order to obtain these effects. Radö wondered why the patient needs "elatants" to relieve suffering? There is, he said, a group of people who suffer from "tense depression" (Ibid., p. 62). The pharmacogenic pleasure-effect can relieve the patient of this painful feeling. This relief leads to a rise in self-regard and an elated feeling of the ego; the ego becomes inflated. The elation is the reaction of the ego to the pleasure effect. In order to demonstrate the need for elation Radö explained the miserable state of the ego, i.e., "the tense depression" (pp. 62–63). Before continuing with Radö's theory on addiction, it might be worthwhile to reflect a little further on the implications of his ideas on the ego, precisely because these ideas summarize the programme for ego-psychology. This programme will influence the thinking on addiction in a profound way for a very long time.

At the very beginning, the ego was full of itself and it believed in its own omnipotence. No desire was left unfulfilled. Then reality began to make an impact and cut the omnipotence down to size. Megalomania disappeared and the influence of the ego was reduced. In order to grow again—this time into a well-adjusted human being with a suitably big ego—the following should happen: narcissistic gratification needs to be found after having been lost for a while. And why does that make the ego feel good about itself? Because self-regard comes from self-love, and self-love, ultimately, comes from narcissistic gratification. Whereas initially, gratification came to the infant automatically, now it has to be worked at and demanded from the environment. In Radö's words: "the ego must make over its psychology from that of a supercilious parasite into that of a well adjusted self-sustaining creature" (p. 62). The ego has to hold its own in order to create a happy relationship with the environment. Only that way can it hold its head high. This ego can be threatened by a reality out there, but it can also be threatened from an internal source, namely bad libidinal development. In the latter case, the ego is overwhelmed by a cesspool of uncontrolled evil drives that threaten to annihilate it. The ego can react to this in a number of ways: for instance, it can develop "tense depression", it can find substitute satisfaction in the form of a neurosis, or it might end up tormenting and reproaching itself. The pharmacogenic pleasure-effect can be a Godsend in these situations. The poor tormented ego can feel good about itself again and is able to return, temporarily, to an original narcissistic state in which it feels, once again, omnipotent.

Drugs can give people a sense of a magical oneness with the world. The problem is, of course, that the effect of the drug wears off, and so the feeling can only be temporary. The sense of guilt and depression will return. In order to get back to the state of elation the ego will search again for the pharmacogenic pleasure-effect. And before it knows what has happened, it is caught in what Radö called a "pharmacothymic regime". This regime only gets worse as the strength of the chemical effect diminishes over time and the ego increasingly needs more to boost and elate itself. This regime intervenes between the ego and other people, colonizing the domain of sexuality and sexual relationships. Sexual objects are not needed or wanted anymore and the addicts now begin to depend on a rich fantasy life. The ego has surrendered itself to the drug regime and it feels increasingly worse about itself. In fact, at this stage it is completely at the mercy of a punishing superego. Radö wrote that by cutting itself off, the following happens to the ego:

> It delivers itself over to that antagonistic instinctual power within, which we call masochism and, following Freud, interpret as a death-instinct. The ego had an opportunity to feel the dark power of this instinct in the initial depression; partly for fear of it then, the ego took flight into the pharmacothymic regime (p. 65).

It is obvious—as will be demonstrated later—that Radö did not follow Freud on the question of the death-drive. For Freud the death-drive is the very essence of life. There are many aspects to it— some of them indeed aggressive, self-destructive or violent—but, essentially, it is not something that the ego can defend itself against by "developing its vitality and thus entrenching its narcissism", as

Radö suggested (p. 65). A thinking that takes place in terms of a simple opposition between a good ego (drive) and a bad death-drive leads to an impasse that most of the post-Freudian thinkers were only too happy not to avoid. The post-Freudian ego-psychology argument is a common sense argument. It argues that the death-drive is a threat emanating from the id, which is ready to destroy the integrity of the ego. It is an aggressive force that needs to be conquered or neutralized. Before coming back to the question as to why the ego can't defend itself against the death-drive by inflating itself, and why a simple opposition between good and bad drives leads to an impasse, the ego-psychology argument about addiction will be outlined and this argument will be illustrated with the rest of Radö's article.

The ego is attacked by aggressive and masochistic forces. In order to defend itself against these threatening forces the ego can find recourse in the use of drugs and alcohol. Or, to paraphrase Radö, the ego can escape into the regime of alcohol or drug addiction. The ego has to fight a serious battle with masochistic tendencies, but the route that addicts choose is a hopeless one. Radö explains why: the chemical elation (inflation) of the ego has reactivated the narcissistic belief in being invulnerable, but this illusion cannot be sustained forever and one day the whole regime collapses (1984[1933], p. 65). According to Radö, there are three ways out of this crisis: (1) a temporary withdrawal from drugs and alcohol in order to restore the original effect of drugs and alcohol such that the addict can re-start the regime of drug taking with a vengeance; (2) suicide, as a surrender of the ego to the masochistic self-destructive forces but, curiously enough, also as an act that should confirm his or her immortality; and finally (3) psychosis, as the result of the pharmacothymic regime breaking down the protective function of the ego, leaving it at the mercy of all kinds of hallucinations and deliria. Towards the end of the article Radö returned to the domain of sexuality which he had considered before, in his article from 1926. However, this time things had changed. Addiction was not a matter of an orgasm of the whole body by-passing the erotogenic zones anymore. Radö now argued that the addiction had driven away eroticism and had played into the hands of masochism. This could result in a number of sexual problems: a homosexual object choice which avoids the fear emanating from a masochistic wish for castration; a passive attitude towards women as a reaction to a loss of potency, or sadism—in order to rescue some masculinity from the place where it was lost.[4] Before turning our attention to Glover, Gross and some more ego-psychology, we will explore the issue of the death-drive being levelled at the ego and the impasse that results from a reduction of the drive-theory into a simple opposition between good and bad drives.

The death-drive versus the ego: the illusion of a mortal combat

The idea that the death-drive can be fought off by a strong ego is based on a misunderstanding of the death-drive. The question of the death-drive and its relation to addiction requires an extensive and detailed exploration which will be undertaken in Chapters 6 and 7.

The ego is not something that fights against the evil, masochistic, and destructive forces of the unconscious. This idea of Radö's was based on a very convenient misconception of the death-drive, a misconception that was perpetuated by most of the post-Freudians. Their argument was that aggression and destruction could be relegated to the field of animal biology because that is also an aspect of human existence. Lacan writes:

> After all, one must eat—when the pantry is empty, one tucks into one's fellow being (semblable). The libidinal adventure is here objectified in the order of living things, and one assumes that the behaviour of subjects, their inter-aggressivity, is conditioned and capable of explication by a desire which is fundamentally adequate to its object (Lacan, 1988a, p. 232).

When Lacan adds immediately that life is not something that wants to be healed, he implies that one of the aspects of life that is sick is the ego. What exactly is this ego that ego-psychologists appear to admire so much? Again Lacan:

> The return to the ego as the centre and common measure is not any way implied by Freud's discourse. Quite the opposite in fact—the further his discourse advances, the further we follow him in the third stage of his work, the more the ego is shown as a mirage, a sum of identifications. Of course the ego is to be found at the rather impoverished point of synthesis to which the subject is reduced when he presents himself, but he is also something else, he also

finds himself somewhere else, he comes from somewhere else, precisely from the point beyond the pleasure-principle at which we can ask—what is it that is caught in this symbolic web, in this fundamental phrase which insists beyond anything we can catch of the motivation of the subject? (Ibid., p. 209).

Lacan makes a distinction between the ego and the subject. The ego is something that the subject can present itself with to others, but the subject and the ego cannot be collapsed into each other. The status of the subject is indeed one of being represented. The status of the subject will be given closer consideration later on in this chapter.

For Radö, and the ego-psychologists, the ego is, by and large, a conflict free zone and mental suffering is the result of a weakness of—or deficiency in—the ego. Consequently, effects of healing come from repairing the damage and deficiencies in the ego, and by making it stronger through the build up of defence mechanisms that protect it against evil forces. In this view, symptoms function as helpers, extensions of the ego. It is this viewpoint that allows Radö to argue that drugs and addiction elate the ego in their fight against the dark power of the death-instinct.

For Lacan, if anything at all can be considered sick in relation to the subject, it is the ego. The ego is a "false connection" with the internal and external world of the subject. It hides the truth from the subject, and because of its connection to the truth, it can be considered to be a symptom. It is important to realize that it is not the drives or the instincts that are aggressive. The drives are only a constant force seeking satisfaction by trying to dissolve themselves. It is when the drives are represented and transformed by imaginary identification that the ego—as the result of this identification—acquires a tendency to dissolve itself. Lacan writes:

> The ego in inscribed in the imaginary. Everything pertaining to the ego is inscribed in imaginary tensions. Libido and the ego are on the same side. Narcissism is libidinal. The ego isn't a superior power, nor a pure spirit, nor an autonomous agency, nor a conflict-free sphere—as some dare to write—in which we would find some support (Lacan, 1988a, p. 326).

Not only is the ego not a conflict-free zone, it is, in fact, in deep trouble, because it wants to dissolve itself. And why should it want to do that? Because it wants to return to an original state of affairs which ultimately implies its own destruction. Aggression is not the defence of the ego against the threat of disintegration and the loss of its unity. Aggression is the attack of the ego on itself as a structure presenting an imaginary, false unity. Aggression desires to shatter this unity in order to get back to the previous state of total fragmentation. This death-drive is unacceptable and it is therefore turned outwards to objects in the world. That is why people are fascinated by violence, mutilations, and destruction, a fact of life which is more than amply illustrated by Hollywood cinema. But the direction of this fascination should not distract us from the real object of aggression.

Thus, not only is there no simple opposition between good and bad drives, there is also no aggression outside the ego which the ego can fight off in a heroic battle. The aggressor is the ego itself and propping it up with therapeutic techniques, and/or drugs and alcohol, might perhaps calm it down or else make it worse. Who is to know? That is precisely Radö's ego-psychological impasse. The effects of drugs are unpredictable and we don't know for whom they will function properly, or for whom they will lead to addiction. Addiction, as a symptom, does not always function as an extension of the ego or, in the words of the Rolling Stones, as "mother's little helper". Radö's conception of addiction as a pharmacothymic regime conveniently avoids an ambivalence situated at the core of addiction and symptoms in general. It makes his theory of addiction incorrect and it leads to a clinical impasse. Addiction and drugs function in ways that go right to the heart of the problem of the symptom in psychoanalysis. A psychoanalytic definition of the symptom is that it is the solution to an underlying conflict. This definition, of course, implies that the solution is not perfect: it does not resolve anything. The symptom is only a symptom in so far as it is repeated. If subjects repeat symptoms, there must be something in the symptom that the subject does not want to let go of, despite the fact that it causes suffering. This is precisely the issue that Freud tried to resolve with his theoretical concept of the death-drive.

It is necessary to be more precise when claiming that addiction is a symptom in the true psychoanalytic sense of the word. If we define the symptom as a symbolically structured formation of the unconscious, and therefore as something that expresses itself in the realm of meaning (although of course it is the unconscious that provides the symptom with its meaning; the symptom lacks meaning in terms of consciousness)—if this is the case then, as addiction is not a symbolic construction, it is not, strictly speaking, a symptom. But then, on the other hand, addiction is the epitome—and clearest illustration—of the symptom in the psychoanalytic sense. As a solution, addiction is at the same time the dissolution of this solution. In words more closely related to the specificity of addiction, addiction is both cause-and-effect. The cause of addiction is related to the effects of drugs and alcohol. These effects are the specific effects sought by addicts; they are the effects they depend on. This means that in terms of understanding addiction, there is neither just the cause of an effect (of drugs and alcohol) nor an effect of the cause in addiction. There is always both and something else. The question is: what is that something else that causes the specific effect and the desire for it? Radö was wrong in one way when he wrote that it is not the toxic agent but the impulse to use it that makes an addict of a given individual. Namely, he was wrong to suggest that the effect is not the cause of addiction. He was right, however, in the sense that addiction relates to a cause or impulse in the individual to use drugs.

The point Radö didn't get is that the cause of the effect which ultimately causes addiction (the effects of drugs and alcohol are crucial to the development of an addiction in the subject) is situated within the subject (the subject being the something else squeezed in between the cause-and-effect dynamic of drugs). This has enormous implications: it means that the cause of addiction cannot be known a priori and that this cause can only be articulated by the subject. One is only able to get to know something about how the effects of drugs and alcohol cause addiction by listening to how the subjects speak about their drug taking and how these drugs effect them. Effects of drugs and alcohol do not exist independently of the subject and subjective structure. Addiction incarnates the essence of the psychoanalytic symptom. Addiction incarnates—and openly demonstrates —the beyond of pleasure that is contained within the symptom; a beyond to which the subject is profoundly attached. Again, this is the point Radö missed when he divided drugs into two categories according to their effect: drugs that provide pleasure and drugs that relieve pain. This division is based on the pleasure principle and it ignores the beyond of the pleasure principle. The position and cause of the subject are closely related to this beyond of the pleasure principle. To try and grasp the cause is letting the effect escape, to try and grasp the effect is letting the cause escape, and to try to grasp both at the same time (in the same movement) is, logically speaking, not possible. The only way out of this impasse is not by trying to grasp either cause or effect (of alcohol and drugs), but by making the "missing link" speak about the effect as cause (of addiction). That is to say, the ultimate cause of the effect is in the subject and it is only this subject that can articulate something about the symptom of addiction.

Glover, Gross and more egological extensions

Glover on addiction: a "borderline" position

Glover's important paper "On the aetiology of drug-addiction" was published in 1932. Before considering the importance of this paper it is necessary to take note of a paper called "The aetiology of alcoholism" which he wrote in 1928 (Glover, 1956[1928]). In this paper Glover argued that alcoholism is a flight from reality into fantasy. This regressive movement allows the alcoholic to satisfy component (infantile) drives that are still active in the subject or, indeed, have been reactivated. This situation results in ambivalent object relations, because the object of the drive can be satisfying in a sexual sense (though predominantly oral or anal in nature) and in an aggressive sense (destruction of the object through devouring it or getting rid of it by rejecting it). Through being fixated at this regressed state of libidinal development, alcoholics have to deal with their own increasing intolerance of a world that is frustrating them, but, alcoholics must also face the intolerance of the world that has been frustrated by them. This impasse of alcoholism spirals out of proportion to the degree that the whole world comes under attack of the alcoholic. Towards the end of the paper Glover indicated the possible connections between alcoholism and other pathologies such as manic–depressive illness, paranoia, and perversion. Like Radö's first paper, this paper by Glover was still to a large degree based on a drive-theory of addiction. This will change to some degree with Glover's paper on drug addiction.

At the start of his paper he mentioned that drug addiction has a close connection with psychosis on the one hand and "sublimatory defence-reactions", as he called them, on the other (Glover, 1956 [1932], p. 188). He related the latter to paranoia, obsessional neurosis, open-air cults, and even the addiction to scented soaps. Apart from the enigma of scented soap, the connection to psychosis is interesting. After his previous paper, Glover had become a follower of Melanie Klein, and she related psychosis to "pregenital sadistic fixation-points". This implies that, according to Glover's point of view, the cause of some addictions must be sought in a pre-oedipal phase of development, whilst the cause of other addictions must be sought in the Oedipal drama. But then he wrote:

> While, therefore, I agree with the tendency of recent attempts to compare drug-addiction with melancholia and obsessional neurosis, I feel that the emphasis laid on the latest Oedipus phase and on early constitutional factors has obscured not only an equally close relation to paranoia, but the possibility of establishing a specific mechanism for drug-addiction. This specific reaction represents a transition between the more primitive psychotic phase and the later psycho–neurotic phase of development (Ibid., p. 201).

Glover proposed that addiction might have its own mechanism; a mechanism that is specific to a transitional state, which is a mental condition that is situated between psychosis and neurosis. Glover came to the conclusion that "noxious" addictions (he recognized the existence of "harmless" habits) represent a reaction to an acute state of anxiety and that the use of drugs is mainly for defensive purposes (p. 212). He showed his true Kleinian colours when he stated that the significance of drug-addiction represents a compromise between projective and introjective processes (p. 213). The effects of drugs can kill off, punish, cure or indulge bad introjected objects which disturb the subject. Drugs can also have a similar effect on bad objects that have been projected into the external world and, indeed, bad objects that already exist in the external world which are disturbing the subject. It is this double action, according to Glover, that explains "the extreme sense of compulsion". In the transitional state the self is experienced to be bad because of the presence of "bad introjected objects" and it is in danger because of the threat of annihilation by the "bad projected objects" from the external world.

The self is confused by the threat of being fused with a bad world. This self is in a narcissistic crisis and it does not feel very good about itself. Certain experiences and developments have resulted in narcissistic conflicts and a weak ego which is unable to cope with affect and ordinary frustration. A crutch enabling it to hold its own in this game is very welcome. Drugs are considered to be a form of self-medication and they are used in order to cope with intense affects. In this object-relations point of view, addiction is thought to be a narcissistic neurosis and it functions as a protective mechanism of the ego. In that sense it does not differ from the ego-psychological point of view and it can therefore be criticized on the same grounds.

Why was Glover's paper so important? It was important because of the introduction of the transitional state. This concept—or rather clinical category—anticipated a category that was first proposed in 1938 by Adolphe Stern in a paper called: "Psychoanalytic investigation and therapy in the borderline group of neuroses" (Kouretas, 1996, p. 46). The Borderline State was born and as a concept it was considered to be a very attractive proposition for mainly two reasons. Firstly, it is based on a very simple and general idea which states that the ego of the borderline patient is weak and therefore unable to fulfil its functions. The reason for the poor state of the ego is a mixture of constitutional factors, traumatic events and disturbed human relationships (Ibid., p. 48). Secondly, the idea is so general that it became the ideal "dumping-ground" for anything that could not be understood or clinically dealt with. No wonder that addiction was dumped there as soon as this category saw the light of day. The problem was that as soon as it was dumped it became a festering mess, because the borderline patients were considered to be untreatable, at least by psychoanalysis or so-called supportive psychotherapy (Ibid., p. 51). Otto Kernberg, the American psychoanalyst who infused ego-psychology with object relations theory, argued that the borderline patient never developed an ego that would be capable of maintaining proper object relations which includes relationships with others. Consequently, the transference will not be able to develop in analysis and proper therapy can therefore not take place.

Another American psychoanalyst, Heinz Kohut, generally considered to be the founding father of a further development of ego-psychology called self-psychology, believed that the very disturbed borderline patients suffer from an extreme lack of self-esteem. Kohut and the self-psychologists moved away from object theory, the economy of the drives and ultimately unconscious processes. Instead, they concentrated on consciousness and the self. This self is not involved in instinctual expression but it seeks relations with others and drives are considered to be the result of a broken and fragmented self (p. 55). The psyche needs to be a cohesive unit that is well suited to harmonious relationships with others and a good adaptation to the environment. Mental problems all stem from deficiencies and failures of this self. Kouretas writes:

> According to the psychology of the self, borderline states involve serious, permanent, or protracted enfeeblement of, and damage to, the self, but complex defences cover this basic deficit and protect the individual from close relationships that might activate the underlying fragmentation. The damage to the self is caused by severe and ongoing failures in parental empathic response to the selfobject needs of the child. Because of the constant threat of loss of cohesion, the child cannot undertake attachments to selfobjects; he or she remains with a chronic and overwhelming sense of dread which contributes to problems in self-regulation, self-control, self-soothing, and maintenance of self-esteem. In later life he or she may resort to compensatory stimulating activities such as *drug abuse* (my italics), indiscriminate sexuality, eating disorders, and so forth (Ibid., p. 56).[5]

In self-psychology addiction is a compensatory activity that regulates, controls, soothes and maintains self-esteem. The addict is an innocent victim of the parental other and carries no responsibility for his or her mental problems or addiction. The problem of addiction has become an objective problem (with the self as object) and that implies that it is a problem without subjective implications (unless affects and feelings are subjective implications). Therapeutically speaking, all that needs to be done is to build up the self so that it feels well. But that is precisely the problem: this self does not want to get well. And because this self does not want to get well the patient is considered to be a borderline patient who is untreatable and who should be handled with care, preferably in an institution.

A reading of the surveys, overviews, articles and books on psychoanalysis and addiction demonstrates that further (ego-psychological and self-psychological) theories on addiction are a variation on the same theme: addiction helps the disturbed individual to cope with themselves and with life. Addiction has been reduced to a transitional or borderline state with the result that it has been separated from the complexities of the subject or subjectivity and isolated from the different clinical structures. This has reduced the problem of addiction to something fairly simple and straightforward, despite the clinical difficulties. The rhetorical question is therefore: who really benefits from this simplification? It is interesting to note that, whilst the trend to throw addiction into the "dustbin category" was initiated by Glover, his thinking on addiction was infinitely more sensitive, complex and interesting than most of the thinking that came after him. To complete the picture one has to mention Ernst Simmel and Edmund Bergler as notable exceptions to the trends of reduction and simplification that characterize ego-psychology, self-psychology and (to a lesser extent) object-relations theory.[6]

The time has come to return to a specific remark in Glover's paper on the effects of drugs and their relationship to addiction. The remark is crucial because it leads into a paper by Alfred Gross that deals with the toxic effects of drugs on the psyche. Gross's paper exemplifies a conception of toxicity that tries to include the psyche, but fails to do this, precisely because it excludes the subject. This psychoanalytic conception of toxicity will also lead to a clinical and theoretical impasse. Glover wrote:

> There is now no doubt that the pharmacotoxic effects of drugs do not play such a specific part in dangerous drug-addictions as is supposed in extra-psychological circles. In certain addiction-cases where a harmless substitute was established (in one case sugar was used in this way), I have observed the same slavish compulsion attach itself to the substitute. And deprivation of the substitute loosened massive charges of anxiety. On the other hand, during the analysis of psycho–neurotics and of neurotic (or psychotic) character abnormalities, I have discovered idiosyncrasies which had the same subjective sense of compulsion and aroused the same anxiety on deprivation as standard drug-habits (Glover, 1956[1932], p. 204).

The connection between addiction, neurosis, and psychosis appears to be related to an object, in fact any object, as long as the subject is deprived of it. It appears that it is the lack of object (drugs, alcohol or other objects) that causes an effect in the subject. If that is the case, then the specificity of the effect caused in the subject by the object (or lack of it) must be related to the way the subject orientates him or herself towards that object or lack. The different orientations of the subject towards the object of lack are defined by Lacan as psychosis, neurosis, and perversion. Each of these subject positions has their own mechanisms for dealing with this lack (foreclusion, repression and disavowal). This is an important element in the possibility of creating a differential diagnosis for addiction. This question of a diagnosis of addiction based on the different subject positions will be investigated in Chapter 8.

But now the question of the toxic effect of drugs on the subject and its relationship to addiction needs to be explored. Drugs do have an effect. That is impossible to deny. The question is: where is the effect located? Is it located in the drug or is it located in the psyche? If it is located in the psyche, what is it in the psyche that drugs react to or indeed interact with? We can advance this exploration with a critical analysis of an article by Alfred Gross that specifically deals with toxic effects in—and on—the psyche. This article is unique because of its subject matter. I am not aware of any other psychoanalytic literature that attempts to analyse the effects of toxicity on the psyche. It will also be extremely interesting to examine the reasons why this article fails to do what it set out to do. It will be worthwhile to analyse this article in some detail.

The benefits of a "Gross" error

"The psychic effects of toxic and toxoid substances" was published in 1935. Gross began by saying that we are subject to toxic effects on a daily basis. He suggested that a "psychopathology of everyday life" exists in terms of toxicity (Gross, 1935, p. 426). Addiction is only one aspect of this vast area. He agreed that we don't know much about addiction, but he argued that this ignorance applies to toxicity in general. Therefore he suggested that it might be helpful to investigate the effects of toxicity on the psyche. Addiction is only one reaction to toxic substances, although it is an extreme reaction (Ibid., p. 426).

Gross wondered whether it was possible to find a formula that included all varieties, multiplicities, and contradictions of toxic and toxoid effects on the psyche. The whole range of effects is so confusing that a formula might perhaps be able to bring some structure. He immediately perceived that the division of the effects of drugs into the categories of pleasure-producing and pain-averting is insufficient, because people react differently to drugs. In other words, there is an individual psychological factor at work. The pleasure principle cannot be the formula that will structure the mess. Gross was of the opinion that there must be a regulating principle at work. First the facts: certain drugs produce certain effects (such as caffeine and heroine), different quantities of drugs produce different effects, people react differently to the same drug, the same person reacts differently to the same drug at different times, means of incorporation produce different effects and so forth. Beneath all this there must be a "principle of multiplicity", something that is able to reduce all the different variants to a number of basic ones. Gross reduced all the variants to five basic principles: (1) the qualitative pharmacogenic variant (the kind of drug used); (2) the quantitative psychogenic variant (how much is used); (3) the individual psychogenic variant (different personalities); (4) the intra-individual or dispositional variant (different possible reactions within the same person); and (5) the method of incorporation (p. 429).

In order to find the common factor in this Gross proposed to investigate two opposite types of toxic actions at a level which is psychological rather than neurological. The common factor between stimulants and sedatives is that they affect the same system, namely the psychic process. The stimulant accelerates a process already there and the sedative slows this process down. This mobilizing or paralysing movement is called the "primary toxic process" (p. 431). He subsequently related acceleration to the psychic experience of intensification and retardation to the sensation of weakening. This introduced the terms of time and energy.[7] Gross did not pursue this any further, but it is hard to resist comparing his ideas to Freud's drive theory. The energy being the source of the drive and the effect of time (the slowing down or speeding up of a process) on the energy must surely be the pressure. It is absolutely remarkable that Gross never referred to Freud's drive theory. It is less remarkable that he does not refer to Freud's work on cocaine (which covers exactly the same ground), because, unlike Freud's work on the drive theory, his work on cocaine wasn't officially published at the time.

Next, Gross introduced analgesics, hypnotics, and narcotics into the investigation. He feels that these drugs relate more to the Perception–Consciousness System (Pcpt–Cs), that is to say, the system that receives and selects stimuli of an auditory, visual or tactile nature. The effects modified by this Pcpt–Cs System are secondary to the primary process. By this, Gross meant that when these stimuli, caused by aforementioned drugs, hit the psychic apparatus "the first result is a purely quantitative change (...) in the functioning of the particular system affected" (p. 431). This quantitative change in functioning can be experienced as pleasure or pain and anything else in between. This makes the pleasure principle a secondary process in the functioning of toxic substances and not a primary process, as Freud would have it. This is relevant in so far as the implication of this is that the outcome of the toxic influence of the drug is unpredictable; it is subject to a primary process which can cause variations in the effects of the drug. This led Gross to say that the psychic impulse to incorporate drugs had nothing to do with the "primary process of toxic action". He wrote: "The impulse to incorporate is an independent psychic act, prior to the primary toxic process, and its aetiology has no more to do with that of the primary process than desire has to do with enjoyment" (p. 432). There are three stages in the process of drugs causing effects that can be put into the following sequence: (1) the impulse to incorporate; (2) the primary process; and (3) the secondary process. It is important to keep in mind that the primary process is independent of the pleasure principle and that the secondary process is subject to that principle. The impulse to use drugs, no doubt, relates to the desire for a pleasure-effect or relief-of-pain-effect. The impulse is also subject to the pleasure principle. It is difficult to know in what direction Gross is moving unless you realize that the primary process, as the first port of call for the action of drugs, is nothing more than the psychic energy. Drugs can transmute psychic energy; this energy can be activated, bound, displaced and concentrated in the psyche. This is reminiscent of Freud's work on cocaine. The difference between Freud and Gross, however, is that Freud tried to locate an energy in the organism that would be affected by cocaine, whilst Gross located the energy exclusively in the psyche. For both, however, this energy is to some degree an unpredictable factor.

Gross then felt that he had found his formula and he put

forward the following three propositions: (1) the sphere of drug action stops at the threshold of the psyche where it evokes the primary process; (2) this process is part of the psychic economy, it employs energy and it is disproportionate to the toxicity of the drug; and (3) the primary process transmutes energy by changing its form and by displacing its quantity. It is most curious that Gross never referred to Freud's primary processes from *The Interpretation of Dreams*, namely condensation and displacement. Freud considered these to be the fundamental mechanisms of the psyche and the formation of dreams. Lacan replaced these terms with the linguistic terms of metaphor and metonymy in order to show that the unconscious is structured like a language. For Lacan, this means that language has a determining effect on the psyche of the subject and also, ultimately, on the distribution of energy for the subject.

With regards to the first proposition, Gross argued that there are two aspects to it, one general and one specific. The general aspect is that a drug is a blind force (like a blow to the head) that produces an undifferentiated effect. It is a force set in motion by the toxicity of the drug, but in itself it is divorced from the toxic dynamics of the drug. In other words, the drug is left outside the internal dynamics of the psyche. The specific aspect is that once the force has taken effect "it is not uniform in its selection of the particular inherent psychic energy with which it works" (p. 434). The force, once set in motion, acquires its own dynamic which is dependent on the energy characteristics of the individual. Again, what springs to mind here is the unpredictable factor that Freud isolated in his work on cocaine.

With regards to the second proposition, Gross said that the psychic energy is not proportionate to the toxic energy, but the latter is, in fact, subject to the five "principles of multiplicity" set out at the very beginning. Gross made four points: (1) psychic energy is the object of the primary process and it is mobilized by the toxic force; (2) quantity of psychic energy is disproportionate to toxic energy; (3) what truly matters in terms of effect is the displacement and form of energy; and (4) the amount of energy available for primary process is variable. Gross's conclusion was that the action of drugs does not differ from any other action on the psyche. Toxic action is only subject to the inherent energy economy of the psyche. Therefore, addiction has nothing to do with the toxic action of drugs.

Gross made clear how he differed from other thinkers on the subject of toxicity: drugs do not generate energy; they liberate energy.[8] Gross now asserts that addiction is not produced by drugs, but by the energy inherent in the psyche that can be displaced by drugs (p. 436). This energy has a limited supply and when this has been depleted the effects of drugs cease to exist. The variations in energy inherent in the psyche of individuals must surely be governed by certain laws. Gross did not know what these laws were. The variability of the energies made him think of a simile that demonstrates precisely the crucial lack in his logic. He wrote:

> Let us picture this psychic energy as a waterfall, say a mountain stream which has only a small volume of water. In order to make a "beauty-spot" for strangers to visit, the people who live on the mountain-side place at a certain point in the course of the stream a dam which they can remove at will and which acts like a sluice-gate, behind which the meagre flow of water collects. When the gate is opened, the damned-up water rushes down with great force. If the dam is left open or opened several times in rapid succession, there will be much less result and finally none at all, because enough water has not collected behind the barrier. Conversely, if the gate is left shut for some time, the spectacle of the waterfall will be renewed, and the longer the interval the more striking will the spectacle be (p. 438).

The flow of water is the psychic energy, the dam stands for the normal or neurotic inhibitions of the psychic apparatus and the force which opens the sluice gate is the toxic substance. According to Gross this simile clarified a number of things: the action of drugs weakens over time; this creates a wish for temporary abstinence; the real source of toxic action is the inherent energy (the drug is only the vehicle for transmutation and displacement); and lastly inherent psychic energy is exhaustible and renewable over time.

These conclusions are utterly sensible. Especially interesting is the implication of the third conclusion, namely that the toxicity is part of the individual and not necessarily part of the drug. In that case, what is needed is a psychoanalytic theory of toxicity, a theory of toxicity that is not based on chemical formulas and chemical effects, but a theory that includes the subject. For the development of such a theory the reader is referred to Part III.

What does not make sense is that the energy is restricted to the psyche and does not include the body, unless the body is included in Gross's conception of the psyche. There can be no doubt that drugs and alcohol affect both mind and body, which is the clearest evidence for the assertion that the difference between mind and body is not to be taken as absolute. If the body is affected (like the psychic energy) by drugs then perhaps there is also an equivalent toxicity of the body? Although I feel constrained to withhold an answer to this question until Chapter 7, it is, however, relevant at this stage to mention that the different transmutations and destinies of (psychic) energy correspond to the different forms of jouissance that Lacan formulated in the latter part of his work.[9]

Paradoxically, the lack in Gross's conclusion provides us with a crucial question. What is the role of the people who want a "beauty spot" for others or, indeed, for themselves? These are the people who want to reap the benefits from the mountain stream of energy, the people who want to enjoy the possibility of the usufruct of this energy and this "beauty spot". They might even want to get themselves out of a "bad spot" this way. Their action or desire will surely be the decisive factor—at least to some degree—as to what happens to the stream of energy and how it can be enjoyed. The people in this simile who desire a beauty spot or, indeed, a bad spot, represent the subject. The sluice-gate, as energy regulator (by displacing and concentrating water) on which drugs operate, represents the laws of language or the function of the signifier. The stream of water that can increase, decrease or disappear altogether, represents jouissance. The dam represents the existence of language, something that is a primordial barrier in the subject. Without this subject the simile does not make sense nor does the rest of the article. The cause of the effect (of drugs or the beauty/bad spot) must be related to the subject. This subject has a relationship to language (the sluice-gate) and jouissance (the mountain stream). The fundamental (but very instructive) error Gross commits is that one can never know how drugs effect someone and that, likewise, one can never know how—and in what way—the beauty/bad spot functions for people, unless one asks these people (the subject) to speak about the effect (of their actions). This subject is the "missing link" in the story.

Conclusion: the necessity for a little "tête-à-bête" and a "missing link"

To study the effects of drugs or alcohol independently of the subject who speaks about them is methodologically incorrect. Magoudi states that the analyst should be concerned with the place of drugs only in so far as it has a place in the discourse of the patient (Magoudi, 1986, p. 105). That is precisely the problem. Gross's simile demonstrates well that drugs try to push the barrier of language as the force operating on the sluice-gate. Nevertheless, it is the only way. As Lacan says, all determination of the subject depends on discourse (Lacan, 1991, p. 178). It is very tempting to describe all the possible effects drugs can have on a subject, but that will only end up in yet another classification of effects that bears no relationship to subjective experience and will therefore not contribute to an understanding of addiction. It is important not to articulate something at the level of the object (drug or alcohol), but to have something articulated at the level of the subject. Only when operating with articulated signifiers is it possible to learn something about the cause of addiction. There is no a priori knowledge available that can indicate a cause of addiction (never mind predict it), no matter how sophisticated the classification systems of drug effects are. It is only speech that can determine the place of the object because the place of the object is determined by discourse. It is language that constitutes the object in psychoanalysis. And it makes no difference whether this is the lost object that makes us desire or whether this is the world of objects to which we relate with our object relations.

If, as was stated in the conclusion to Part I, addiction is the waste-product, or (lost) object, of psychoanalysis, then psychoanalysis has to listen to how the object drug speaks in the subject. Only the spoken signifiers can determine the place of the drugs and their effect in the structure of the subject. In other words, there is no essence to drugs and addiction. This is implicit in Freud's thinking considering the fact that addiction can be related to virtually all his meta-psychological concepts in some way or another. This was even stated explicitly by Freud: "the most interesting methods of averting suffering are those which seek to influence our own organism" (Freud, 1930a, p. 78). Drugs are not essential precisely because suffering is essentially subjective, and the implication of this is that it is only through the subject that we might gain access to the place of drugs and alcohol in the lives of people. And there are as many places to be occupied by drugs as there are subjects.

Does that mean that one cannot speak about addiction? In a manner of speaking one can't: the subject is the only agent who can indicate the place of the object he or she is addicted to. All people are addicted to this object (the lost object–cause-of-desire) and the problem is that the place of this object is ultimately always empty. No drug can fill this place to make it essential. To situate drugs and alcohol only in relation to the drives leads to an impasse, because the trajectory of the drive circles around the object. This trajectory misses its aim because the object is a void. The object and the drive cannot be connected through an essential link. There is always a "missing link" and it is precisely that "missing link" that designates the place of the subject. The "missing link" is the subject.

To place the object drug or addiction only in relation to the ego is as problematic as relating it to the drive. The ego is an image, an identification of an image with the body. If the drug supplements a default in the ego, then one needs to know precisely what a body is. Neither the drive oriented theorists, nor the ego-psychologists, relate addiction to the "missing link" of the subject and the body. For an understanding of these one needs Lacanian theory. When one considers the ego, i.e., an image of the body, one has returned to the drive. That is to say, one has returned to an image of the drive which Freud named libido. The drives originate in the body and they demand representation by the psyche. They are a demand "upon the mind for work" (Freud, 1915c, p. 122). The problem is that not everything of the drive and the body can be represented. Not everything can be represented because the representation is through language or the discourse of the Other, and these are incomplete, which always leaves a remainder.[10] The subject who is designated by language and represented by the signifier has to live with this remainder, which is the unrepresented aspect of the drive of his or her demand, and the cause of his or her desire. This demand insists and the desire is ongoing. The cause of the desire is the cause of suffering and therefore the cause of our discontent in civilization. That is exactly why drugs are so effective, but it is important to keep in mind that they are effective in relation to something unrepresentable. Drugs and alcohol have an extreme and massive effect because they function outside the realm of language and they push against the limits of language. Having said this it needs to be stated that although drugs and alcohol function outside language, this by no means implies that there is no relationship between language and the effects of drugs and alcohol. The nature of this relationship is a crucial element in a psychoanalytic understanding of addiction and will therefore be considered later on.

It would be unjust to say that the drive theorists and the ego-psychologists were completely wrong, but each thought that they had told the whole story. However, this does not imply that in order to complete the story all that is necessary is to combine both positions so that one can complement the other. It is rather that someone needed to bang their heads together so hard that it would produce an irreducible remainder.

The "missing link" between drive theory and ego-psychology is the subject. Who or what is this subject? Gross's simile serves us well again here. It can be supposed that the subject is the one for whom the energies in nature, such as a mountain stream, can take on significance. The possibilities, laws and energies in nature presume a subject. It is not possible to say: "the possibilities, laws and energies that exist in nature", because that would mean that they do not suppose a subject. It would be ridiculous to think that a mountain, a stream, an energy, could suddenly realize its own potential as a possible beauty spot, and then transmute itself in order to create such a spot. The subject is the cause who wants to effect transmutations, do calculations, and who desires to create something new, different, or remain the same at all costs. The subject cannot be equated with the individuals who live on the mountain who want a beauty spot. It is something more than that. Or perhaps it is better to say, that it is something within them that causes them to think that there is something more (to them and to others). This subject is not essential, but it exists and its existence is extremely well demonstrated by dreams, parapraxes and jokes. These are all aspects of everyday (night) life that overcome people and that do not belong to their individual personalities. They come to the conscious ego and catch it by surprise; they come from the subject of the unconscious.

A reading of the *Interpretation of Dreams*, *The Psychopathology of Everyday Life* and *Jokes and their Relation to the Unconscious* demonstrates very clearly the difference between the ego and the subject.

The subject is the very split between the ego and the unconscious. It is therefore neither the false sense of self nor the language that marks the subject and directs his or her life without them knowing it. In other words, it is not the discourse of the Other in the subject. The subject is exactly what makes sure that the false self and the discourse of the Other do not meet. Put another way, if the subject wasn't there to separate the two, the result would be absolute madness. An ego that is the discourse of the Other is speaking in tongues. The unconscious is constituted in the camp of the Other. The ego comes about via an image outside itself. The subject is the one element in human existence that truly does not belong to an outside camp. It is the exception. This can also be put in an inverted way: everything in human existence belongs to a particular camp. This camp can be collected in the set of outside camps. If the limit of this set is defined by that which is not Other, then it is the subject who defines this limit. The subject is the exceptional element which defines the limit and therefore the set itself. This is not just a mental exercise for its own sake. The subject is a necessary assumption. If everything in human existence is an indication of otherness there has to be a point for which—or in relation to which—this otherness is there. There has to be a point against which something is other. This point is the subject. It is that element in us which causes us to say that we don't quite feel ourselves. The irony is that we need that distance from being truly ourselves. We need the distance of representation, i.e., we need the imaginary and symbolic to distance ourselves from ourselves. If that is not the case one will experience the uncanny deep familiarity of the psychotic-like moment of depersonalization, an experience that occurs to people close to death or in utter trauma. When people say after such experiences, that they have always kind of known this (which is often said), they are already beginning to take a distance by trying to symbolize the utterly familiar, yet most alien, part of themselves.

The subject can only be known in so far as it produces effects in the very material that causes this subject. The material that causes the subject is language, but it is important to keep in mind that the relationship between language and the subject is not straightforward and transparent. Freud had sensed this complication very well when he wrote *The Interpretation of Dreams*. He made it very clear that there is no point to finding a meaning in the dream. The dream means absolutely nothing in itself. It is only after the dreamer has spoken about the dream that the significance of the dream might be revealed. What matters is not what one dreams, but how one speaks about it. And when the dream is being put into words, there will always be a point where these words come to a halt. Freud called this point the navel of the dream, the precise point from which the dream originates. This point is the cause of the dream and it is the location of the subject. The subject is located outside—or between—signifiers and words. The cause of the subject can only be indicated through effects in language.

As mentioned before, to link the effect to a cause without supposing the "missing link" of the subject, leads to an impasse. In terms of Gross's example this impasse can be explained as follows: the desire for a beauty spot cannot be located without the subject who speaks. Without speech all that can be located is the effect, i.e., the beauty spot. Without the speaking subject the effects of drugs (including addiction) cannot be related to a particular cause. This cause is particular because it belongs to the subject and it is only via the subject that it produces effects. Cause and effect can only be grasped via the subject. If the cause of the subject is located in language and if the effects of the subject (symptoms, dreams, parapraxes, etc.) are expressed in language, then one must logically come to the conclusion that it is only the subject who can articulate something about the effects of drugs and the cause of these effects. But that entails a difficulty: the effects of drugs do not express themselves in language. Effects of drugs are always in the real. The therapeutic challenge is to try and get addicts to replace these effects by language. But that leads to the following question: how can language have an effect if the effects of drugs are outside language? Language can have an effect precisely because the cause of the specificity of the effects of drugs is related to language. Language (or the signifier) constitutes the subject and his or her specificity and that includes the specificity of the effects of drugs (the individual variations in the effects of drugs or the "variable factor" from Freud's cocaine studies).[11] The causes of the effects of drugs can be approached by language. That is why it is important in the treatment of addicts to move from the effect to the cause via the medium of articulation, so that the speech (about the cause) of the subject can change the specific effect that causes the addiction. The hope is that this effect, which is an effect in the real, changes its nature in such a way that it doesn't cause addiction anymore. That is the difficult movement from avoiding words to the choice of words: from a-diction to diction.

What can be learned about addiction from Lacan? This question will be the subject matter of Part III. What is certainly known already at this stage is that he wasn't very good at a-diction: he produced an extraordinary amount of spoken seminars. Part III concerns some of the relevant aspects of Lacan's vast body of work.

Notes

1. Yorke mentioned papers by Ferenczi (1911), Birstein (1913), Burger (1912, 1913, 1916), Tausk (1915), Clark (1919), Marx (1923) and Hartman (1925) (Yorke, 1970, p. 146).
2. Yorke writes: "Only Sachs (1923) considered the addiction to alcohol and drugs together in search of a common pathology and found in these conditions a compromise between the perversions and the compulsion neuroses" (op. cit., 1970, p. 146).
3. Mijolla (de) and Shentoub write that Kielholz (1923, 1925) refers to narcissistic neurosis and manic-depressive states and that Ferenczi (1911) mentions paranoia (1973, pp. 56 & 59).
4. Radö promises to discuss the conditions in women in another article (Radö, 1984[1933], p. 67).
5. Incidentally, indiscriminate sexual behaviour is now considered to be an addiction to sex, whilst bulimia and anorexia are addictions to food and the lack of food respectively.
6. Simmel had a great interest in addiction and he set up a psychoanalytic sanatorium ("Schloss Tegel") for those suffering from "morbid cravings", as he called it. He wrote an excellent account of the treatment of addiction in this sanatorium (Simmel, 1929). He has written a number of other articles on alcoholism and drug-addiction. Also Bergler has written a number of articles and books on addiction. One of his books is on the addiction to gambling. This excellent book is a standard work on compulsive gambling (Bergler, 1957). For a complete list of references and a more detailed survey of the later non-Freudian psychoanalytic literature the reader is referred to the aforementioned works by Ferbos and Magoudi (1986), Limentani (1986), Mijolla and Shentoub (1981), Yorke (1970), Rosenfeld (1964). An interesting article that deals with an overview of the differences

between drive-theory and ego-psychology was published by Kamran Ghaffari (Ghaffari, 1987). An excellent collection of classical, standard, and recent papers on psychoanalysis and addiction was edited by Daniel Yalisove (Yalisove, 1997). A book by Leon Wurmser on the psychodynamics of compulsive drug use should be mentioned (Wurmser, 1995) and there is also a book by Louis Berger on treatment approaches and cultural beliefs about addiction and addiction treatment (Berger, 1991). These are only some of the books and articles dealing with the topic of psychoanalysis and addiction. There are many more, but as indicated before, often they are no more than variations on the same theme without being able to make any new contribution to our understanding of addiction. As an illustration of this it is useful to read an article by Morgenstern and Leeds (Morgenstern & Leeds, 1993, pp. 194–206). Excluded here are the Lacanian texts dealing with addiction because they will be referred to in the third part of this work. The reader is advised to avoid the later texts on psychoanalysis and addiction, but to read Freud and the "classic texts" referred to in this chapter.

7. Acceleration and retardation indicate the decrease and increase of time spent moving from one point to another, whilst intensification and weakening refer to the accumulation and decrease of pressure concerning an energy.

8. Again, we must assume that he was not familiar with Freud's ideas on the action of cocaine.

9. Despite an exploration of Lacan's concept of jouissance in Part III (and a brief mention of it in Part I), it might be of help to the reader to have some more information about this difficult concept at this stage. We alluded before to the fact that Freud's drive theory contains an energistic element. The tension or energy from the erogenous zones seeks release in the form of satisfaction, but that process is inhibited by repression. Some of this energy will, indeed, be discharged, whilst the rest will be retained and accumulated. There is a third possibility which is not a reality for the human being and that is a complete and full discharge of all the energy. That complete satisfaction would annihilate the subject. A partial discharge of energy (a limited form of pleasure) is called phallic jouissance by Lacan. He calls this phallic because this form of satisfaction is limited by language and it is the identification with the phallus that hooks the subject to language. The rest of the energy that will be retained in the psyche of the subject is called a surplus-jouissance (a more-to-be-enjoyed) by Lacan. It is a surplus because it is accumulated, ready to be used, but not actually used. This jouissance is maintained and built up in the erogenous zones. The total

satisfaction is called the jouissance of the Other by Lacan, because the subject supposes that this possibility exists, but always somewhere else. It supposes it in the Otherness of elsewhere and of course it does exist in the Otherness of death.

10. The incompleteness of language and the Other will be discussed in Part III. The structural incompleteness of language as the discourse of the Other is an essential aspect of Lacan's theory. There are aspects of human existence that are doomed forever to remain outside the realm of language and are therefore deeply disturbing and traumatic for people. Lacan names this aspect of ex-istence the real. This completes the triad of the real, the imaginary and the symbolic. The three orders that define the human subject and its reality.

11. The theoretical framework of reference for the study of addiction in this work is related to research in the area of language. However, it seems obvious, when I propose that there is a connection between language and the subject-specific effects of drugs, that empirical research on the relationship between neuro-biology and language in the field of addiction studies could be considered in the future. Colwyn Trevarthen's work on autism, language and biology is perhaps leading the way in this area (Trevarthen et al., 1998).

PART III:
ELEMENTS FOR A LACANIAN THEORY (AND TREATMENT) OF ADDICTION: THE ADMINISTRATION OF TOXICITY

Introduction

Lacan hardly ever referred to drugs or addiction. One could conclude from this that he wasn't interested at all or that he didn't think addiction was important. But, it is important not be too hasty. Hugo Freda has indicated that Lacan made six references to drugs or toxicomania.[1] In 1938 in *Family Complexes in the Formation of the Individual* Lacan suggests that addiction is related to a "lost universal harmony" and that it is an attempt to rediscover the "imago of the mother" (Lacan, 1938, pp. 12–13). In 1946 in "Propos sur la causalite psychique" he relates it to the attempt to resolve the "primordial discordance between the ego and being"; "an unfathomable concession to freedom", he calls it (Lacan, 1966[1946], p. 187). In 1960 in "Subversion of the subject and the dialectic of desire in the Freudian unconscious" Lacan claims that "the experience obtained under the influence of hallucinogenic drugs" has something to do with wanting to undo the division of the subject, and it pertains perhaps to reaching a state of pure thought, by eliminating the dimension of jouissance. This is something that is akin to Platonic enthusiasm or Buddhist meditation (Lacan, 1977[1960], p. 294). In 1966 in "La place de la psychanalyse dans la médecine" he says that scientific discourse confers a new status onto "tranquilizers and hallucinogenics" (Lacan, 1966, p. 767). The legislators of medical practice impose two duties: "controlled use...of drugs" and "an ethical dimension which moves into the direction of jouissance" (Ibid.). Lacan's remarks in this round table discussion also imply that toxicomania is following the path of (medical) science and is becoming increasingly dependent on, what he calls, an "epistemo-somatic relationship" to the body (Ibid.). In 1973 in his Seminar *Les Non-Dupes Errent* Lacan says that "hash is superfluous" and when one considers the immediate context of this remark it actually suggests that hash is not a source of knowledge (1974, lecture from 18 December 1973). In 1975 in the "Culture aux journees d'études des cartels" he makes his most famous remark: "there is no other definition of a drug than this one: it is something that permits the separation from the marriage with the 'little willy'" (Lacan, 1975a, p. 268, my translation).

The implications of this last remark will be explored further on in this work. The other five remarks are certainly not groundbreaking. The first three indicate that Lacan's thinking is not much different to Freud's. Toxicomania is the attempt to undo a loss, to eliminate discomfort and to reach a more agreeable state of mind. The fourth remark is more interesting in that he indicates that medicine and toxicomania collude, whilst the fifth remark in a way confirms Freud's discovery that there is little to be expected from drugs with regards to knowledge about them in terms of the people who use them.

There is another remark made by Lacan which was not mentioned by Hugo Freda. Jean Pierre Dupont paraphrases Lacan when he says "in any case speech always addresses toxcicomaniacs".[2] That is a curious remark. It implies that everyone who speaks is an addict and that addiction has everything to do with language. It is perhaps not so curious if one relates this remark to the previous one. The idea that drugs help to undo the marriage to the "little willy" means nothing other than that drugs allow someone to break away from the restrictions put on us by the phallus, i.e., drugs are an attempt to escape the consequences of castration. Once one lives and functions in language one is poisoned by a passion for something else.[3] Language employs us and enjoys us (Lacan, 1991, p. 74). People might wish to escape this situation from time to time. But once one escapes the limits and limitations of language one finds oneself in the realm of the death-drive.

INTRODUCTION   135

Chapters 6 and 7 deal with two different aspects of the death-drive. In these chapters it is argued that the death-drive cannot be equated with a simple death-wish, as is so often proclaimed in psychoanalytic circles. It is demonstrated that addiction has various connections to the death-drive. Chapter 6 is more specifically concerned with the symbolic and the imaginary as the representational aspects of the death-drive. From this angle it is possible to investigate how death can bring pleasure and how this relates to the attempt to master death.

Chapter 7 is concerned with the real aspect of the death-drive: the realm that is situated beyond symbolic and imaginary representation, but also beyond normal daily pleasure. This is a toxic realm and this realm will also be related to the body. When something of the body is not represented in the symbolic/imaginary realm, one is faced with a toxicity of the body. This is an aspect of the body that suffers in the real. This idea introduces a new psychoanalytic theory on toxicity. Why a psychoanalytic theory of toxicity? Because one can expect very little from drugs in the way of a knowledge about how the subject becomes addicted to them. A conception of toxicity that includes the subject and the body will bring us closer to the true nature of addiction.

Chapter 8 is concerned with psychopathology and addiction. A psychopathology that is exclusively based on empirical, positivist or descriptive science will run into difficulties in terms of understanding the complexities involved in addiction. In this chapter it is argued that, if one is to further an understanding of addiction, and if one is to intervene more efficiently in the field, addiction will need to be related to the different clinical structures and as such, incorporate the complexities involved in this field of work. The incorporation of complexities happens precisely by not excluding the subject from research and clinical practice. The idea proposed here is to build the foundation for a differential diagnosis for addiction by introducing a concept that functions as a hinge between the clinical structures and addiction. This concept distinguishes between toxicomania and the ordinary use of alcohol and drugs. This concept is named administration for a variety of reasons that will be demonstrated in the text. However, a brief mention at this stage of how the etymology has again been kind to us, might be appropriate. The word administration comes from the

Latin administrare, which means to minister to. This in turn comes from ministrare and that indicates to serve. A minister is a servant. The term administration is very appropriate as addiction is enslavement to enjoyment (jouissance), as well as to language. Addiction is a matter of the subject being caught, as minister or slave, between two masters and it is characterized by the choice of the subject for (going "lock, stock and barrel" for) the One (of jouissance) rather than the Other (of language).

Chapter 9 considers addiction to be a particular social bond. The consequences this particular bond might have for a moral attitude towards—and treatment of—addiction, are investigated. In comparing the discourse (or social bond) of addiction with the discourse of science it is demonstrated that there is a dangerous complicity involved, as both exclude the subject from any say in the matter. Hence, the relevance of the involvement of a discourse that aims at the responsibility of the subject is argued in this chapter. However, in confronting the discourse of analysis with addiction, a similarity rears its ugly head. The addict has a tendency to turn the therapeutic or analytical relationship into an idealized relationship with hypnotic qualities. If that is the case, what is one to do? This question will be taken up again in the conclusion.

Notes

1. These six references were compiled by Carlo Vigano in his article "Les nouveaux symptomes et la question préliminaire: l'example de la toxicomanie" (1999, pp. 49–51).
2. This remark was made in a roundtable discussion on toxicomania published under the title Discours de la Toxicomanie (Dupont, 1984, p. 51).
3. According to Plato language and passion can be poisonous to man (Plato, Laws II, 935a).

CHAPTER SIX

The pleasure before death: the symbolic, the imaginary and jouissance

"As mortals we are afraid of everything, but we desire everything as though we were immortal"

La Rochefoucauld, *Maxims*, 1959, p. 105

The moral of a story

Toxicomania (alcohol and drug addiction) often leads to an early death. That is an observable and well-established fact. But does that therefore mean that toxicomaniacs desire death? This question is not so easily answered, because desire is not necessarily observable and its object is difficult to establish.

The problematic nature of this question can be illustrated with a well known story: Someone goes up to two alcoholics and says to them—with the best of intentions—"Do you know that alcohol kills you slowly?" They look at each other, and one of them answers: "Ah, well, we're not in a hurry."

The interesting thing about this story is that the well-meaning person wants to inform the two alcoholics about the objective fact of the lethal dangers of drinking, and so is communicating at an educational level. However, the good intentions and the educational facts are completely swept aside by a reply which is communicated at an entirely different level. The answer does not respond to the fact that drinking leads to an early death but, instead, deals with the question of how and when to die. It is thus an answer on the level of the desire of the subject, and represents the desire not to end things too quickly. At the same time, it appears to refer indirectly to an enjoyment which might be there before the end comes—"Life is short so let's enjoy it while we can". The essential point is that the alcoholic's answer implies the acceptance of a life which is profoundly mixed-up with death. The informative question of the well-meaning person—meanwhile—aims at separating death from life, by avoiding the former as long as possible. This attitude reflects the attempt of the positivistically orientated human and medical sciences to ignore as far as possible the fact that life is conjoined to death from the very beginning. Indeed, it is this ignorance which takes the place of truth in scientific discourse. Lacan suggests that life-insurance is the translation of the fact of our mortality into the discourse of science. In other words, "death", in science has no other significance than a calculation of probabilities (Lacan, 1973, p. 32).

This aphorism should not be taken to suggest that alcoholism or toxicomania, in general, implies an unproblematic acceptance by addicted subjects of their relationship to death. In fact, this will prove to be far from unproblematic. What this story emphasizes is the surprise one encounters in the addict's answer and that therefore only by refusing to ignore the speech of the subject will one come to know something about the conjunction of life and death.

The speech of the subject reflects the desire of the subject, and his or her relationship to enjoyment. Lacan constantly draws attention to the fact that there is a close relationship between desire, death and enjoyment (or jouissance as he calls it). An exploration of these relationships is of crucial importance for an understanding of toxicomania. The reason is that this clinical condition—more than any other—seems to centre precisely upon the complex entanglement of life, death and jouissance. A consideration of toxicomania will—in turn—allow the illustration of the function of the death-drive in human existence, because this concept indicates the pivotal point around which the entanglement gravitates.

The meaning of life and a sense of death

According to Lacan it is the Freudian dialectic, through its emphasis on the realm of meaning, which has led us to consider human existence as the zone where life and death are conjoined. He says:

> That is what life is—a detour, a dogged detour, in itself transitory and precarious, and deprived of any significance. Why, in that of its manifestations called man, does something happen, which insists throughout his life, which is called a meaning? We call it human, but are we so sure? Is this meaning as human as all that? A meaning is an order, that is to say, a sudden emergence. A meaning is an order which suddenly emerges. A life insists on entering into it, but it expresses something which is perhaps completely beyond this life, behind the drama of the passage into existence, we find nothing besides life conjoined to death (Lacan, 1988a, p. 232).

When meaning enters the realm of life we pass into human existence and—simultaneously—death joins life. This is because language—which is the locus from which meaning is determined—introduces something into the subject, something which can be considered to be the cause of the subject. The cause of the subject is the signifier; consequently, no subject can be its own cause, as Lacan says in "Position of the unconscious" (Lacan, 1995[1964], pp. 265, 269). So, if the subject is indeed constituted by the signifier of the Other (that is, by language), then the subject is alienated from itself. The subject disappears under the signifier which, from now on, will merely represent the subject. This implies that the subject is a cause in the real as it is excluded from the symbolic in which it is only represented. The effect of the cause of the subject is death, but, as will be demonstrated, it is also desire.[1]

The conjunction or union of human life and death divides the subject, because it imposes a choice which has the logical structure of an "either/or". This is what Lacan calls the "vel of alienation". The conjunction of life and death causes a logical disjunction which is illustrated by certain demands. As speaking-beings, confronted with the desire emanating from the field of the Other, one understands the significance of these demands only too well. They can be articulated as follows: "your Money or your Life" and "Liberty or Death". With regard to these two choices Lacan writes:

It is merely a question of knowing whether or not (*sic aut non*) you want to keep life or refuse death, because, regarding the other term in the alternative, money or liberty, your choice will in any case be disappointing. You should be aware that what remains is, in any case, diminished: it will be life without money and, having refused death, a life somewhat inconvenienced by the cost of freedom (Ibid., p. 270).

In other words: in order to live you have to lose something, and it is this loss which causes desire for that which one can not have—unless, of course, one is prepared to lose life. The irony is that—in the end—death arrives anyway, and also that one is fully conscious of this fact. This, then, is the meaning of life.

Language and meaning introduce death into the life of the subject. For the speaking being, life carries within it the dimension of death (Lacan, 1975a, p. 32). Death can be imagined, thought, ignored and feared. Death is (re)presented by the signifier, and therefore can also be desired. In this sense, it is possible to say that it is the (re)presentation of death which inaugurates the possibility of a death-drive.

It is this representational sense of "death" or "death-drive" which plays a prominent (though, as will be seen, by no means the only) role in the clinical picture of addiction. Hence, it is important to comment on this sense of "death" which provides us with an image of something "beyond" life.

Life, death, God, woman and...

At the end of *Thoughts for the Times on War and Death* Freud gives us a little bit of advice: "If you want to endure life, prepare yourself for death" (Freud, 1915b, p. 300). This is obviously a very difficult thing to do because, in life, it is our own inevitable death that is feared above all else. The fear of this certainty is so great that, unconsciously, one is convinced of its opposite. Unconsciously one does not believe in one's own death and one behaves as if one is immortal (Ibid., p. 296).[2] Previously it was asserted that meaning provides us with an image of death. It must now be conceded that this image of death as "beyond life" is of a paradoxical nature. Indeed, everything seems to indicate that—in fact—we want to eliminate death from life as much as possible. Freud wrote:

It is indeed impossible to imagine our own death; and whenever we attempt to do so we can perceive that we are in fact still present as spectators. Hence the psychoanalytic school could venture on the assertion that at bottom no one believes his own death, or, to put the same thing another way, that in the unconscious every one of us is convinced of his own immortality (Ibid., p. 289).

One can now understand the paradoxical nature of the image of death beyond life: consciously you know for sure that you will die, but unconsciously, we all believe in immortality. Perhaps Lacan's remark, that the only true formula of atheism is "God is unconscious" (Lacan, 1979, p. 59), can also be understood in this way. The only means by which it is possible to circumvent the certainty and fear of death is by introducing the illusion of a choice, to believe in the religious representation of an after-life, which reduces life before death to a mere preparation for another life. However, it is perhaps better to say that this choice is forced; mortals do not "choose" death in the unconscious.

In *The Theme of the Three Caskets* Freud solved "a small problem", —as he put it (Freud, 1913f, p. 291). This small problem is actually nothing less than the relationship between choice and death. To solve the problem, Freud interpreted the reoccurring theme of "the choice between three sisters", which one finds in myths, fairy tales and classic literature, such as Shakespeare's King Lear. There is an apparent contradiction in this theme "of choice" because—every time—it is the third sister who is selected. Freud concluded that this third sister represents either the Goddess of Death, or else Death itself.

Although Freud's resolution to his problem was quite straightforward, his method of resolving it gives rise to a subsequent problem. The choice always falls on the woman who is apparently characterized by silence, dumbness or a remarkable pallor. These characterizations are all representations of death, indications of what lies beyond the signifier and the pleasure principle. The question is: if one is free to choose, then why choose death? Freud's answer was—again—quite simple. A substitution has taken place. The Goddess of Death has been replaced (by a reaction-formation) with her very opposite, namely the Goddess of Love. Freud wrote: "The third of the sisters was no longer Death; she was the fairest, best, most desirable and most lovable of women" (Ibid., p. 299). But, as always, the replacement maintains its relationship to the substituted element. The mother-goddesses are creators and destroyers, they represent both life and death. It is precisely this double representation that provided Freud with the simple answer to his question. On this representation of the conjunction between life and death he wrote:

> The same consideration answers the question how the feature of a choice came into the myth of the three sisters. Here again there has been a wishful reversal. Choice stands in the place of necessity, of destiny. In this way man overcomes death, which he has recognized intellectually. No greater triumph of wish-fulfilment is conceivable. A choice is made where in reality there is obedience to a compulsion; and what is chosen is not a figure of terror, but the fairest and most desirable of women. (...) The free choice between the three sisters is, properly speaking, no free choice, for it must necessarily fall on the third if every kind of evil is not to come about, as it does in King Lear (Ibid., pp. 299–300).

The "small problem" that Freud resolved here, then, concerns the enigma of our imaginary "mastery" over the Absolute Master: belief in a free choice has provided people with the illusion of a conquest over death. It will be demonstrated that this imaginary relationship between death and choice is also characteristic for toxicomania, but in a rather specific way.

However, one aspect of the problem, which Freud resolved, remains problematic: why should these representations of death be attached to the woman? Freud's last sentence of his paper may provide the beginnings of a possible answer: "... it is in vain that an old man yearns for the love of woman as he had it first from his mother; the third of the Fates alone, the silent Goddess of Death, will take him into her arms" (Ibid., p. 301). There is only one woman who loves unconditionally, and that is Mother Nature who—we can be sure—will always receive us in death—men and women alike. Mother Nature does not make any distinction: her love knows no conditions, because she effaces all difference. She is the only One who can guarantee Oneness and total happiness.[3] Greek mythology has represented her as the third of the Fates, named Atropos, who cuts the thread of life.

In classic literature, mythology and art, death is often represented in the form of a woman. What is the connection between woman and death? Why is she so often placed at the conjunction between life and death? Death is what is radically "other" in human existence. The terror of this radical otherness stares one in the face and captures one's gaze, due to the fascination for this realm beyond life. Lacan suggests that the function of desire stands in a fundamental relationship to death (Lacan, 1992, p. 303). Man has to defend himself against wanting to enter "the unspeakable field of radical desire that is the field of absolute destruction, of destruction beyond putrefaction" (Ibid., p. 216). Man has to defend himself against his desire for annihilation and death. Is the aesthetic beauty of the feminine figure one possible barrier against this terrifying otherness? If the appearance of beauty can disarm this lethal desire (Ibid., p. 238), then the beautiful can be a protective shield against the realm of death.

Why the feminine figure? In Encore Lacan says:

It is in so far as her jouissance is radically Other that the woman has a privileged relation to God which is greater than all that has been able to be stated in ancient speculation according to a path which has manifestly been articulated only as the good of mankind (Lacan, 1975a, p. 77, my translation).

If the jouissance of woman is defined by both the relationship to the Other, and to what is situated beyond this Other, then her image is ideal for representing the intersection between the symbolic order and the real of death which lies beyond. She incarnates this radical division of her jouissance, which maintains a link with what is situated beyond life. Nevertheless, her figure can protect one against death if this division is "stitched up", and she is presented as One and All. Perhaps it is possible to say that the third sister is always chosen because, as the sister of death, she has been substituted by a particular representation of what Lacan calls "The Woman" (Lacan, 1975a, pp. 68 & 75).[4] She is chosen because as, One and All, she is both decoy and illusion of truth. The belief in "The Woman" is, as Lacan says, precisely what analysis will ultimately reveal through lifting the veil from God, who is a manifestation of "an Other of the Other" (Lacan, 1976, p. 39). This is a construction that the human race apparently cannot do without.[5]

It is well known that the discourse of toxicomania—by which is meant its associated literature, poetry, lyrics, art and jargon—contains many references to death and its connection with woman. For instance, it is well accepted that Coleridge's famous poem, *The Rime of the Ancient Mariner*, was influenced by his opium use. Here are two verses from that poem:

> Are those her ribs through which the Sun
> Did peer, as through a gate?
> And is that Woman all her crew?
> Is that a DEATH? And are there two?
> Is DEATH that woman's mate?
>
> Her lips were red, her looks were free,
> Her locks were yellow as gold:
> Her skin was as white as leprosy,
> The Night-Mare LIFE-IN-DEATH was she,
> Who thicks man's blood with cold (Coleridge, 1993, p. 227).

Toxicomania, gambling or the fascination with— and mastery of—death

Toxicomania, gambling, symptoms and death

Drug cultures display a remarkable fascination for an aesthetics related to death. Fernando Geberovich writes:

> The junky aesthetic, is in fact, obsessed with the idea of a ravaging fusion with death. Their relationship to the drug and to the syringe is compared in their poetry and in their music to a gaze captured by the image of a woman dressed with an icy, faultless beauty, of an irresistible herald of death; the imaginary of the junkie has dressed ruination with a post modern and fantastic Moirea. Apocalyptic angel, pale and mute Goddess, inevitably chosen companion, always the same, for dancing "The Last Waltz" which in the mean time one would want to start eternally (Geberovich, 1984, p. 94, my translation).

The junky aesthetic in drug culture is a flirtation with death. It eroticizes and provokes death. It derives enjoyment from the image of death. The New York journalist, Ann Marlowe, wrote a very interesting and informative book about her own heroin addiction.

In relation to the aesthetics involved in heroin addiction she wrote the following two passages:

> The love of heroin is a way of expressing love for an aesthetic as much as anything else. The visual style of heroin is of course different for each user, but in my subculture it was often Gothic—dark, wasted, wan, solemn. And Gothic is popular in youth culture for good reason. It invokes the authority of death and the glamour of danger, laying their beauty and power as a gentle mantle over one's insecurity or even misery (Marlowe, 1999, p. 156).

> There was a beautiful man leaning against a wall, smoking, and I nudged David. "Who is that? Who does he hang out with?" "Oh you mean Stuart? He hangs out by himself. Everybody he used to hang out with is dead." And Stuart acquired an extra layer of glamour for me with David's words. To be so hip that all your friends were dead: that was the deepest layer of cool (Ibid., p. 80).

What is important, however, is that none of this necessarily represents a wish to die but, rather, an attempt to defy death. The junky's proximity to death provides the fantasy of being able to master it. Walking this timeless interzone between life and death, the junkie is disinherited from a history, and curiously enough, also from a future. It is as if this lack of destiny gives him or her the illusion of a free choice between life and death, through which he or she is psychically able to avoid the reality of death. Again Ann Marlowe.

> You could just as well argue that repetition is a device for keeping death at bay. The more your days resemble each other, the less you notice time's passage. This is another way that the constraints of dope life are precisely what the user is after (Ibid., pp. 262–263).

> When I turned to heroin I wanted to halt the flow of time, not so much out of a desire to remain young, but out of a fear of the injuries time might bring: more painful relationships, more loneliness, an incurable disease like the one that devoured my father's nervous system. I acted out of impulses that had been with me my whole life, so unconscious that it outlasted a psychoanalysis. And for a while heroin worked. It gave me some years free of pain, in which I was able to start writing. And then it gave me some more years free of pain, free of most emotions too. Distracted by the high, when you begin to do heroin you don't even notice that part of the appeal is the cessation of anxiety, especially anxiety about the

future. You just feel free of burdens you were never conscious of before. For a short while this freedom can be a revelation. It can make you more productive, and more open to other people. But that anxiety was put there for a reason by evolution: it separates us from the other animals. Living in an eternal present is not good for us, however much we want it (Ibid., p. 295).

Despite the symbolism involved in addiction that is alluded to in some of Ann Marlowe's quotes, the toxicomanias qua symptom are mostly not symbolically structured, nor do they represent an attempt to address the Other via signifiers. Their movement seems to take the form of an exclusion of the Other. Toxicomanias can be considered as immediate and radical means of attempting to undo the lack as the cause of our desire. In this sense toxicomania concerns a jouissance which is predominantly oral in nature. It is jouissance which is total, which can be administered immediately at will, and is able to avoid the risk of the encounter with the desire of the Other.

It is interesting to note some of the differences and similarities between the toxicomaniac and the compulsive gambler. Avoiding the risk of the encounter with the desire of the Other is not an essential component of the clinical picture of gambling. Gambling is about taking risks or chances, which suggests a different kind of jouissance. So what is compulsive gambling from a psychoanalytic perspective and what is its relationship to death or the death-drive?

Gambling is often considered to be dangerous in the same way as drugs and alcohol: it is something to which one can become addicted. The destruction and deterioration caused by addictions reveal a similar pattern and are expressed on a physical, psychological and social level. The unifying nature of their manifestation is reflected in the uniformity of the description of their symptomatology. This has led to the development of treatment models, which make hardly any distinction between addictions or addicts.[6]

Several questions arise when looking at the addictions from a psychoanalytic perspective. Are different psychological mechanisms at work in compulsive gambling and the toxicomanias (alcoholism and drug addiction)? Does this concern different kinds of enjoyment? Does this concern different ways of coping with the questions of death and one's destiny?

The relationship between the subject and his or her symptom is a central clinical problem in psychoanalysis. The subject speaks through or with symptoms in the sense that symptoms are a way of trying to appeal to an other; they are an attempt at communication. The difficulty is that the symptom conveys a meaning, which the subject refuses, but it is a symbolic construction nevertheless and that opens the possibility for analysis and interpretation. The toxicomanias are mostly not symbolic constructions and also they always lead to secondary problems which will eventually come to determine the stereotypical clinical picture of the addict.

As stated before, addiction in the form of toxicomania is able to avoid the risk of the encounter with the (desire of the) Other. This is not the case with gambling. Gambling does not exist without taking risks. Strictly speaking, compulsive gambling is not a toxicomania because it is not based on the incorporation of a drug which causes immediate jouissance independently of the Other. The gambler plays a game of chance in which the possible outcomes are winning or losing. This excludes another kind of game, namely, the game which depends on pure skill or reasoning. An example is chess. The only limit here is one's inability to oversee all possible strategic moves. A gambler is rarely addicted to a game of pure skill. The gambler is mostly interested in games of chance, like roulette and throwing the dice, or games in which skill and chance are combined, such as card games, betting and stock market speculation.

A description of compulsive gambling

Compulsive gamblers take chances with their stake out of habit, they learn nothing from their loss, never stop when they win, always risk too much and get a peculiar kind of enjoyment out of this; a thrill. According to Eric Laurent, this thrill or enjoyment is very reminiscent of the enjoyment Balint mentioned when he described the phenomenon of the funfair (Laurent, 1986, p. 44). He distinguished between three forms of entertainment. Two of these contain a component of oral aggression, namely, to stuff oneself with sugar based food and aggressive games of destruction or violence. The third form of entertainment is different. The games here are connected to the sensations of vertigo and feeling overwhelmed. These sensations are based on a certain kind of anxiety: a mixture of anxiety, pleasure, hope and faith in the face of an external danger. Moods and anxieties of that nature seem to express themselves in the discourse of compulsive gamblers when they talk about their experiences and the chase for their enjoyment. The cyclical moods and the chase for this enjoyment are very specific characteristics of the gambler.

Another characteristic of compulsive gamblers is that they quite often try to develop a strategy to play their game. Despite this, they lose eventually and their debts accumulate. Compulsive gamblers never appear able to escape an extraordinary sense of guilt, often co-existing with a feeling of depression.[7] This raises questions about the connection between the accumulation of debts and this burden of guilt. In his essay on Dostoevsky, Freud wrote that the neurotic's sense of guilt can take tangible shape in the form of a burden of debt (Freud, 1928b, p. 190). Freud quotes one of Dostoevsky's letters: "The main thing is the play itself. I swear that greed for money has nothing to do with it, although Heaven knows I am sorely in need of money" (Ibid.). Dostoevsky was addicted to gambling, he lost everything and it ruined his life. The "masochistic" project of compulsive gamblers comes across as a form of self-punishment. When all money is lost they promise everyone that this was really the last time. This promise is always broken, more humiliation follows, and the inevitable downward spiral continues. The conscious rationalizations of compulsive gamblers for repeating their game are based on the illusion that fate will eventually provide a big win which will wipe out all debts. Meanwhile, however, they feel worthless because they lose their stake and fate is not paying out anything. The burden of debt and the daily conflicts of compulsive gamblers can become so bad that they attempt suicide.

Again, one is faced with a number of questions. What does the stake represent for the subject of the gambler? What enjoyment do they get from this game of chance? What keeps them imprisoned in these repeated acts, this passion for the game? These questions aim at what lies beyond a description of gambling as an addiction. They aim at the subject of the gambler and the gambler's relationship to the game of chance as a symptom. Forrester writes "What else could one expect from the detailed examination of the soul of a gambler but the anatomy of a neurosis" (Forrester, 1990, p. 260). But what kind of neurosis? In order to be able to answer this question

THE PLEASURE BEFORE DEATH   149

properly it might be helpful to have a look at the theory of games from a psychoanalytic perspective.

The subject of the unconscious and the theory of games

In the *Écrits*, Lacan compares the course of a cure to the development of a game of bridge.

> One cannot regard the fantasies that the analysand imposes on the person of the analyst in the same way as a perfect card player might guess his opponent's intentions. No doubt there is always an element of strategy, but one should not be deceived by the metaphor of the mirror, appropriate as it may be to the smooth surface that the analyst presents to the patient. An impassive face and sealed lips do not have the same purpose here as in a game of bridge. Here the analyst is rather bringing to his aid what in bridge is called the dummy (le mort), but is doing so in order to introduce the fourth player who is the partner of the analysand here, and whose hand the analyst, by his tactics, will try to expose: such is the link, let us say the abnegation, that is imposed on the analyst by the stake of the game in the analysis (Lacan, 1977[1958b], p. 229).

To illustrate the analytical cure this metaphor of the game of bridge can be grafted on to Lacan's L-Schema, which is a representation of the analytical situation as a structure (Lacan, 1977[1958a], p. 193).

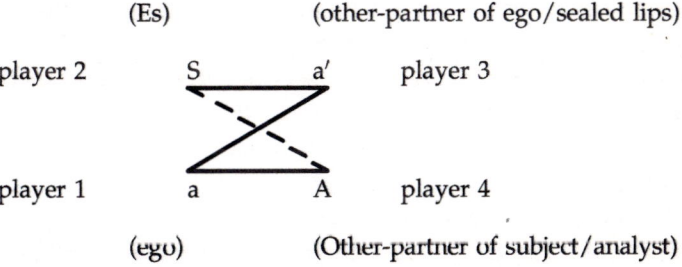

	(Es)	(other-partner of ego/sealed lips)
player 2	S a'	player 3
player 1	a A	player 4
	(ego)	(Other-partner of subject/analyst)

The "dummy" (or *le mort*) as aid of the analyst allows the transference to unfold. Lacan continues the bridge metaphor: "But what is certain is that the analyst's feelings have only one possible place in the game, that of the "dummy", and that if he is re-animated the game will proceed without anyone knowing who is leading" (Lacan, 1977[1958b], p. 230). The feelings of the analyst belong to the realm of "death" for the subject and because of this strict structural situation the unconscious of the analysand will get a chance, eventually, to reveal its cards, i.e., the truth. Nathalie Charraud writes "the metaphor of the game to describe the analytical situation is only there to reveal another game which is much more radical; this is the game of the destiny of the subject who has entered in a game of strategy with an Other, intimate partner of the party who plays" (Charraud, 1987, p. 24, my translation). Freud compared the analytical structure to a game of chess. Although the moves are dependent in part on the other player, the game is, at least in theory, determinable. The fact that Freud uses chess and that Lacan adopts bridge as his metaphor for psychoanalysis is not incidental, according to Charraud. Chess is determinable, the moves are on the chessboard, but in bridge the players do not know the other's cards. The knowledge of the bridge player is incomplete. Bridge is therefore not determinable and contains an impossibility; it shows a lack (Ibid., p. 25). Lacan's position remains quite close however to Freud's. He retains the idea that the course of the subject's destiny will unfold in a fairly strict way. But what needs to be established is what Lacan hoped to achieve by introducing the bridge metaphor. Lacan introduces into psychoanalytic theory the concept of a symbolic order which is incomplete. This Other is lacking (Ø). When Lacan introduces the Other as lacking in psychoanalytic theory, he is forced to posit that the subject, who is introduced into this Other, cannot be completely determined by it. Something is left over from this division of the subject by the Other; the object a (cause of desire) as an unconscious remainder. The discovery of this object a has turned analytical truth into something that can be approached only indefinitely; a limit in the mathematical sense of the word. This implies that the game between subject and Other is not a *fait accomplie* because it contains an impossibility, or a lack, around which the game is structured. Where does that leave the subject of the gambler?

The question of the subject of the gambler and his or her object of desire

Gamblers are very interested in the game of pure chance. What is their passionate interest in this game? Lacan says, "the gambler's passion is nothing but that question asked of the signifier, figured by the automaton of chance" (Lacan, 1988b, p. 51). The automaton of chance is a repetitive procession of pure signifiers, which have acquired the status of a sign for the gambler in the sense that they have come to represent something for him or her. The gambler's question is asked of the signifiers, which are devoid of meaning. These signifiers are pure signifiers, like the writing on a dice which has no meaning in itself. In Seminar II, Lacan says, "In the game of chance no doubt he will test his luck (chance), but also he is going to read his destiny in it. He has the idea that something is revealed there, which belongs to him, and, I would say, all the more so given that there is no one confronting him" (Lacan, 1988a, p. 300). For gamblers, the Other exists in the form of a game of chance. The operation of the structure of the game, i.e., the rules of the game in their purely symbolic form, produces a subject; a subject of the game which comes as an effect of the points or moments of irreducible impossibility inherent in the playing of a symbolically structured game. When the subject puts the question of his or her existence to the Other, it is as a game: can you tell me who I am? He or she wants certainty and is prepared to take enormous risks to achieve it.

So far only the symbolic dimension (the structure and rules) and the real dimension (the points of impossibility) of the game have been referred to. There is also an imaginary dimension to the playing of games. The subject who plays or gambles apparently cannot escape this dimension. Lacan illustrates this with the help of a game of even and odd in Seminar II (Ibid., pp. 179–185). He wonders what sort of strategy is needed to play with a machine and why the machine always wins. He begins with the example of a game from Poe's Purloined Letter (Ibid., p. 179). Dupin, a character in the story, relates the tale of a guessing game. In this game someone has to guess whether the adversary has an even or odd number in his or her hand. To do this, the subject will take up a mirror position through imaginary identification with the other, which is supposed to give access to the truth by eliminating the element of chance as much as possible. This method always presupposes a dimension of intersubjectivity, in the sense that the subject has to know that he or she is dealing with another homogenous subject (p. 180). The form this method usually takes from the second guess onwards can be worded as "I think that he or she will think that I think ... etc.". The game unfolds between one ego and an alter ego on the level of a dual relationship, that is, on the level of the imaginary axis (this is the relationship between player 1 and 3 from the adjusted L-Schema). This game will lead to an impasse when the aim is the truth in the form of guessing correctly.

Lacan proposes to play this game with a machine which can produce pluses and minuses (p. 182). The subject might attempt to develop a strategy which allows him or her to figure any regularities in the production of plus and minus by the machine. As a consequence, the game has become one of predicting patterns (p. 184). It is not intersubjectivity that we are dealing with here, but with the subject's strategic behaviour at an imaginary level, and it is this that is supposed to guarantee winning. The highly intelligent strategy of the subject is countered by the idiotic production patterns of the machine. The subject's strategy of predicting patterns to enable him to guess correctly will only lead to an impasse when confronted with a machine that is wholly unpredictable. The only way out of these impasses is to play at random. This will prove impossible for the subject. Freud has shown us that every apparently random choice is always unconsciously motivated (Freud, 1901b, p. 240). Every choice obeys the laws of the unconscious and in the context of a game, the adversary (or machine when it is complex enough to be able to keep count of previous attempts) will detect the unconsciously motivated patterns of choice. There is only one way out for the subject when the employment of strategy leads to an impasse, when the choice of the Other (machine) is unpredictable, and when playing at random appears unconsciously motivated: to have choice dictated by, for instance, the game of heads or tails. The only way to play a game of chance is to rely on the calculation of probability (Charraud, op. cit., p. 27). For example, in a game of 50% chance you can base your moves on the flicking of a coin. That is, the gambler must match the probability of his or her moves to the probability of the outcomes of the game. Ultimately then, the game is totally determined, but this is absolutely not what interests gamblers; they want to take chances or risks.

The imaginary/dual aspect of playing games usually takes the form of developing particular strategies such as patterns of choice, intimidation, misleading your adversary or guessing. The combination of this imaginary dimension with the way games of chance are structured always leads to loss for the compulsive gambler. Gamblers frantically push or force the real out of the symbolic. According to Charraud, gamblers provoke the real, the *tuché*, over and beyond the structure of the game, which will provide an answer to their question, an answer which is immediate and as such avoids a long detour (Ibid., p. 28). *Tuché*, a concept Lacan borrows from Aristotle, stands for the encounter with the real in Lacanian psychoanalysis. This encounter is the trauma in Freudian theory and is the result of an accidental external event; pure chance.

In the section on the Purloined Letter from Seminar II, Lacan shows that the real can be determined in the symbolic as a point of the inevitability of certain successions of unities, or to put it differently, as a calculation of impossibility. For Lacan, this point of the real as trauma is determined, but in a negative way, as something impossible in a series of possibilities; an inevitability (op. cit., p. 193). This implies that the real (or trauma) can be calculated and located. The trauma seems to fit the neurotic, often remarkably well ("I'm not surprised this happened to him or her"). Access to this point of truth, however, often requires a lot of analytical work. Gamblers force an immediate answer to the question of desire. They avoid as such the long road of the psychoanalytic cure (Charraud, op. cit., p. 28). Gamblers have no time or money for a long winding detour, for working through the fantasy to gain access to the truth (cause of desire) which structured it. Instead they take a short cut, so short that they create a short-circuit. Indeed gamblers often appear to be living in a state of frantic activity and of timelessness.[8] They cannot unmask their fantasy and will not be able to establish an effect in the real of their existence. Compulsive gamblers are imprisoned in their passion and they oscillate between anxiety and guilt or loss and debt, often accompanied by a cycle of mood-swings, ranging from fear to depression, via excitement and agitation. Subjects who are addicted to the game of chance live under the illusion that the "big win" is attainable through increasing the stakes. The game therefore contains for gamblers an object (not cause) of desire which can generate an enjoyment. The object cause-of-desire is the object of the stake of the human subject, which must be given up so that the subject can partake in human culture.

Fundamental to the structure of toxicomania and compulsive gambling is the illusion that worldly objects of desire can be substituted for the object cause of desire. There is a marked inability to accept that our object cause of desire is forever and irretrievably lost. In Seminar II Lacan writes:

> You mark the six sides of a dice, you roll the dice—from this rolling emerges desire, I am not saying human desire, for after all the man who plays with the dice is captive to the desire thus put into play. He does not know the origin of his desire, as it rolls with the symbols written on its six sides. Why is it only man who plays with dice? (op. cit., p. 234).

What is the desire to which the gambler is captive in this game of pure signifiers? It is a (psychoanalytic) fact that (symbolic) castration is the condition for the humanization of desire. It prohibits and it makes the primordial jouissance of the (m)Other impossible. Anxiety and guilt feelings always stem from incestuous desire for that primordial prohibited jouissance. What is important to realize, however, is that these feelings are not just related to this lost enjoyment but also relate to the impossibility of being able to respond to the lack of the mother; to answer the question "What does she want?" (Verhaeghe, 1997, pp. 180–183). Coming face to face with this question causes anxiety because one is stuck for an answer of one's own. This is the moment when the subject disappears under the signifiers of the Other (afinisis), and constitutes itself in that field, in a process which Lacan calls alienation (Lacan, 1979, p. 211).

At this point of imaginary castration the subject does not yet have any desire of its own, but is captive to the desire of the Other; it wants to be the object which fulfils that desire. This is not yet human desire in the aforementioned sense. In this process of alienation the subject will arise as meaning and disappear as (pure) being (Ibid.). This process takes place around a central lack, which is the very cause of this process. As stated earlier, this lack is due to the fact that something of the subject cannot be fully represented in—or determined by—the Other. In the process of subjectivation the subject has lost the state of pure being, but is caught in a desire to complete this lack in the Other: it wants to be a desirable thing for the Other. To play the game of partaking in human culture, the first stake the subject puts up is its being. The subject will have to formulate an answer to the loss of its being and to the consequences of its disappearance under the signifier (into the demand) of the

Other. It will have to answer with its own lack through a process of what Lacan calls separation (Ibid., pp. 213–214). This is the acceptance by the subject of another lack; a lack on the side of the subject. So now, neither subject nor Other is considered complete anymore. The necessary condition for separation (or symbolic castration) is the installation of the function of the Name-of-the-Father. When this has taken place the subject is not completely dependent on the question of the Other anymore, but can develop a desire of its own (Verhaeghe, op. cit., p. 175). The lack in the Other is answered with the lack of the subject. The subject has to let go of his stake, but this implies the death of his being. He or she enters the field of meaning and gains an awareness of finality; death has become an integral part of his or her existence. Life, as a game of signifiers, is indeed a game—because it has a stake (Charraud, 1986, p. 45). It is a game of loss and gain. What is lost is being, what is gained is desire and access to language, but also a conscious awareness of death and an unconscious wish to master it.

When compulsive gamblers are only able to chase the provocation of the real out of the symbolic, namely the loss of the stake, then maybe it is possible to understand what Charraud means when she writes that the enjoyment of the gambler flows out of the identification with his own loss and the stake is "being" itself, in the sense of litter (Ibid.). Loss has to win, and the end will eventually come. This is the radical answer gamblers are demanding. It can also be put as follows: compulsive gamblers (like rabbits caught in headlights) find themselves frozen in a position as passive object of jouissance for the Other, thereby completing this Other. This leads to what Lacan refers to (in Seminar X) as a "lack of lack" which causes anxiety for gamblers (and neurotics), as a warning signal that they are disappearing as a subject.[9] Compulsive gamblers are not able to accept the consequences of symbolic castration. The Oedipal situation does not resolve itself in a symbolic solution, but grinds to a halt in the imaginary. Symbolic castration implies the ability to accept the lack in a movement of separation, but for most neurotics and gamblers this lack is unbearable and causes anxiety.

A possible way out of the impasse of this imaginary prison is the use of a symptom as a barricade against the desire of the Other. The symptom emerges as a form of resistance and sometimes as a true rebellion. Rebelling and agitating are common features of the compulsive gambler. The solution compulsive gamblers have acquired, as a way out of this imaginary impasse, is as follows: they install an imaginary fate, which functions as an absolute master, and it inflicts a lack or a loss on them as a form of punishment, without them knowing why this happens. The result is a symbolic (financial) privation in the "lack of lack", instituted by an imaginary agent (fate) through a real act (the repeated acts of gambling). Gamblers are trying to do away with anxiety by accumulating debts. They exchange anxiety for guilt (through the tangible form of debt) because they cannot be for the (m)Other what they think she wants them to be. They feel guilty or indebted and try to absolve themselves by paying off the debt. Being unable to do this often leads to a state of depression. This way the cyclical drama unfolds. Compulsive gamblers look to fate, as a projection of the father, to provide them with a loss in the form of a privation.[10] They hand themselves over to fate, abdicate responsibility and their destination comes to them as if by chance (*zufall*). This goes hand in hand with the illusion of omnipotence, so characteristic of compulsive gamblers, which expresses itself in the wish to be master of their destiny. These illusions are rooted in the identification with the omnipotence of the phallic mother (the mother with a "lack of lack") (Verhaeghe, op. cit., p. 210). Sometimes illusions can touch reality. On occasions when compulsive gamblers win, they can become overexcited and even maniacal. Some remarks made by Charles Melman when he was talking about depression seem relevant to situate this phenomenon.

> If things are too successful I may become maniacal, and I have the feeling that nothing can stand in my way any longer. I can do anything, and I am very rich, and I have this feeling possessing an inexhaustible fortune, which is linked at that moment to the manic subject and to the emergence for him of this imaginary phallic agency, whose possession he thinks gives him all power (Melman, 1990).[11]

These are the moments compulsive gamblers live for, but they are not the truth which drives them. The passion of the gamblers is a passion for ignorance, because they do not want to know about this truth.

Take away the game from the compulsive gambler and what emerges is anxiety as a reaction to the appearance of the real with the possibility of "acting out" or *passage à l'acte*.¹² What does one do? Leave gamblers to their game? Leave them to accumulate debts as the price for their "being-unto-death"? Death is the radical answer to the question of their destination, and that is what the game will eventually reveal to them. Schopenhauer wrote the following about life and death as a game of chance: "Admittedly, we know no greater game of chance than the game of life and death. Here every decision is faced with supreme suspense, concern and fear. In our eyes, it is all or nothing" (Fingarette, 1996, pp. 144–145). However, that is only half the story, because according to Freud, whilst indeed everyone is always playing games, the unconscious is at work. Unlike the ordinary gambler, the compulsive (or addicted) gambler, leaves nothing to chance: the chase for the final answer is completely determined.

To briefly summarize this rather long discussion on the relationships between gambling, addiction, and death it is possible to say the following: compulsive gambling is not a toxicomania because it is not based on the incorporation of a drug which has—as its effect—a jouissance procured independently of the Other. It seems, rather, that gambling represents a head-on collision with the Other. Compulsive gambling as a symptom is symbolically structured; that is, it addresses the Other, but in a way that is so frantic and confrontational that, like the toxicomanias, it functions in that timeless zone. Compulsive gamblers do not know whether they have received, or are bereft of, an answer from the Other. Gamblers want to force an immediate answer to the question of the cause of their desire, as well as to the question of the destiny of life. Compulsive gamblers chase the provocation of the real out of the symbolic. Loss has to win in their game. The end of the game will eventually arrive, and this end is the answer they demand. Death is the radical answer to the question of their destination, which is what the game will eventually reveal for them. As the essential part of every game of pure chance, the element of choice (including the choice of strategy) provides the gambler with the illusion of power over the inevitability of their destiny—that is, death. The illusion of a mastery over death is what the gamblers have in common with some of the toxicomaniacs, but their style or aesthetic is quite different. The discourse of gamblers is permeated with all kinds of references to fate, destiny, death, mastery, and tempting of the gods.

The relationship of gamblers to their game is of a deeply religious nature. Having total faith in revelation and ultimate redemption, in "the big win" as their ultimate guarantor, gamblers stake everything on "Lady Luck", but—through the way they persistently continue to play the game—she will eventually become the herald of their ruination. The choice of the gambler falls on the third of the Fates. She is the silent Goddess of Death, in the guise of the heralding Goddess of Love.

Drugs, drink and gambling as evidence of the lack in the world

The junky aesthetic—in contrast—is a flirtation with the image of death. This conceals the underlying fantasy of a being able to take on death as an erotic and equal partner, who can be fought until the end. The style of the gambler indicates a defiance of fate which relates to the fundamental fantasy of his omnipotence—so characteristic of his psychology. Within this fantasy of omnipotence is the belief in the ability to overpower the fear of being devoured by the ultimate destiny. In order to situate the alcoholic, it might be helpful to quote from that extraordinarily sensitive alcoholic writer, Marguerite Duras, whose comment on her drinking was that it was the sickness of death:[13]

> Alcohol has been made to support the emptiness of the Universe (Belot-Fourcade, 1989, p. 13, my translation).
>
> Alcohol does not console at all, it only replaces the lack of God (Ibid., p. 17, my translation).
>
> It is from a certain point onwards that one has a choice: to drink to insensibility, the loss of identity or to stick with the rudiments of happiness; to die of sorts every day or else to live (Ibid., p. 18, my translation).

Renate Günther made the following comment on Duras's alcoholism in relation to her work:

> From 1964 onwards, Duras's work became a progressive movement towards emptiness, a movement which reveals lack and absence as the paradoxically hollow core of existence, and which highlights the illusory nature of her character's initial quest for unity and

completeness, both within themselves and in their relationships with others. If God fills this empty space for some people, for Duras alcohol has taken the place of God, as she herself wrote in L'Amant. It seems, therefore, that while her writing creates an ever-increasing vacuum, drinking compensates for this sense of void and alleviates the fear it inspires (Günther, 1994, p. 200).[14]

To live life is to accept that in it there are only fragments of happiness. This is not enough for the alcoholic. The effacement of emptiness and the substitution of God seem to indicate the alcoholic's fantasy—that there exists the possibility of the universal fusion of the One. This is a belief in the existence of Eros as divorced from Thanatos, a hope for the ideal of wholeness in the Universe and indeed in the sexual relationship. This hope can only be realized in the ultimate sexual relationship.[15] The aim of the fantasy of the alcoholic converges on the mystic experience; its structure is close to that of a natural religion. It shares some of this aim with the use of other drugs—such as certain religious or mystic uses of opium, cannabis, mescaline, LSD, and so on. Aiming for the One rather than the Other is a death-drive, in the sense that reaching this aim would annihilate the Other and—therefore—the subject who is constituted in its field. The result of chronic alcoholism is indeed, as Marguerite Duras suggested, a loss of identity or, to put it differently, an effacement of the subject. Literature inspired by drugs often demonstrates the impossible dynamic between beauty and total despair as an aesthetic and emotional aspect of the death-drive.[16]

As there are many ways of drinking and many different forms of alcoholism, it seems important to mention at least one other, which appears to organize itself in a fairly coherent clinical picture. This is the alcoholic described by Charles Melman in a series of three essays. It concerns a style of drinking associated with working-class men. He writes:

> The stereotypical quality of the subjective drama validates the unpleasant necessity of having to consider the alcoholic as a class without concern for the individuals who would give this class its particularity. The reason for this consideration will be found in alcoholics generally sharing a fantasy that can perhaps be isolated (Melman, 1993, p. 235).

This alcoholic wants to be a master in his own home, but he has chosen a partner who is a threat to his hegemony. He has chosen her as a mother whose son he has subsequently become. She has a terrifying, omnipotent presence for him, which drives him out of the home and into the arms of a brotherhood of fellow drinkers who will receive him openly as all identify with him. This virile group identity functions as a phallic barrier against what awaits him at home, which is—Melman suggests—precisely the underlying fantasy which determined his choice of partner, as though:

> he could do nothing other than to pursue an archaic feminine fantasy: that of a God whose infinite bounty would leave no prayer unanswered and who would thus be the true therapist of castration. As Other, a mother always seeks to embody this God (Ibid., p. 245).

Why is this so terrifying? Precisely because her presence demonstrates to him his monstrous fantasy as measured against the dread of his castration. This alcoholic is able to avoid the questions of life and death, not just through trying to drink the desired, ultimate "last one", which would totally satisfy him—and therefore never comes—, but also (and especially) by metaphorically drinking "the One" which unifies his first and last drink, and anything that comes in between. Consider, as an illustration of the connection between alcoholism, woman, wholeness and castration, the following two poems by Redgrove who, as a poet, had a real interest in alcohol and alcoholism:[17]

> The quiet woman: the pub where men sat suckling
> In the silence; a joke against wives. She was headless
> Yet her benefits flowed; she was tongueless
> Because we would not listen to her. A joke
> Against drinkers. The Son it was
> Who listened, whom the womb magnified from his dot,
> Who entered shining with it, and returned, the Word
> Arising always from the liquid mind, again,
> There, as you see it, again there,
> The Ever-Coming One, the same
> Again please
> (Roberts, 1994, p. 154).

> To endeavour by drinking to condense
> As far as possible the all-pervading
> Mother-body of water, to become

One of her whole and rounded bald glisters.
As the web drinks the dew
And displays its coruscations

So the body brims
With burning internalized
Self-interest, like light in drops
(Ibid., p. 156)

The secret fundamental fantasy of this drinker is to erase all difference. The great unifier for this alcoholic is "The Woman", who remains married to him in a lethal bind, till death does them part. The choice of this alcoholic reveals the death-drive in a specific way. His belief that he has chosen his partner freely allows him to think that he is master over his life. In the end, however, it only exposes his impotence in relation to death. But he cannot allow himself to know anything about this, and that is why he lives in the timeless illusion of having conquered death.

To illustrate the theme of the combination of fascination and mastery in relation to death—in a much more direct way—we can use the examples of two very different luminaries of drug culture, Aldous Huxley and Timothy Leary. Michael Gossop wrote of the former:

> Aldous Huxley was so profoundly impressed by his spiritual experiences after taking mescaline that he asked to be given the drug as he was dying. His wife gave him two doses of mescaline during the day and as he lay in bed he said little but gazed at his wife with an expression of love and happiness. His wife wrote of his death, "is his way of dying to remain for us, and only for us, a relief and a consolation, or should others also benefit from it? Aren't we all nobly born and entitled to nobly dying?" (Gossop, 1993, p. 130).

It seems as if Huxley wanted to combine his spiritual drug experiences with the experience of death. This seems to involve a fantasy of acquiring knowledge about death through the process of dying. It could be argued that this fantasy is also evident in scientific discourse. Science is also concerned with knowledge in relation to death—namely, an accumulation of knowledge (or a calculation of probabilities) as an insurance against the truth (or real) of death. This knowledge runs away from death; it does not want to know about it.[18] Or perhaps Huxley's fantasy represents a desire he shared with certain mystics, namely to open the doors of perception onto a realm beyond reality and life, called either "infinitude" or "immortality".

As far as "nobly dying" is concerned, the American LSD guru Timothy Leary expressed the wish that his death should be visible to everyone; he wanted to have it broadcasted via the internet. Is this not an example of Leary trying to represent in the Other something of that which is situated beyond it; the attempt to give an image of death in life? Or is it rather his attempt to keep something alive after death? The answer to these questions will never be known, but they all seem to be related to different forms of attempting to master the Absolute Master. The important thing to keep in mind is that there is a fundamental ambiguity at the heart of the death-drive in the form of mastery of death. One could argue that if the subject attempts to master death then one cannot speak about a death-drive, unless the death-drive is interpreted as being driven away from death. Leaving the last interpretation aside, it is quite correct to speak about a death-drive in this context, because the result of having mastered the absolute master, or the very realization of creating a oneness in the universe, would be, precisely, the death of the subject.

Toxicomania, alcoholism and also gambling teach us that "there is no Other of the Other", and that "The Woman does not exist". In other words, they teach that there is no ultimate authority beyond language which would speak a reassuring truth about death, nor is there a "third sex" which would harmonize the (sexual) relationships between the sexes. If alcohol, drugs, and gambling have been created to support the lack in the world, then those who indulge in them do so because they are lacking. The results of the fantasies of toxicomaniacs, alcoholics and compulsive gamblers, as they find expression in concrete reality, show this more openly than any other clinical picture. The death-drive, considered from its representational point of view (symbolic and imaginary), allows, in one respect only, the unification of the field of addictions (toxicomania, gambling, etc.) on the basis of one particular signifier, namely the signifier mastery. Addiction is a form of mastery and, ultimately, it is an attempt to master the ultimate master. However, that is not all there is to addiction and mastery. In this chapter it has become clear that there is something that makes the master a fragile figure. There is the real and it makes all the difference. The time has come to consider this other aspect of the death-drive; an aspect which is not unrelated to the representational aspect. This aspect, which will be the subject of the next chapter, comes as a consequence of the representational aspect; after all, the signifier is the cause of the real in the subject. The real shatters any illusion of unity for the subject and it shatters any illusion regarding the unification of the field of addiction.

Notes

1. In Lacan's work a distinction must be made between physical death and death that results from the introduction of the subject into the field of language. This introduction into language condemns the subject forever to symbolic existence thereby causing the death or loss of "pure being". This loss makes the subject long or desire for that previous "state of being". There is however another meaning to death as it is used in this context. The introduction of the subject into language results in a conscious awareness of the inevitability of physical death at the end of the life of the human being.
2. Freud must have been influenced by the philosopher Arthur Schopenhauer. Schopenhauer wrote the following: "...the feeling forces itself upon us that the world is no less in us than we are in it, and that the source of all reality lies within us. The result is actually this: Objectively the time when I will not be will come, but subjectively it can never come..." (Fingarette, 1996, p. 146). Already just from this quote it is possible to detect that Schopenhauer's influence on Freud stretches beyond the question of death. "The source of all reality lies within us" goes straight to the heart of Freud's thinking.
3. One and Oneness are written here with a capital O to indicate that the meaning of one in this context is one of totality and completeness and not the "one" of a series, such as the series of ones (one and one and another one and so forth, which is what Lacan calls "there is something of one") or the one of counting (one, two, three and so forth). The One is the Absolute Master and indeed paradoxically death.
4. Lacan says that we cannot really speak of "The Woman" (see chapters 6 & 7 of Seminar XX, 1975a). The "The" and the capital letter "W" would suggest that there is such a thing as the essence of femininity or womanliness that can be precisely indicated and articulated. However, for Lacan "The Woman does not exist" and he writes this by crossing

out the "The". There is no signifier in the symbolic order that can signify the essence of Woman. In Chapter 1 of Seminar XX Lacan says that woman is "not-all" (Ibid., p. 13). In other words, there is something in women that cannot be subjected to the universality of the phallic signifier. My understanding of "The Woman" as a concept is that it indicates an illusion or a fantasy in both men and women which functions as a protection against the discomfort or even anxiety provoked by the lack in the symbolic order.

5. It was stated before that the human subject is constituted in the field of the Other. This process of constitution is necessarily incomplete as this field is structurally lacking. There are always signifiers lacking in the chain of signifiers that make up language. In the previous footnote, for instance, it was indicated that there is no signifier for woman. This lack in the Other implies that one will always try to grasp something from "the beyond of this Other" in order to ground and guarantee reality. On numerous occasions Lacan states firmly that "there is no Other of the Other". There is nothing outside language—for instance, a metalanguage—with which one would be able fill in the lack in language and gain access to an absolute truth. This lack of ultimate grounding for truth leads to a—often desperate—search in the human subject for a figure (such as "The Woman", "The Primal Father" or God) which might guarantee the completion and stability of truth.

6. Examples of these are the 12-step programmes of self-help groups such as Alcoholics Anonymous, Narcotics Anonymous and Gamblers Anonymous.

7. Bergler writes about guilt feelings in gamblers in his excellent book *The Psychology of Gambling* (1957, pp. 96 & 151).

8. See also Forrester when he writes the following: "The world of the convict and the gambler are similar-lives withdrawn from life, a world of timeless crisis time, of the final moments of consciousness before execution or suicide" (1990, p. 281).

9. See lecture from 28 November (Lacan, 1963).

10. In his work on Dostoevsky Freud writes the following: "For every punishment is ultimately castration and, as such, a fulfilment of the old passive attitude towards the father. Even Fate is, in the last resort, only a later projection of the father" (Freud, 1928b, p. 185).

11. In November 1990 Charles Melman gave a talk called, "On Depression", to The School of Psychotherapy in St Vincent's Hospital, Elm Park, Dublin. Only an unpublished typed version of this talk exists.

12. See Lacan's Seminar X, *Anxiety* and more specifically the lecture from 23 January 1963, for an exploration of the relationship between "acting out" and *passage à l'acte* as reactions to a confrontation with the real.

13. These quotes were taken from an article by Pascale Belot-Fourcade on Marguerite Duras' relationship to alcohol (Belot-Fourcade, 1989).
14. Günther's article is extremely interesting. There is a passage that deals more directly with the connections between Duras' distress, her writing and her alcoholism (Günther, 1994, pp. 202–203). A particularly interesting aspect of this passage is where the female character in Duras' book remarks to a young man that his fear of feminine "otherness" is not only cause of his "sickness of death", but also symptom. The implication of feminine otherness being a symptom of death, surely must mean that her other jouissance (her otherness) is related to death. This was commented on in the section entitled *Life, death, God, woman and . . .* in this chapter. This feminine other jouissance is troublesome for both men and women.
15. In Confessions of an English Opium Eater, Thomas de Quincey writes that his dreams were "the true objects" of his book (1986, p. 147). He finishes one dream with the following words: "and with a sigh, such as the caves of hell sighed when the incestuous mother uttered the abhorred name of death, the sound was reverberated—even lasting farewells! and again, and yet again reverberated—ever lasting farewells!" (Ibid., p. 113).
16. When Thomas de Quincey comments on his dreams that were fuelled by opium he writes the following: "For this, and all other changes in my dreams, were accompanied by deep-seated anxiety and gloomy melancholy, such as are wholly incommunicable by words. I seemed every night to descend, not metaphorically, but literally to descend, into chasms and sunless abysses, depths below depths, from which it seemed hopeless that I could ever reascend. Nor did I, by waking, feel that I had reascended. This I do not dwell upon; because the state of gloom which attended these gorgeous spectacles, amounting at least to utter darkness, as some suicidal despondency, cannot be approached by words" (1986, p. 103).
17. These two poems were quoted from an article by Neil Roberts on the poet Peter Redgrove (Roberts, 1994).
18. In order to clarify and illustrate this statement I will quote from the last couple of pages of a book by Ernest Becker called *The Denial of Death*. This quote goes right to the heart of the argument put forward here. "Creation is a nightmare spectacular taking place on a planet that has been soaked for hundreds of millions of years in the blood of all its creatures. The soberest conclusion that we could make about what has actually been taking place on the planet for about three billion years is that it is being turned into a vast pit of fertilizer. But the sun distracts our attention, always baking the blood dry, making things grow over

166   THE SUBJECT OF ADDICTION

it, and with its warmth giving the hope that comes with the organism's comfort and expansiveness. *Questo sol m'arde, e questo m'innamore*, as Michelanchelo put it. Science and religion merge in a critique of the deadening of perception of this kind of truth, and science betrays us when it is willing to absorb lived truth all into itself" (Becker, 1973, p. 283). For more of Becker's thoughts on science and death (or the death-drive), see also the next two pages.

CHAPTER SEVEN

The death of pleasure: the real, the body and jouissance

"Neither the sun nor death can be looked at steadily"

La Rochefoucauld, *Maxims*, 1959, p. 40

"If writing, according to the king and under the sun produces the opposite effect from what is expected, if the pharmacon is pernicious, it is so because it doesn't come from around here. It comes from afar, it is external or alien to the living, which, is the right-here of the inside, to logos as the zoon it claims to assist or relieve"

J. Derrida, "The Pharmakon", p. 104

Freudian foundations for a psychoanalytic theory of toxicity

An overexcited or under-excited psyche

In 1885, when speaking to the Psychiatric Society of Vienna about the general effect of cocaine, Freud refers to those afflictions of the nervous system which are not based on organic lesions. Here Freud puts forward the idea of psychic lesions or processes as the possible cause of suffering and pathology.

Chapter 2 detailed that the year after Freud wrote his last paper on cocaine, he published an article on hysteria. In this article he considered the prescription of a narcotic drug in the case of an acute hysteria to be a serious technical mistake. The reason for this was that he was then of the opinion that hysteria was the result of the formation of excess stimulation in the psychic organ caused by an irregularity of the nervous system; therefore, the increased stimulation produced by the administration of a drug would only aggravate the hysterical condition. As cocaine is a stimulant, this must have been the drug he was talking about; a depressant would result in a dissipation of the excess stimulation. However, he did recommend the administration of cocaine for conditions that are in need of stimulation; conditions he described as states of mental weakness. Neurasthenia was one of those conditions.

In this article, Freud suggested that hysteria was the psyche in an overexcited state caused by a somatic anomaly in the organism. This implies that the soma and the psyche are two interconnected areas. As to the precise nature of this connection, Freud was not yet very clear.

His work on hypnosis and on the relationship between suggestion and psychic treatment, led Freud to concentrate increasingly on the psychical processes as a factor in the aetiology of hysteria. The further away from medical practice he moved, and the more he began to rely on listening instead of observation, the more he began to realize the importance of the factor of sexuality in the aetiology of hysteria. As established earlier, he did initially consider a sexual trauma to be the cause of hysterical symptoms, but he realized later that this was not always the full story.

Meanwhile, however, Freud had become interested in the relationship between psychical processes, and he isolated sexuality and anxiety as the symptoms that were central to hysteria and neurosis; but he did not seem to be able to see this relationship with any clarity. In order to improve this deficiency, he began to develop a structural psychopathology from 1892 onwards. On the one hand, he established the category of the "psychoneuroses of defence" which, a little while later, he would separate out into hysteria, phobia, and obsessional neurosis. On the other hand, he developed the category of the actual neuroses, which contained both neurasthenia and anxiety neurosis.

With the "psychoneuroses of defence", Freud broke away from the conventional psychopathology of his time by basing his explanation of the neuroses (such as hysteria) purely on the psychical processes. The precipitating cause of the neurosis lies in the psychic field and is based on a mechanism of defence, whose purpose is to ward off incompatible and unpleasurable representations from consciousness. Once the incompatible representation has been excluded from consciousness, the tension (or energy), having no escape route, accumulates, thus causing displeasure, and so becomes pathogenic. The therapeutic effort will consist of bringing the representation back into the normal chain of associations, so that the accumulated tension can be drained away and thus reduced. This appears to be the perfect solution, but can only be seen as such within the strictures of a functioning pleasure-principle. This perfect solution does not apply to the actual neuroses, and it had already come to be noticed that Freud had failed to arrive at a perfect solution in his work on cocaine.

It is important to realize that Freud had already defined pleasure here in an essentially negative way. The accumulation of tension results in pain and suffering. It is only in the escape from this condition, through the reduction of tension, that pleasure is produced; which ultimately aims at an unattainable state of complete lack of tension (pure happiness). Pleasure is built on pain and cannot exist without it. In order to build a proper foundation for a psychoanalytic theory of toxicity, we will need to revisit Freud's ideas on the actual neuroses, more specifically neurasthenia and anxiety neurosis. It is necessary to question Freud's ideas on these matters. After all, he never fully developed his ideas on the actual neuroses (and indeed addiction), despite the fact that he kept referring to these ideas till the end of his life.

Neurasthenia

Freud's treatment of the actual neuroses also represented a break away from conventional psychopathology. The main authority on neurasthenia was an American neurologist named Beard. He defined neurasthenia in terms of a degeneracy of the nervous system, which led to symptoms such as weakness, fatigue, irritability and pain.[1] Armstrong gives the following description of Beard's ideas on neurasthenia in an interesting article called "Addiction, electricity and desire":

> He saw neurasthenia in electrical terms, as a depletion of the body's neuro-electrical energies, to be treated by stimulants of various kinds, including drugs and techniques of bodily electrification like "central galvanization". Beard, with A.D. Rockwell, was also the author of the standard text on electricity and medicine in the period, in which he pictured the body as an electrical system with a set level of energy, like the voltage of a battery. Even more importantly, he saw the body as plugged into other energy systems: the major causes of neurasthenia are the demands of the modern world—transport, technology, the telegraph, speed and the inventions, in particular, of his friend Edison. The self was thus not isolated, but implicated within a technological structure which determined its equilibria, energy levels, and perhaps even its desires (Armstrong, 1994, p. 138).

It is curious to note that some of these ideas are still being put forward as explanations for the malaise generated by the modern world. One is, however, inclined to wonder how Beard would have survived in today's world. The important thing is the difference between Beard and Freud: that difference concerns the sexual factor.

Freud defined neurasthenia in an entirely different way. He claimed neurasthenia was the effect of an actual sexual problem. This was a problem which was based on the sexual reality of the patient and has no subjective psychological history. The example Freud used was sexual exhaustion through, for instance, excessive masturbation. Freud thought that masturbation led to a false discharge, in which the tension had accumulated, and so become noxious, as it had been diverted away from the possibility of being psychically processed. He wrote in Draft E: "It may be that the neurasthenic nervous system cannot tolerate an accumulation of physical tension, since masturbation involves becoming accustomed to frequent and complete absence of tension" (Freud, 1894, p. 82). In other words, because the nervous system must be able to tolerate a certain amount of tension, the neurasthenic becomes vulnerable to illness as he has fallen victim to the habit of trying to completely avoid any amount of accumulated tension. The neurasthenic symptomatology is based on a lack of tension and this lack (or deficiency of something) which cannot be psychically processed, becomes toxic. But Freud could not remain within the framework of the pleasure principle when he tried to explain the mechanisms underlying the clinical phenomena of neurasthenia here. A reduction of tension becomes toxic whereas it normally would produce pleasure. Similar impossibilities and contradictions in his work on cocaine led him to abandon his project of finding a universal panacea for human suffering.

Three years later in the famous letter from December 22, 1897 to Fliess (this is the letter in which he wrote about masturbation being the "primary addiction") Freud established in the aforementioned quote a relationship between hysteria, addiction and neurasthenia. But, he also expressed a fear that these last two might not be curable (Masson, 1985, p. 287).

Anxiety neurosis

Although neurasthenia was already established as a neurological concept, it had been completely redefined by Freud; whereas, anxiety neurosis was a totally new concept, but because of the way it had been defined by Freud, it represented a rupture with the thinking on psychopathology at the time. Jonckheere and Verhaeghe consider the actual neuroses to be an important turning point in psychoanalytic nosology (Jonckheere, 1988, pp. 102–103; Verhaeghe, 1993, pp. 72–73). As will be indicated, Lacan's later theoretical elaborations turn around this nodal-point. In his research on anxiety, Jonckheere shows how Freud was able to limit his definition of hysteria through the development of a separate aetiology for anxiety neurosis as structurally distinct from hysteria and the other neuroses (op. cit., p. 108). The way Freud defined anxiety neurosis (as well as neurasthenia and toxicomania) not only limited his theoretical field but also his therapeutic field. On that point, it is especially important to question and challenge Freud.

What is anxiety neurosis? In 1894 Freud defined it as follows: "... the mechanism of anxiety neurosis is to be looked for in a deflection of somatic sexual excitation from the psychical sphere, and in a consequent abnormal employment of that excitation" (Freud, 1895b[1894], p. 108). In this definition, Freud stated that this neurosis was not caused by psychical processes, and he implied that, like neurasthenia, it was based on the actual reality of the sexual life of the patient. For a variety of reasons (such as being distracted through conscious repression of, and ignorance about, sexual activity) the psyche is not able to process sexual somatic energy. This sexual energy cannot find a psychical representation and thus becomes toxic. This toxic chemical substance transforms into anxiety. This process can be put into the following sequence: there is an accumulation of endogenous sexual tension (that is, the somatic sexual drive or physical libido); this reaches, but does not go beyond, a certain threshold (if, indeed, it was capable of going beyond this threshold, it could enter into relation with groups of ideas which form the psychic libido); so, for various reasons, psychic linkage does not happen and the physical tension becomes a toxic substance (anxiety). The terminology and logic Freud used here was reminiscent of his work on cocaine (toxicity, increase and decrease of energy). But this was not the only connection with this work.

In the *Cocaine Papers*, as mentioned before, Freud had not been able to explain why an effect of toxicity only occurred in some people. Neither had he been able to explain the phenomena he was investigating within the laws of energetics, or its Freudian equivalent of the pleasure-principle. As regards anxiety neurosis, Freud had not been able to find a satisfactory answer to the question as to why "one would come to grief from one's own body", as he worded it in the letter to Fliess from 1 January 1896 (Masson, 1985, p. 161). He had not explained why certain people fell victim to anxiety neurosis (he described actual sexual practices without giving a structural explanation, and he ignored the possibility that some of these might be psychologically relevant), nor did he understand how, like neurasthenia, anxiety neurosis defied the pleasure-principle; increased tension is not reduced to result in pleasure, but is transformed into something else, which in turn then causes anxiety.

Freud's attempt to ground a theory of the actual neuroses led to the same impasse as his work on cocaine. His explanations for neurasthenia, anxiety neurosis and addiction were dependent on the idea of the existence of a toxic factor which has its effects within a vague domain forming the connection between the soma and the psyche. These three clinical phenomena remained largely unexplained in Freud's work. What little he did explain related to what was actual and incidental in the sexual life of a patient. Freud kept the actual neuroses and addictions out of the field he created because he didn't have the theoretical tools at his disposal. With Lacan, the actual neuroses can be brought back into the field of psychoanalysis via his conceptualization of the real as an effect of the signifier. This real is a structural element of every neurosis because it refers to the kernel of human subjectivity. Verhaeghe suggests that the actual neuroses are an immediate reaction to this real kernel, whilst the psychoneuroses are a defensive signifying process as a mediating answer to this real and, as such, a containment of a structural actual neurosis (op. cit., p. 73–75).

In order to advance these ideas, and in order to include the toxicomanias in the theoretical and clinical field of psychoanalysis, it is necessary to develop a psychoanalytic theory of toxicity. However, in order to do this properly it is crucial to return to the related concepts of jouissance and the death-drive and to introduce the question of the status of the body in the theory of Lacanian psychoanalysis.

Towards a psychoanalytic theory of toxicity and the body

A lack of meaning in life and the non-sense of death

The very last sentences of Burroughs's book *Junky* read as follows:

> Kick is seeing things from a special angle. Kick is momentary freedom from the claims of the ageing, cautious, nagging, frightening flesh. Maybe I will find in yage what I was looking for in junk and weed and coke. Yage may be the final fix (Burroughs, 1977, p. 152).

In an article he wrote for The British Journal of Addiction (included as an appendix in his book *Naked Lunch*, 1993) Burroughs writes that yage is a hallucinogenic drug which deranges the senses, induces a state of conscious anaesthesia, and produces what he describes as: "a shift of view point, an extension of consciousness beyond ordinary experience" (Burroughs, 1993, pp. 199–200). Burroughs is looking to escape a dying (ageing) body in turmoil, through the different viewpoint of a consciousness beyond consciousness. Yage may be the final fix, but what would it "fix" for him? It seems as if Burroughs is looking to settle, once and for all, a problem in relation to his body, through the medium of what we might call a "meta-consciousness". Something of his body needs to be pacified, and he hopes to do this through a manipulation of his mind and senses.

There are two very striking aspects in these statements about drugs made by Burroughs, a toxicomaniac. Firstly, the connection he makes between mind (or consciousness and senses) and body is not only a cause of much agony, anxiety and turmoil for him, but it is also theoretically problematic. Secondly, he fantasizes about a final solution to the disturbing effect of this cause, in the form of an ideal object or drug.

To cast light on these statements, it is useful to consider the question of the body in Lacanian psychoanalysis and the relationship of the body to the subject. The second statement touches upon the most obvious characteristic of toxicomania. Toxicomania might be defined as follows: it is the search by the subject for an object which can be administered at will, which would satisfy desire and regulate or keep jouissance at an ideal level. "Administration at will" implies that this object can function for the subject in a way which is largely independent of the Other.[2] Every encounter with the Other, no matter how fleeting or minimal, is also an encounter with desire. The desire of the Other is problematic for addicts; indeed, as we have seen, they choose to avoid desire (through seeking this total satisfaction which would annihilate it) and instead they take the side of jouissance.

A more precise definition of jouissance may enable one to understand why the toxicomaniac sides with it. Jouissance can be defined in relation to the Freudian conception of "pleasure". Pleasure, according to Freud, is the reduction of tension to an agreeable level —this is the pleasure principle. Pleasure is regarded by Lacan as a very specific form of jouissance—that which, at a later stage in his work, he termed "phallic jouissance".[3] Evidently, then, there are varieties of jouissance, although the word can usually be taken to refer to the realm which Freud situated beyond the pleasure principle. This is the realm of the death-drive, which expresses itself in the form of negative therapeutic reactions, repetitions of trauma, nightmares, children's play, masochism, and so on (Freud, 1920g). This aspect of jouissance is unpleasant, harmful and disturbing, yet one is hooked into it by one's symptoms. It disturbs the equilibrium of the pleasure principle. It would make more sense to avoid this form of jouissance, however, as Freud discovered, there are certain forms of satisfaction which are not based on the reduction of tension and the avoidance of pain.

It seems that the kind of pleasure based solely on a reduction of tension leaves us with a longing for a realm beyond. This realm beyond pleasure is not "desirable" for the human subject, because it would eventually destroy him or her. Nevertheless, this longing for an undesirable something that would destroy the subject constitutes the death-drive. The jouissance of this realm is "too much", but at the moment it becomes "too much" the pleasure principle comes into operation again and so the subject withdraws from it. Hence, the subject oscillates between a "too much" and a "never enough". This lack of equilibrium is the failure of the pleasure principle. However, the most important point, in this context, is that pleasure acts as a barrier against jouissance. Lacan writes:

> But we must insist that jouissance is forbidden to him who speaks as such, although it can only be said between the lines for whoever is subject of the Law, since the Law is grounded in this very prohibition. But it is not the Law itself that bars the subject's access to jouissance—rather it creates out of an almost natural barrier a barred subject. For it is pleasure that sets the limits on jouissance, pleasure as that which binds incoherent life together, until another, unchallengeable prohibition arises from the regulation that Freud discovered as the primary process and appropriate law of pleasure (Lacan, 1977[1960], p. 319).

Pleasure and jouissance are thus not the same thing; the former makes the latter impossible. If it is pleasure that makes life coherent and which forbids jouissance, then it must follow that it is jouissance which is annihilating and lethal. Jouissance is therefore the death-drive, and pleasure its barrier. However, according to Lacan, pleasure is not the only barrier. In the passage quoted above, Lacan refers to the Law which prohibits jouissance. This Law is the law of symbolic castration, and functions as a prohibition of the jouissance of incest. The loss of this jouissance is the cause of our desire. This desire which cannot—should not—be satisfied is also a barrier against jouissance. Lacan writes: desire is a defence (dèfense), a prohibition (dèfense) against going beyond a certain limit in jouissance (Ibid.,

p. 322). It is interesting to note how desire and pleasure work together to prohibit a lethal jouissance. However, it is not at all the case that pleasure and desire are one and the same thing, for instance, one can desire pleasure; it is even possible to say that one desires jouissance. But is it possible to say that one "enjoys desire", or that one has "pleasure in desire"? That is not so certain. Desire is somewhat uneasy: it is always for something that one does not have, and thus leaves one with a sense of dissatisfaction. However, what one can say for sure is that ultimately one desires to desire. It is what keeps people going. It is clear, then, that desire, jouissance, and pleasure (or enjoyment) are related to each other, but that these relationships are far from being simple, proportional and unequivocal. In other words, they are full of discord. Lacan notes:

> What analytic experience shows is that, in any case, it is castration that governs desire, whether it is normal or abnormal... Castration means that jouissance must be refused, so that it can be reached on the inverted ladder (*l'èchelle renversée*) of the Law of desire (Ibid., p. 324).

Here Lacan indicates the existence of different forms of jouissance. It is desire, as a result of castration, which forbids one form of jouissance, whilst at the same time creating the possibility of another form.

It was suggested earlier that toxicomaniacs have found a way of avoiding the desire of the Other and their own desire. Braunstein writes that addiction is "something which allows a nearly experimental connection with jouissance and it takes a shortcut with regards to the Other and his desire" (Braunstein, 1992, p. 263, my translation). One can now see that, in doing so, toxicomaniacs run the risk of enjoying a jouissance which is lethal and impossible, because this jouissance is not regulated by the law of desire. With regard to the subject's relationship to his or her object, this law does not function for—or rather, is circumvented by—the toxicomaniac. This is a reiteration of a previous intimation that the toxicomaniac's relationship to the object of his or her jouissance reveals the illusionary character of every object. It demonstrates the impossible abyss of what lies behind the illusion.[4]

The relationships between desire, pleasure and jouissance are extremely problematic for the toxicomaniac. But then, for whom are

THE DEATH OF PLEASURE   177

they not? People have their ways of managing this situation. When one says that toxicomaniacs run the risk of a lethal jouissance, which escapes both the regulatory function of the law of desire, and the limitations of what constitutes a "normal" or conservative pleasure, a question forces itself upon us: can all toxicomania be considered a death-drive? Unfortunately, the answer is not at all as obvious as these investigations so far might suggest. The reason for this is that not all toxicomanias aim at this other jouissance beyond pleasure.

The jouissance of the body as death-drive

Lacan comments that for jouissance one needs a body, and that the dimension of jouissance for the body is the dimension of the descent towards death (Lacan, 1972, lecture from 4–11–1971). In other words, the jouissance of the body is the death-drive. In order to understand this, it is relevant to look at Lacan's difficult theoretical elaborations concerning the body, dating from the last period of his work.

In very early infancy, the body of the child is experienced as a living organism, a real body, full of alien impulses and fragmented sensations. These impulses and sensations are the real drives of the infantile body. These drives are evoked and provoked in the real body of the infant by the first encounters with the Other. This Other is the one who has taken it upon herself to look after and take care of the infant. This Other feeds, holds, touches, and desires the infant. The infant as real body is itself an object of desire and jouissance for this Other. In this sense, it is completely at the mercy of the Other. The different manifestations of care by the Other for the infant can be considered as specific forms of seductions. In other words, the infant is a sexual and seducible object for the carer and this, in turn, will ultimately begin to sexualize the body of the infant. Freud wrote:

> A child's intercourse with anyone responsible for his care affords him an unending source of sexual excitation and satisfaction from his erotogenic zones. This is especially so since the person in charge of him, who, after all, is as a rule his mother, herself regards him with feelings that are derived from her own sexual life: she strokes him, kisses him, rocks him and quite clearly treats him as a substitute for a complete sexual object (Freud, 1905d, p. 223).

Before sexualization of the body takes place, the seductions of the (m)Other will already evoke and establish a jouissance in the body, in the form of drives, which are not yet attached to a representation. These are real drives causing a non-sexual jouissance of the body. They are non-sexual because they have not yet been subjected to castration. Frédéric Declerck writes as follows on these drives:

> In the pre-oedipal period the subject encounters his drives. Due to a lack of representation to which these drives could be attached, they cannot be abreacted and they manifest themselves consequently as a massive (anxiety neurotic) breakthrough of anxiety. This real jouissance will occasionally be called the Other jouissance (*L'Autre Jouissance*) by Lacan—"Other" because it cannot yet be qualified as sexual as it has not yet come under the primacy of the phallus (Declerck, 1997, p. 211, my translation).

In the period before castration—that is, in the period before the introduction of representations and signifiers into the life of the subject—the infant is a passive object for the Other. It is like a sponge soaking up this jouissance of the Other. It is important to mention that this process is already different for every infant: the way in which the infant soaks up this jouissance of the Other is dependent on how the desire of this Other is structured by fantasy. In other words, the pre-oedipal differences regarding the jouissance of the Other are the result of interactions with particular others and their fantasy structures. Lacan relates these differences to what he calls a "knowledge in the real". This seems to indicate a knowledge (like traces) that is deeply unconscious, but which, nevertheless, has a determining effect on the subject. This concept will be considered in more detail in Chapter 8 and in the Conclusion as it is specifically relevant to the different effects of drugs on the subject. It is clear that the fantasy structure of the Other has important consequences, especially for the relationship of human subjects to their body. Passivity is the starting-position of the human subject, and sexuality makes its entrance only after the influence of the Other. Before the conscription of the subject into the ranks of the Other—that is, before the signifier enters the real body, thereby producing a subject who from then on will have a body—the infant is nothing but passive object which the Other enjoys. Declerck argues that this reduction of the subject to object as real body (which the Other enjoys) supports Freud's notion of "passive trauma", although he argues that this is not necessarily to be taken as a case of the child as innocent victim of perverse intentions. It is rather the case that every infant as subject is subjected to the desire and jouissance of the mother/carer, as expressed in her physical contact, touches and caresses (Ibid., p. 213).[5] Trauma and anxiety are now the result of the child having been at the receiving end of the desire and jouissance of the mother (or carer), whereby the passive nature of this trauma comes as an effect of everything she has done to the child. That is why Lacan calls this "other jouissance"—occasionally—a "jouissance of the Other" (Ibid., p. 213).

What is a human body? A human body is a "reality". However, we are not born with the reality of a body, but as a living organism or real body—that is, as flesh and blood, bone and tissue. The only reality we have is the reality of language and if our body is a reality than it is a body of language. The introduction of language into the real of the body does not only produce a subject, it also produces a body for this subject. The invocations of the Other call a subject into being and, at the same time produce a body for this subject which he or she can "have" from then on. Language therefore constitutes a subject and a body, but not in the same place—the subject is not the body. Where the subject is, we find no-body; and where the body is, we find no subject. Despite this fundamental disjunction there is a relationship but it is problematic in nature. Before continuing to explore Lacan's later conception of the body in relation to toxicity, the real, jouissance, the death-drive and addiction, it might serve the reader to summarize how he developed his thinking on the body.[6]

The body played a major role in Lacan's work from the very beginning. The body is something that can be disturbed and it is also a place in which symptoms can be inscribed. A lot of the symptoms of Freud's patients from the *Studies on Hysteria* (1895d) were bodily symptoms. Not too long before the Studies Freud had in fact discovered that hysterical paralyses had nothing to do with the laws of anatomy or neurology.[7] So the idea of a body speaking through symptoms is certainly not a recent one. However, what is relatively recent is Lacan's idea that the body has to be considered as something separate from the organs or the organism. The body is a reality that is constructed (Soler, 1996, p. 8). For Lacan, reality is constituted by a combination of the symbolic and the imaginary. So where does that situate the real of the body?

The idea that the body is a constructed reality implies that it is based on an identification with something outside the subject, and that the body is the locus for this identification. In a first period of his work which runs till 1953, this is the period before the Rome Discourse, Lacan puts quite a lot of emphasis on the imaginary and initially he privileges the identification with an image as the crucial factor in the constitution of a body. The "Mirror Stage" is the process of the constitution of the ego and the body on the basis of an identification with an image. What is needed for this process is two things: a living organism and an image (Soler, op. cit., p. 10). Put the two together and the body becomes something that the subject can see as a co-ordinated unity. Before the mirror stage, the body was a fragmented mess (at least that is how it is seen from a later point of view). A sense of body (and a sense of self) comes from outside. That means that we have a body that is not really our own. Already at this stage what is ours and what is Other is profoundly mixed-up. At the start of this period the symbolic doesn't play a major role in Lacan's thinking on the body. The body is predominantly the function of a visual gestalt and it covers the real of the organism. The real at this stage is to be considered as a lack in biological maturity (the organism in bits and pieces) which necessitates unification by the image, but it also something that expresses itself in the threat of fragmentation after unification has taken place. The body is a coating of the real of the organism and its organs with the material of an image. The threat of fragmentation is always there precisely because the mirror-image or coating leaves something of the essence of the body outside its grasp. That is where anxiety and aggression are situated. Something is left for real in the process of representation of the body. But what is the place and function of the symbolic?

It is the (parental) Other who helps and encourages the child to recognize its image in the mirror. That means that there is already a presence of something else (besides the fragmented body and the image) for the child; a third element that can function as a reference point. In his article on the mirror stage from the *Écrits* Lacan refers to a symbolic matrix and he explains that this symbolic matrix precipitates the formation of the I before this I is able to identify with the other and before language constitutes an actual subject (Lacan, 1977[1949], p. 2). Lacan's use of the expression symbolic matrix is a precursor of what will later become a trait in the Other; an ideal point, I(A), of identification for the child. It is the introjection of this trait that will provide a symbolic position or angle from which it can look into the mirror. The moment the child recognizes itself, an ideal image is constituted, namely an image of the ideal other, i(a). The child not only recognizes itself, but also the other as equal to him or her. A world opens up for the child and it happens on the basis of a dynamic with the Other. It is the speech or gaze, as materializations of the desire of the (parental) Other, that direct the child to an image of itself which provides it with a sense of unity. The child is orientated towards the desire of the Other; it wants to be and do what it thinks the Other wants. In fact, it is already caught up in the dialectic of the desire from the very beginning. The trait that is introjected by the child is nothing other than a representation of the enigmatic desire of the Other. When the unary trait of the Other becomes the foundation stone for the dialectic between the child and the Other, the imaginary moves into second place as the "designer" of the body. The imaginary is something that operates within the matrix of the symbolic and it is in the parameters set by the symbolic that it can have its effect as a kind of "inertia" in discourse and relationships. Where does that leave the gestalt as the totalizing and captivating aspect of the mirror stage?

This captivating aspect has become an important element in the dynamic between the child and the Other and it is expressed as the imaginary in that relationship. The Other begins to function like a mirror for the child. The child tries to see itself from the point it thinks the Other might want to see it from.[8] The child wants to be the kind of child that is loved by the Other. The child searches in the Other (as mirror) for a reflection of itself as a loved object, and this search produces an imaginary identification. Now the body is the symbolic result of an encounter with the desires, demands and signifiers of the Other with which the child has identified. This identification provides the child with an illusory sense of coherence that only hides a fundamental lack, namely the true essence of the desire of the Other.

Throughout the 1950s the function of language is pushed to the forefront and this began to influence Lacan's thinking on the body more and more. In fact, Colette Soler argues that Lacan made a u-turn in his thinking on the body from the time he delivered the Rome Discourse when he claimed that the signifier introduces discourse into the organism (op. cit., p. 11). The signifier and the organism have switched roles to a large degree in this "second period" of Lacan's thinking. Soler writes: "The common point between the two periods is that, in any case, there is discord. There is discordance. And in the second period Lacan came, on the contrary, to think that the organism itself has a unity at its command. It is a cohesion. And it loses this cohesion because of the signifier" (Ibid., p. 11). In other words, the body is torn apart by the signifiers of the desires and the demands of the Other. These signifiers cut the body in parts and it is the function of the signifier in a chain of signifiers that is able to "stitch" these parts together. The organism is a "thing" in the real that remains hidden behind the parts and the stitches of the symbolic body. At times it might rear its ugly head. Increasingly, Lacan begins to emphasize the role of the real in this second period. For a detailed exploration of the second (and third) period in Lacan's work on the body the reader is referred to Paul Verhaeghe's article "Subject and body—Lacan's struggle with the real" (1999).[9] The second period comes to an end by 1970. In the third period in Lacan's thinking on the body, this real element will again find its place, but it will be articulated and situated differently.

In a text from 1970 called *"Radiophonie"*, Lacan argues that the body of language, which in itself is a source of potential jouissance, is incorporated by the subject (Lacan, 1970, pp. 60, 61). It will be demonstrated shortly how this incorporation has a number of consequences for the subject and the body. One of these consequences is what one might call a "toxicity" of the body. The thesis proposed here is that this "toxicity" is responsible for the problematic relationship that exists between the different forms of jouissance. The incorporation of the signifier changes the real of the organism into a body which the subject can take possession of, but which, strictly speaking, does not belong to him or her. This body belongs, as it were, to the Other. For sexual enjoyment of the erogenous zones the subject can now borrow "body-parts" from this Other, but the subject cannot be unified with this body anymore.

Sexual enjoyment is partial and situated outside the body, then, because the incorporation of the signifier results in the signifying cut of castration. Castration cuts out the erogenous zones from the rest of the body and transports them outside its immediate realm. This happens by way of the transactions between the subject and the Other. The moment the organism becomes a body is also the moment the signifiers of the demand of the Other begin to push the jouissance of the real body into the anatomical rims and sexual objects outside the body. Language "phallicizes" the body by transforming this real jouissance into a sexual or phallic jouissance which is situated outside the body. There it can be enjoyed in the limited way of our human sexuality. Sex has a beginning and an end, which is why it is never completely satisfactory, and it is why one keeps longing for that Other (more total) jouissance. Once the real drives of the body, through the process of symbolization, have become attached to signifiers or representations, they take on a different dimension. The drives are now split. They aim at the other as sexual object for their satisfaction, while at the same time they aim at the recuperation of the total jouissance beyond language. This latter aspect is the reason why—as Lacan says—every drive is also a death-drive (Lacan, 1995[1964], p. 275). The incorporation of language causes entropy, because it devitalizes the body of jouissance by exteriorizing this jouissance through the sexual drives, thereby making the body barren for jouissance. The tension between a sexual jouissance, which is only available in limited quantities, and the desire for an all comprehensive (but lost) jouissance is nothing other than the cause of the failure of Freud's pleasure principle.

The incorporation of language, otherwise known as the process of symbolic castration, will lead to the reality for the subject of having a symbolic body, which is emptied of jouissance. There are two interdependent reasons why this process of symbolization is incomplete and can become problematic. The process is incomplete because language (or the symbolic order) is in itself structurally incomplete. This lack in the Other is expressed in the demand of (and on) the subject; it is the signifier of this demand which provokes and channels the drives of the body. This lack in the Other and the consequent possibility of an inconsistent demand will result in—respectively—a division of jouissance, and an often problematic economy of jouissance for the subject. Incorporation and symbolization will therefore not only lead to the reality of a symbolic body with psychically processed sexual drives, but it will also leave a remainder in the form of a real of the body, with unprocessed real drives. This real part of the body contains a jouissance which is an effect of the defect of the signifier, and of the problems and inconsistencies in the signifying articulations of the demand of the Other. This jouissance is situated outside the immediate reach of the signifier, and therefore cannot be pacified by language and speech. Consequently, it cannot be poured into the sexual objects via the symbolic channel of the sexual drives. Lacan remarks that:

> You have to make a distinction between phallic jouissance, which prevails in the speaking being, and a jouissance of the body which is of a different order than phallic jouissance (Lacan, 1974, lecture from 21–5–1974, my translation).

The jouissance which emanates from the real part of the body is jouissance of the body. This is an asexual jouissance, because it was never phallicized. The relationship between phallic jouissance and jouissance of the body is of the same nature as the relationship between the pleasure principle and what lies beyond the pleasure principle, namely the death-drive. The real jouissance of the body—therefore—is the death-drive, because our relationship to it is of a lethal nature. The absence of this jouissance of the real creates the illusion of the possibility of a total satisfaction. However, its presence would be "too-much" or "toxic", because it lies beyond the normal confines of pleasure and human reality. In other words, in the presence of this jouissance of the body we would disappear as subjects. Our relationship to the death-drive and the real of the body is an impossible one:

> The death-drive is the real in so far as it can only be thought of as impossible—that is to say, that every time it peeps round the corner it is unthinkable. We cannot hope to approach that impossibility, because it is unthinkable; it is death, of which the foundation of the real is that it cannot be thought (Lacan, 1976, lecture from 16–3–1976, translation Luke Thurston).

The real jouissance of the body cannot be thought or comprehended, but its extimate being causes a death-drive in the human subject.[10] It is phallic jouissance and the enjoy*ment* of the signifier which safeguard against this toxic jouissance. The toxicity referred to here is the toxicity of the real of the body. This is a psychoanalytic conception of toxicity. This toxicity is not at all the same as the toxicity of chemical intoxication; it concerns instead a jouissance of the body which would annihilate us if there was not the (sexual) jouissance of the signifier to curtail it. The subject can make drugs and alcohol act as "flood-gates", regulating the jouissance of the Other, by forming barriers against the pressure of its (lethal) attraction. Toxicomania can function as a defence against anxiety which results from being inundated with this Other jouissance.

To return to the question of whether or not toxicomania is a death-drive: not all toxicomanias are a death-drive. Some toxicomaniacs do indeed aim at this Other jouissance beyond pleasure. Others, meanwhile, use drugs and alcohol as a protection against the death-drive of the jouissance of the body. For instance, Burroughs wrote:

> If all pleasure is relief from tension junk affords relief from the whole life process, in disconnecting the hypothalamus, which is the centre of psychic energy and libido. It seems more probable that junk suspends the whole cycle of tension, discharge and rest (Burroughs, 1993, p. 41).

These two sentences by Burroughs are absolutely crucial for an understanding of the paradoxical nature of toxicomania. Drugs can allow one to suspend the pleasure principle. However, it is important to note that this does not imply, in his case, a tendency to want to move to a "beyond of the pleasure principle". Indeed, it seems instead that the regulating and containing effect of the pleasure principle was insufficient to pacify something in him. He did not want relief only from tension; he wanted relief from the whole life-process. And is this "process of life" not exactly (as Lacan suggested) the "jouissance which conjoins life to death"? (Lacan, 1974, lecture from 19–2–1974). Burroughs wanted to escape the "cautious, nagging, frightening flesh" (Burroughs, 1977, p. 152); he wanted to protect himself against the jouissance of his body. There are indications in Thomas De Quincey's writing of a similar cause for his addiction to opium. He wrote that, in relation to the often asked question as to how he became an opium-eater, he responded once as follows:

> (Yes, by passionate anticipation, I answer, before the question is finished)—was it on a sudden overmastering impulse derived from

bodily anguish? Loudly I repeat, Yes; loudly and indignantly—as in answer to a wilful calumny. Simply as an anodyne it was, under the mere coercion of pain the severest, that I first resorted to opium; and precisely that same torment it is, or some variety of that torment, which drives most people to make acquaintance with that same insidious remedy (De Quincey, 1986[1821], p. 140).

Summary and a conclusion

After this long detour on the body it seems appropriate to summarize Lacan's thoughts on the "body of jouissance" and to include in this summary the arguments put forward as to how the constitution of the subject in language is able to represent "certain ways in which our organism is regulated", as Freud said (Freud, 1930a, p. 78), but also how it is deregulated. Freud's trajectory was based on hope in science; he had a strong belief in science and its positive outlook. Some of the blindness of this hope restricted him from exploiting his own discoveries. It might be interesting to start this summary from a different point of view, namely with a comparison between Freud's hopeful idea of a "vital energy" from his "Cocaine Episode" and Lacan's concept of jouissance.

In his Addenda to *Über Coca*, Freud writes that the only constant effect of cocaine he found was an increased capacity for work. Cocaine appeared to be able to release an otherwise unavailable vital energy in the organism which could be used for work. The nature of the relationship between cocaine and this vital energy remained an enigma for Freud. In seminar XVII, *L'envers de la Psychanalyse*, Lacan says that signifying articulation or knowledge (S2) is the means of jouissance; when it is at work it produces entropy and this point of entropy is the only regular point of access to jouissance (Lacan, 1991, pp. 56–57). Lacan's argument is that the material of signifying articulation causes a loss of vital energy in the body, an entropy of jouissance, which cannot be retrieved anymore, but a small amount of which can still be enjoyed in a limited way via the material of language. However, one way or another, something is lost. Entropy is a concept from physics (more specifically thermodynamics) and can be understood as virtual energy that is lost and in that condition no longer available for work. In his work on cocaine, Freud expressed the hope that this vital, but lost, energy could be made employable and useful again. It is only with his discovery of a beyond of the pleasure principle that he understood that this hope was in vain. He also realized then that not everything in the economy of what drives humans is useful.

In Seminar XX, *Encore*, Lacan says that jouissance serves nothing (Lacan, 1975a, p. 10). In other words, it exists beyond the possibility of a useful deployment of its vitality. Therefore it cannot be reconciled with the pleasure principle because it does not lend itself to the production of pleasure; to being reduced to an acceptable and necessary level. It is good for nothing and it is a form of enjoyment which must be called to a halt in order to limit its effect. Unlike Freud's idea of an employable positive energy, from *Über Coca*, the vitality of Lacan's jouissance is essentially negative and divided.

There is a division in jouissance, because castration prohibits it and gives access to it elsewhere in a different form. One enters reality with the apparatuses of jouissance and the only actual apparatus is language. Language is itself a form of jouissance, a kind of enjoyment that is different from the jouissance of immediate experience and total vitality. The introduction of the signifier causes jouissance and tears it apart at the same time; sexual (or phallic) jouissance and a jouissance of the Other are the result. In the important aforementioned text, "Radiophonie", Lacan refers to language as a "first body". This is a body of potential jouissance and instead of being introduced into it, the subject incorporates this body. The incorporation of the signifier does not only produce a differentiation of jouissance; it also produces a subject, allows it to speak and turns the being of a real organism into a body. Freud's starting point was that the constitution of the human subject is not a very successful process and Lacan made the point that this failure also applies to the body. Language, or the signifier, is structurally incomplete and because of that fact it constitutes an only partially symbolized body in language. These real (unsymbolized) parts of the body can become cause for suffering and in that sense they have a toxic effect.[11] Consequently, it is possible to say that the incorporation has a number of important consequences, one of which is poisonous or toxic, and which will be responsible for a relationship of impotence between the different forms of jouissance. The previous remarks on language, the body and jouissance can be condensed into the following three points.

The incorporation of the signifier grasps the being of the organism and turns it into a symbolic body which the subject can have from then on, but which does not belong to him. For the enjoyment of pleasure zones the subject can only borrow parts of this body from the Other, but it can no longer be united with it.

The incorporation of the signifier leads to a cutting out of these pleasure zones from the body. This brings them outside the body, where they soak up its jouissance and where they can be sexually and only partially enjoyed in a movement of build-up, climax and come-down. Sex has a beginning and an end which is why it is never completely satisfactory and makes us long for another jouissance; a *plus-de-jouir*. This sexual (or phallic) jouissance causes entropy because it largely devitalizes the body of jouissance, rendering it barren for enjoyment.

The signifier is structurally incomplete and its incorporation will therefore not only lead to a symbolized body, but it also produces a remainder in the form of a real body. This real part of the body contains a jouissance which also comes as an effect of the signifier but lies outside its symbolic realm and cannot flow into the sexual objects via its symbolic channel. This is a jouissance of the body of the Other and it is asexual because it is not phallicized.

This real jouissance of the body is paradoxical because on the one hand its presence is beyond the pleasure of sexual jouissance, i.e., it is "too much" and therefore toxic, whilst on the other hand, its absence creates a mirage of absolute satisfaction, in other words, a "never-enough". It is the sexual jouissance of the signifier which forms a barrier against, and an enclosure of, this other toxic jouissance. When the signifier produces a body which is divided between real and symbolic, it also causes a subject who will feel torn apart. That is the destiny of the human subject. As long as the subject is able to stake its claim and as long as it is able to maintain enough differentiation between the real body and the symbolic body by keeping the former at some distance, it will retain some consistency and not disappear into the gap of anxiety in the clinical phenomenon of depersonalization. In seminar XXII, *R.S.I.*, Lacan says:

> Apart from tearing it to pieces, one does not really know what one can do with an other body. I mean a body which is human. That justifies, that, when we seek how to enclose that jouissance of the

other body, in the sense that it surely creates a gap, what we find is anxiety ... Anxiety, what is that? It is that, which is interior to the body, and ex-ists when something wakes it up, torments it (Lacan, 1975b, lecture from 17-12-1974, my translation).

It can happen that language does not function for the subject in such a way that it is able to keep the real body at a distance. The toxicity of the jouissance coming from the real body may be unbearable for the subject when the signifier does not do its work.[12] The effects of drugs can compensate for the lack of the function of the signifier; it regulates jouissance and keeps anxiety at bay. However, it is important to keep in mind that this is not the only function of toxicomania.

As mentioned before, the signifier also creates a lack in the subject by cutting him or her off from a primordial jouissance which characterizes the dual unity with the mother/universe (Freud's oceanic feeling). This symbolic castration leaves the subject unsatisfied because it will desire something more than ordinary pleasure or jouissance. Yet when this desire threatens to be realized, the subject will panic and this heralds his or her annihilation. But for some, even the threat of annihilation, the threat of something beyond ordinary daily reality, might be attractive in an ambiguous kind of way. Dollimore's comment on Bataille's work is relevant here:

> The fact that life is riven with loss, mutability, death and destruction is, for Bataille, a source of human anguish. But this same fact is also, more fundamentally and remarkably, the cause of exhilaration when we recognize it as the condition of life itself; anguish is overcome when we profoundly—that is, sacrificially, masochistically—identify with, rather than disavow, this truth of being (Dollimore, 1998, pp. 250–251).

And Bataille himself:

> Anguish, which lays us open to annihilation and death, is always linked to eroticism; our sexual activity finally rivets us to the distressing image of death, and the knowledge of death deepened the abyss of eroticism. The curse of decay constantly recoils on sexuality, which it tends to eroticize: In sexual anguish there is a sadness of death, an apprehension of death which ... we will never be able to shake off (quoted in Dollimore, Ibid., p. 154).

The realm beyond ordinary life is the realm of the death-drive. Drugs and alcohol can function as attempts to break with ordinary (thus limited) pleasure (or phallic jouissance) and produce something more or indeed, occasionally, they can function as barriers against the lethal or toxic domain beyond ordinary pleasure which threatens to annihilate the subject. In the latter case, the toxicity is not situated in the chemicals, but in the subject. On top of this, the introduction of the signifier leads to speech which never reaches its full potential.[13] For all these reasons it is inevitable that the subject not only desires bigger things, smaller things—always better things—but will also suffer and experience anxiety. In a Lacanian conception of the subject, drugs and alcohol can function differently for different people in terms of their relationship to jouissance, pleasure, anxiety, pain and their body. In this chapter it has been demonstrated that the real of the body can be disturbed in various ways. These various disturbances require different forms of management or regulation. That is the reason why drugs and alcohol function differently for people. It is undoubtedly the case that this has consequences for treatment, as the effect of alcohol and drugs, will be (at least to some degree) determined by the way they function for the subject.

In concluding, it is crucial to state immediately that when one talks about the function of drugs as a floodgate for regulating the jouissance of the Other (or toxic real of the body) one is only referring to one possible form of toxicomania here. However, it is nevertheless a crucial step towards a differential diagnosis in the psychopathology of addiction. It is also a necessary step for a treatment based on an ethics of psychoanalysis, that is, an ethics that concerns the problem of the subject's relationship to jouissance. The question of the possibility of a differential diagnosis in the psychopathology of addiction based on an ethics of psychoanalysis is the main subject matter of the next chapter. In order to develop such a differential diagnosis it is necessary to explore first the problems that seem to be inherent in a scientific or medical based psychopathology. In other words, it is necessary to investigate the extremely problematic relationship between science and psychoanalysis. The real that psychoanalysis talks about and operates upon, the real that makes the subject speak, or rather complain, is not the real that science produces or is indeed in any way concerned with.

Notes

1. Beard was an important man in the history of psychiatry in America. What is often forgotten is that he was also interesting in terms of his thinking on addiction. He was one of the first people to develop a psychological explanation of alcoholism, according to Ellenberger. Armstrong writes the following: "He (Beard) postulated that drinking was linked to levels of nervous energies, and to the discrepancy between the amount of nervous force which they felt within themselves and the effort which they had to furnish in their lives. It is thus a way of artificially restoring those energies drained off by modern life, a product of the energy-grid which is the modern city" (Armstrong, 1994, p. 138).
2. The concept of administration will be investigated in detail in Chapter 8 in terms of its theoretical and clinical implications.
3. Lacan discusses his concept of "phallic jouissance" extensively in seminar XX, *Encore* (Lacan, 1975a, pp. 13, 14, 26, 40, 56, 61, 75.).
4. The relationship between toxicomaniacs and their object drug or alcohol demonstrates very well—and in an exaggerated way—the dynamic between the illusion of phallic objects and what lies beyond this illusion. Drugs and alcohol can function for some people—especially addicts—as artificial providers of happiness, satisfaction, fulfilment and instant gratification, whilst the lack of these objects always leads to the horrors of withdrawal, pain, misery and suffering for these people.
5. Freud writes: "A mother's love for the infant she suckles and cares for is something far more profound than her later affection for the growing child" (Freud, 1910c, p. 117).
6. Three texts (I know of) that have been written on Lacan's conception of the body and that make a distinction between different periods in his work are the following: Katrien Libbrecht, "De problematische verhouding van het subject ten aanzien van het lichaam" (1991); Colette Soler, "The body in the teaching of Jacques Lacan" (1996); Paul Verhaeghe, "Subject and body, Lacan's struggle with the real" (1999).
7. In a footnote to the letter from May 28, 1888, from the Freud–Fliess correspondence one can read that Auden wrote to Jones the following with regards to the article *Some Points for a Comparative Study of Organic and Hysterical Motor Paralyses*, Freud had written in 1888: "You give a wonderful example of his historical insight when you tell how he pointed out to Charcot that the regions affected in hysteria correspond, not to anatomy, but to popular ideas of anatomy. And how typical of the time that Charcot wasn't interested" (Masson, 1985, p. 22).
8. Libbrecht summarizes the result of the introjection of the ideal point in the Other as follows: "The introjection of this trait, the incorporation of

this point which represents the desire of the Other, permits that the child, who is assigned a place through speech—the voice—or in being looked at—the gaze of the Other, will manoeuvre in such a way in front of the mirror of the Other that the mirroring in this Other allows the child to perceive itself as a unit (of Love) of the Other (Libbrecht, 1991, 49, my translation).

9. There one can read the following relevant passage: "As long as the accent was put on the determining influence of the symbolic order, the body could only be considered as a mere effect, that is, as a signified body, as imaginarized body. Indeed, we have a body as an effect of language. From the moment that Lacan takes the real seriously, another body enters the game, one for which the signifier 'body' is not very useful anymore. If one takes the real as starting-point, it is not the body that is operative, but the organism, the organs. Lacan provides this with a psychoanalytical significance by understanding this with the drive and with the Freudian division inherent in the drive: somatic (real) and psychical (symbolico-imaginary)" (1999, pp. 95–96).

10. In an article entitled "Extimité" Jacques Alain Miller writes that the term "extimacy" was coined by Lacan from the term "intimacy". Miller develops the term further and he does so principally for two reasons. Firstly, because he wants to devote himself to the question of the real in the symbolic and the term "extimacy" designates the problematic relationship between the real and the symbolic. Secondly, he writes that "this expression extimacy is necessary in order to escape the common ravings about a psychism supposedly located in a bipartition between interior and exterior".

According to Miller, Lacan invented the term "extimate" in order to indicate that in the analytic experience the most interior has a quality of exteriority. "Extimacy" is not the contrary of intimacy. Extimacy says that the intimate is Other—like a foreign body, a parasite. What is truly Other for the subject is jouissance, thus "it is in relation to jouissance that the Other is really Other" (Miller, 1994b, pp. 74–79).

11. It might help to remind the reader that in Seminar XX, Lacan calls the jouissance related to this real aspect of the body, the jouissance of the body or the jouissance of the Other (Lacan, 1975a, p. 11). He calls the ordinary (sexual) pleasure or jouissance, phallic jouissance (Ibid., p. 13).

12. It is important to re-emphasize that this work insists on the fact that a psychoanalytic conception of toxicity does not necessarily consider toxicity to be inherent to alcohol and drugs, but can indeed indicate anything that is detrimental to the subject. Toxicity, in this view, is therefore an inevitable aspect of human existence. It is nevertheless something from which the subject has to distance him or herself as far

as he or she can. Toxicity in psychoanalysis includes the real (of the body), the realm of the death-drive beyond the pleasure-principle, but also, for instance (as will be indicated later), suggestive words spoken in a hypnotic relationship. For a detailed consideration of the possibilities of a psychoanalytic conception of toxicity see also Sylvie Le Poulichet's book, *Toxicomanies et Psychanalyse* (1987, pp. 7–171).
13. This full potential is the ideal of communication which is the ability to say it all so that nothing needs to be said anymore.

CHAPTER 8

Science, addiction and diagnosis: a question of administration

> "Whereas Freud took it upon himself to show us that there are illnesses which speak (unlike Hesiod, for whom the illnesses sent by Zeus descended on mankind in silence) and to convey the truth of what they are saying, it seems that as the relationship of this truth to a moment in history and a crisis of institutions becomes clearer, so the greater the fear which it inspires in the practitioners who perpetuate its technique"
>
> J. Lacan, "Intervention on transference", 1982[1952], p. 63

Modern science, human science and the subject of science

The tearing away of concepts and humans

Towards the end of *Civilization and Its Discontents*, Freud had a question which he felt he could not evade. After contemplating the similarities between the development of civilization and the individual he wonders whether it is possible to make the diagnosis that "under the influence of cultural urges, some civilizations, or some epochs of civilization—possibly the whole of mankind—have become neurotic?" (Freud, 1930a, p. 144). He immediately points out the danger implicit in making this kind of diagnosis by saying that "we are only dealing with analogies and that it is dangerous, not only with men but also with concepts, to tear them from the sphere in which they have originated and been evolved" (Ibid., p. 144). This is a very important remark. Sometimes man has no choice in being torn away from the place he originated and grew up. There are perhaps certain problems attached to that, but it is not impossible to avoid or overcome these. A human life is after all to some degree a process of coming to terms with the loss of one's original place and position.

Sometimes, in order to explore a new field or a particular phenomenon for which there are as yet no conceptual tools, the man or woman of science has no choice but to tear concepts away from their original place and position. This must be done with great sensitivity to both the area explored and the area from which the concepts have been borrowed.

When concepts and theories are transported from one area of study to another, they sometimes undergo radical changes depending on their object of study and the context they have been taken from. This process can lead to confusion and the criticism that this new application is based on a misunderstanding of their original meaning and application. This form of criticism is grounded in a particular conception of science which implies that concepts refer to a particular reality or to particular objects in a straightforward and unproblematic way. These concepts belong specifically to the objects or reality studied and should not be detached from them and deployed elsewhere.

The foundation for this conception of science is a belief that nature contains laws and an order which exist independently of the researcher. Scientific knowledge is the observation, registration and systematization of this "order of things". There is no doubt about this "order of things" in nature and all hope for the future is pinned on completing the task of observation until accumulated knowledge about the empirical environment has conquered the universe, that is, until all the "hard scientific facts" have been established. Modern science represents a very optimistic and hopeful approach which does not take kindly to any doubt or criticism. There has been criticism though, namely from the human sciences. Jacques Alain Miller argues that modern science has produced a humanist protest. This is a protest which does not desire the kind of mechanical, mathematical and objective knowledge from the so-called "hard sciences". It desires something else. He writes:

> A humanity which desires to concern itself with truth, beauty, goodness and badness, and which even acquires, in that respect, a certain jouissance of ignorance in relation to scientific knowledge. This humanity persuades itself that the essence of humanity escapes scientific knowledge, that it has nothing to do with knowledge in the real, that the book of man is not written in mathematical characters. That is the price to be paid for the *docta ignorantia*, that is to say, an ignorance which knows more about it (i.e., the essence of humanity) than scientific knowledge does (Miller, 1994a, p. 41, my translation).

The humanities react against the claim that there is a concrete human reality which can be grasped simply by naming the objectively observed facts and data. They feel that this scientific method does not capture the essence of humanity. Miller claims that the human sciences embody "the rejection of the desire of science in the name of the question 'what about Man?'" (Ibid., p. 42). The human sciences react against the modern sciences by ignoring their knowledge, and therefore managing to avoid the connection to the death-drive. Why is that the case? The knowledge of modern science seems to have a life of its own, because the signifier—being its basic constituent—performs its work independently of the subject, like a cancerous growth. This aspect has led Miller to the idea that the modern sciences are related to the death-drive. He writes: "one does not occupy oneself with the consequences that science has for the subject, and, for instance for his living being" (Ibid., my translation). The work and processes of modern science drone on without regard for life. This is related to the death-drive in the sense that the signifier—as a support of these modern sciences—carries on by itself once it is set in motion, often to the detriment of the human condition and civilization. The human sciences produce a knowledge which functions as a life assurance against the threat of death. It has been argued in the previous two chapters that ignoring the questions of death or the death-drive is not necessarily helpful in terms of understanding psychopathologies such as addiction.

Another problem with the human sciences (the so-called soft sciences) is that the aforementioned essence of humanity is never defined, except in aspirational terms. It is precisely this aspiration that is shared with modern science (the so-called hard sciences): science (both human and modern) is progressively moving towards a complete understanding of the human and physical world and the only problem, or limitation, is the immensity of the task facing the scientist.

Whereas criticism of modern science took shape in the form of the humanities, doubt about the validity of objectivity in modern science arose from a place where one would least expect it, namely from within the ranks of modern science itself. For instance, certain developments in quantum physics, Einstein's theory of relativity and Heisenberg's uncertainty principle introduced the notion of subjectivity into the "hard sciences". It was discovered that the subject not only decides the object of research, but also affects the outcome. Heidegger wrote:

> Modern physics is not experimental physics because it applies apparatus to the questioning of nature. The reverse is true. Because physics, indeed already as pure theory, sets nature up to exhibit itself as a coherence of forces calculable in advance, it orders its experiments precisely for the purpose of asking whether and how nature reports itself when set up in this way (Heidegger, 1993, p. 326).[1]

In other words, nature has to comply with the subject of the scientist and not the other way around, meaning that the scientist should comply with the laws and "order of things" in nature by merely calculating or describing these. A clear distinction between the hard and soft sciences seems to fade when the subject of science throws a spanner in the works of science.

Lacan calls the laws and the "order of things" in nature, which supposedly exist independently of the human subject, a "knowledge in the real". In Seminar XXI, *Les Non-Dupes Errent*, Lacan described a "different kind of knowledge" which, he claimed, is situated in the real. He stated:

> ... there is a *knowledge in the real* which functions without us being able to know how it is articulated in the way we are used to seeing

this happen (Lacan, 1974, lecture from 25-5-1974, my translation and italics).

He adds that this kind of knowledge is not attributable to a subject who could preside over its order and harmony (Ibid., lecture from 25-5-1974). This knowledge is entirely different from the knowledge of the human sciences—which is produced by people for people—because it is apparently able to organize itself without a subject and does not directly relate to people.

The knowledge referred to here is the object of the modern sciences (as opposed to the human sciences). The modern sciences are logic, mathematics, and all the other sciences based upon these—such as mechanics, energetics, and physics. According to Lacan, logic can only be defined as "a science of the real" (Ibid., lecture from 12-2-1974). The notion of "science of the real" is Lacan's answer to the problematic question of what is "natural" and, therefore, "true" to nature. On the same question Quackelbeen writes:

> Koyré proved in a masterly fashion the way physics, since Galileo, was constructed on the basis of mental experiments... and how mathematical coherence was the decisive factor, and not empirical verifiability (Quackelbeen, 1991, p. 104, my translation).

In "Television" Lacan considers whether energy is, in itself, "natural". He comments that the fact that a dam stands in a landscape does not imply that the energy it generates is "natural" (Lacan, 1987[1974], p. 34). It seems rather that the manipulations of signifiers, numbers and mathematical constructions which led to the construction of an artificial dam created an effect in the real called "energy".

It must be recognized that "knowledge in the real" requires the desire of a subject to set it in motion. Lacan calls this "the desire of the subject of science". In his article "La passe de la psychanalyse vers la science: le désir de savoir", J. A. Miller writes:

> The subject makes the signifier work and the result is a knowledge which is transmissible without the subject ... One can do science simply by ordering signifiers, drawn on a blackboard or a sheet of paper (Miller 1994a, p. 42).

For Lacan this characterizes modern science ever since Galileo and Newton were able to calculate and write these (mathematical) laws. This Lacanian conception of modern science is crucial. It evokes his remarks on the subject of science from "Science and truth". He indicated there that modern science, which was born in the 17th century, was the precondition for the discovery of the subject of psychoanalysis (Lacan, 1989[1966], pp. 6–7). How is one to understand this? Knowledge which exists in nature (knowledge in the real) presupposes a subject for who this knowledge is meaningful. It also implies a subject who has a desire to possess this knowledge. This subject is called the "subject of science" and it is the subject upon which psychoanalysis operates. Modern science made the decision to find certainty in the object and concentrated its efforts exclusively there. Freud discovered a doubting subject underlying this search for certainty, and he set himself the enormous task of studying the relationship between this subject and the object. In this task he stumbled upon the problem of meaning and language as the elements which connect the two, but which also obscure their relationship at the same time.

Towards the end of the 19th century Freud realized that language was an important part of the human psyche. He observed that the psyche was structured and that using language in certain ways can establish a change in people. He asked people to "free associate", and found that although their talk centred around a nucleus, the emphasis appeared to be forever shifting. One thing always led to another and never settled into something specific. Freud had discovered displacement as one of the mechanisms of the psychic apparatus. He had also discovered that this psychic apparatus was centred around a lack which people avoid. He defined this lack as the object that is lost when we have to tear ourselves away from our place of origin; it represents an original satisfaction that is gone forever. Initially, it can only be represented through hallucinations, but later with words. Freud had no conceptual tools at his disposal to ground these discoveries in a theory of language; a theory that could include the subject and this object. Not that this theory didn't exist in his lifetime, he just did not know about it.[2]

Torn apart and the lack of object(ivity)

These conceptions of the object, the subject and language have far reaching consequences for our understanding of science and the question of diagnosis in clinical work. The relationship between the subject of science and his or her object of study is of an impotent nature, because every progressive step in scientific research leads to the further retreat of its ultimate object. Science, as a cumulative symbolization process, will always move around or away from the "thing" it tries to reach.[3] For instance, advances in neuroscience and neuropsychopharmacology only seem to lead to the discoveries of ever more neurotransmitters and newer forms of interactions between them, whilst none of these discoveries bring us any further in our understanding and treatment of psychopathology.[4] But that is not all. The further the object of science retreats, the more the subject of science tends to step forward. This situation is absolutely antithetical to the ideal of scientific objectivity. A remark by John Hughes, Professor of Neuropharmacology at Cambridge University, might serve as an illustration of this point:

> You know you have to be convinced, you really have got to be convinced in science that you are right. This business about the impartial scientist assembling facts in order to disprove a hypothesis is absolute balderdash. Karl Popper could never have been further from the truth. You have got to be convinced. Yes, and I think most scientists are deluded (Healy, 1996, p. 545).[5]

One could conclude from this remark that, as a scientist, Hughes does not have much time for the painstaking and meticulous work of gathering data using the empirical method of objective scientific research which, according to Popper, should lead to progress in one's scientific work providing that this happens on the basis of continuous falsification of hypotheses. The implications of Hughes' remarks are that scientists can be convinced about the truth before research is done and that science only has to prove that they were right in their conviction. Science, in that case, is only a matter of what the subject of the scientist intuitively knows already.

Nevertheless, modern science has made enormous progress in terms of understanding and mapping the brain. Likewise, human science has allowed us to describe and categorize enormous complexities of human behaviour and thought processes. However, in the area of psychopathology modern and human science have spectacularly failed. Something keeps interfering.

Clinical diagnosis in psychiatry and psychopathology: a history of impasse and little change

A new found object(ivity) in the 19th century and its limit

Most of Michel Foucault's book *The Birth of the Clinic* (1963) centres around the description of how an epistemological shift led to the birth of modern clinical medicine towards the end of the 18th century. Eighteenth century medicine was characterized by a highly systematized, organized and hierarchized classification of diseases, their symptoms, and signs, not unlike the great botanical taxonomies of the same period. This classificatory medicine represented a particular ideal of objectivity in which systems of diseases exist independently of the diseased bodies of the individuals which manifested them. Anything else, including individuals and their bodies, were considered to interfere with the process of objective registration of diseases.

Suddenly, towards the end of the 18th century, a mutation of discourse takes place and with it came a new kind of objectivity. If the 18th century can be characterized by a code of knowledge, or a mythological description, which obscured the body and consequently dictated how things should be seen, the 19th century can be characterized by an opening up of possibilities of what could be seen rather than what should be seen. At the beginning of the 19th century a new visibility of the body emerges. Sheridan writes:

> Suddenly doctors were able to see and to describe what for centuries had lain beneath the level of the visible and the expressible. It was not so much that doctors suddenly opened their eyes; rather that the old codes of knowledge had determined what was seen (Sheridan, 1980, p. 39).

This new 19th century body is a body-in-depth and not just a surface-body emulating mythological science. The classic intervention of the early 19th century scientific physician was to "open up a few corpses", and in the process of doing this he produced an anatomical morphology.[6] In this way the body was reconstituted as the unity of functional systems and sub-systems (such as, for instance, the cardio–vascular system and the endocrine system). That meant that diseases became disorders of these functional systems. The causes of disease was now located within the body and it was the investigation of corpses that paradoxically allowed the scientific physicians to trace the morbidity in the tissues and organs of the living body.

The history of psychiatry in the 19th and 20th centuries is the history of the continuous attempt and failure to make this same epistemological transition, to isolate the functional area of the psyche which would give a conceptual unity and clarity to the differential clinic of psychopathological disorders. This failure causes psychiatry to revert back to the relative security of the nosological systems and classifications that, supposedly, grasp a clinical reality. The security provided by nosology and classification is the offer of control and mastery over something which is unknown or not understood, but it is of course an illusion; indeed, it is doubly so because nosological names not only have no correspondence to empirical reality but, in fact, they rather obscure that reality (Verhaeghe, 1994, p. 62). The latest and perhaps best known of these classifications is the DSM system (I-IV), the *Diagnostic and Statistical Manual of Mental Disorders*. In relation to current diagnostic classification systems, Dany Nobus writes:

> The categories of mental disorders included in the diagnostic manuals function as prototypical examples of states of psychic illness that can be determined through observation and deduction. Nevertheless, the univocal empirical recognition and delineation of mental disorders remains a psychiatric sign, since a perfect objectivity and a fully adequate categorical system are impossible to realize. Current diagnostic systems for mental disorders have many epistemological shortcomings, which are often acknowledged by psychiatrists themselves, but they continue to be used, in many cases because professionals are convinced that there is nothing better available. Of course the question is what this better thing would be: a more guaranteed objectivity through a system with more or less differentiations, or a radically different approach? (Nobus, 1997, p. 53).

It is very important to look at the possibility of developing a radically different approach to our understanding of psychopathology and especially to addiction which, of all the mental pathologies, is arguably the one that occurs most frequently. This radically different approach is a necessity, because the attempt to find certainty in the object (of clinical reality), through naming and categorization, will only lead to a further retreat of this object and a further separation between subject and object. But there is the other danger, namely of hoping that a similar epistemological shift will take place in psychiatry and psychopathology as took place in somatic medicine towards the end of the 18th century.

Positivist science depends on the observation, naming and classification of empirical reality; but it nevertheless assumes that in properly constituting itself as a science, it will make a similar transition as that which characterized the emergence of modern clinical medicine. What this means is that it hopes to move from a classification of observations to the postulation of an underlying functional dynamic of which these observations are only the visible manifestations. What the history of psychopathology shows is an oscillation between elaborate classification systems, such as the DSM, and the attempt to isolate from this a differential clinic based on functional unities. The attempt to establish a differential clinic based on functional unities has failed to sustain itself in the domain of psychopathology.

Material and moral reductionism and their limits

Paul Verhaeghe has divided the thinking on psychopathology in the 18th and 19th century into two broad categories (Verhaeghe, 1994, pp. 74–97). Some aspects of the two categories will be outlined here because, in some respects, the ideas put forward in this important, but untranslated, Dutch text, converge with the history we have just sketched and, more importantly, will lead to similar conclusions. Verhaeghe makes a distinction between the anatomical-pathology paradigm, or what he calls the "wishful dream of positive-science" and the *"traitement moral"*, or moral treatment paradigm.

The first is the paradigm of reductionist materialism, and has roots that go back to Democritus, who postulated that everything can be reduced to some fundamental particles. The basic premise, propagated by Bayle, is that every psychopathology should have one specific organic cause (or be based on a disorder in one specific functional unity) and should therefore be organically treatable. The accidental discovery of neuroleptica in the early 1950s gave new impetus to the idea of organic causation. The logic was as follows: if chemical substances can have an effect on pathological behaviour, then the cause of this behaviour must surely be chemically based as well. One of the consequences of this scientific way of thinking is that the subject is excluded. The illness is defined as a nosological essence and the patient is only its vehicle. In fact, even as a vehicle, the patient is an interference in the understanding of the nature of the disease. The subject is a passive victim of an organic agent and carries no responsibility whatsoever for his or her mental problem or disease.

The second paradigm (the moral paradigm) has roots in the fifth century before Christ, when the sophist Protagoras postulated that all perceptions could be reduced to their subjective determination and can therefore only contain an individual truth (for instance, two people seeing the same thing does not mean that they experience it in the same way). Despite this position, Protagoras does accept that certain perceptions are better than others: the perceptions of healthy people are better than those of sick people. Better perceptions are those that have better factual consequences. This leads to a paradox, namely, Protagoras starts from the point of view that perceptions are always subjective, yet some perceptions have better "factual" (objective) consequences than others. The inevitable consequence of this paradox is that, despite the aspect of subjectivity, one depends on an authority, or a master who knows, for knowledge about the difference between good and bad perceptions. The relevant consequences of this concept were the special institutions created, such as psychiatric asylums and hospitals, which were headed by a master or "*chef de clinique*" who would know what is good for the patient. Essentially, diagnosis and treatment within the moral paradigm come down to this: people become mentally ill as a result of sick-making perceptions or ideas, and treatment is done in a healthy environment with the help of a masterful figure. In other words, treatment takes place within a totalitarian discourse in which, yet again, there is no place for the choices, desires and responsibilities of the subject. This paradigm is strongly reflected in today's social/psychological approach.

It is striking that both paradigms rely on external factors. In the first paradigm the environment is responsible for the problems of the subject. Consequently, the subject is an "accidental" component in the therapeutic mechanism and the treatment takes place despite his or her responsibility.

Who suffers?

The lack of certainty in the unity of words and things

Psychopathology has not managed to reduce itself in any stable way to the functional systems of the brain and their disorders, nor has it managed to grasp clinical reality in a perfect and unequivocal language, reminiscent of the famous statement of the 18th century sensualist Condillac, who said: "Une science parfaite serait une langue bien faite" (a perfect science requires a clear language). It is as if psychopathology refuses to separate itself from subjectivity, language and culture. What the history of psychopathology shows, above all, is the constant attempt to exclude the subject and subjectivity (of both clinician and patient) from its full investigation. Psychopathology tries to find certainty in an unstable object of study and in the process it manages to ignore the relationship between subject and object and between subject (of the clinician) and patient.

In terms of a scientific conception of psychopathology and treatment of psychopathology, what the aforementioned paradigms—including classificatory medicine and functional (or somatic) medicine—have in common is the fact that the subject (of both patient and clinician) stands excluded in relation to the cause as well as in relation to the treatment. That surely must lead to an impasse, because is it not the subject who is happy or unhappy, who has pleasure or pain, who suffers or manages to avoid it, who will have to die and accept this or not, who will be confronted with the otherness of—and within—the Other sex and, who, ultimately, is the only one who knows—whether he or she is consciously aware of it or not—the true nature of their relationship to these sensations, feelings, thoughts, experiences and responsibilities? Can we believe that these thoughts, experiences and their causes exist independently of us? Or can we be told precisely how to go through—or live with—these experiences by persons who are subject to these experiences themselves? What is interesting about these questions is that they defy both an objective and a moral answer, but instead demand an ethical response. For instance, to die can be neither positively known nor is it good or bad. All we know is that we will have to come to terms with the fact that death will come and that this fact is beyond good or bad. The ethical response is to allow subjects to reconcile themselves with this fact, irrespective of the successful outcome of this process, because success implies having reached an external objective or ideal.

Freud shifted emphasis from the eye to the ear in his clinical practice. The difference between seeing and listening is quite enormous. What you see is what you see, but when you listen you can hear things that are hidden from the eye, things that have meaning or—when not understood—can cause distress. What Freud heard was that meaning is not always obvious, and neither was the language that produces it. Freud heard the existence of the unconscious. This discovery of the unconscious allowed him to generate a psychopathological clinic based on the dialectical interaction of subjectivity and clinical structure, thus undermining any attempt at strict differentiation and separation of subject and object in the psychoanalytic arena. This dialectical interaction transforms the classical psychiatric nosography and provides it with the possibility of a theoretical unity. This is however a form of unity that is not acceptable to the pretensions of objective and empirical science who prefer instead the unity of the observable object and the unity of word or concept and thing. The preference for this kind of unity in objective and empirical science, so prevalent also in the domain of psychiatry and psychopathology, has led to an impasse, especially in the area of clinical diagnosis.[7]

The failure to create a diagnostic system that classifies symptoms and syndromes of mental disorders on the basis of a precisely locatable causation, an uniform aetiology and an accurate prognosis for each disorder, i.e., the failure to create a diagnostic system that matches perfectly well with clinical reality, has become blatantly obvious in clinical practice. Moving away from diagnosis and treatment, psychiatry, to a large extent, has become a practice of patient management and patient care. And where this transformation has not taken place (yet), psychiatry and clinical diagnosis are largely a practice of intuition based on personal experience. Verhaeghe writes:

> Every clinician has experienced in his life a certain amount of anxiety, depression, relationship problems, problems in growing up, etc. As long as what he encounters in his client, is situated within the limits of his own experience, he will consider this more than likely as "normal". However, if what he encounters in his

client is situated outside his quantitative field of experiences, he will suddenly diagnose it as pathological and if it is situated outside his qualitative field of experiences, the diagnosis will become psychosis (Ibid., p. 35 my translation).

There are simply no absolute criteria available that would neatly indicate the quantitative and qualitative differences between the different categories of mental illness and pathology. The reason for failing to develop these criteria—and criteria in this case are ultimately nothing else than points of reference which determine the difference between normality and abnormality—is based on the fact that there is nothing outside language that can guarantee the absolute validity and truthfulness of these criteria. Therefore the unity between clinical category (or concept) and clinical reality (or object) cannot be established.

The certainty of a lack in the unity of psychoanalytic theory: the subject suffers

In psychoanalysis there is really only one point of reference, or one criterion for truth, and that is when the constitution of the subject in language confronts the subject with the trauma of a lack. All subjects, in their own way, try to come to terms with that fact, but there are no absolute tailor-made terms available to do this for them. Everything the subject does, whether in language or outside language, is to be understood as the attempt to live with this trauma of the lack.

Considering the impasse in clinical psychiatry and psychopathology in terms of failing to develop a coherent clinic of diagnosis and treatment (in psychiatry, treatment is to a large extent dependent on making the correct diagnosis), it might be worthwhile to look at the possibility of applying the theoretical unity of psychoanalysis to the clinical area of addiction. In no other clinical area is it more obvious that the relationship between subject and object can be very problematic and extremely disturbed. For this reason it makes sense to apply a theory that is based on the relationship between the subject and object and to apply a psychopathology that centres around the different structures, modalities and avatars that characterize this relationship. The attempt to establish a differential diagnosis of perversion based on the description and classification of sexual behaviours, their consequences and the contexts in which they occur, ultimately failed precisely because it ignored the clinical structure of the relationship between the subject and the (sexual) object (Nobus, 1994, pp. 132, 142; Temmerman, 1994, pp. 126, 127; Verhaeghe, 1994, pp. 242, 243).

Another reason why it makes sense to consider the possible contribution psychoanalysis can make to the area of addiction is that the contributions made by objective and empirical science or psychiatry have so far only led to unsatisfactory results that show an alarming inconsistency. A coherent diagnosis of addiction—based on the description of addictive/compulsive behaviours, drug taking, alcohol consumption, addictive/toxic characteristics of drugs, alcohol and their effects on psyche, soma, and social environment, course and development of the addictive disorder/disease—has not been successfully realized. Nor has it been possible to establish a precise cause-and-effect relationship between addiction and specific psychological characteristics, social factors or medical/organic anomalies that would explain the phenomenon of addiction in a uniform way.[8]

As mentioned in the introduction to Part II, it appears that something in relation to addiction is indeterminate. In other words, it is very difficult to positively define both addiction and drugs themselves (including alcohol). Coffee, tea, tobacco, sugar, water, food, prescription drugs, illegal drugs, can all be incorporated and may even act as drugs. A lot of people are addicted to alcohol, but can one say that it is a drug? Yes, one usually does for good reasons, but alcohol nevertheless causes a lot of ambivalent feelings in people, and it is by no means the only drug that does.[9]

Equally ambivalent is the relationship between drugs and medicine. Does a drug become a medicine when it is made available only by medical prescription (it seems that marijuana is now going to be used for the medical treatment of glaucoma, whilst amphetamines travelled the other direction by crossing over from being legal to being illegal) and what exactly is the difference between Prozac and ecstasy besides the legal aspect? (Lenson, 1995, p. 4). The history of legislation of drugs shows that, in terms of the function and effects of drugs, the law is arbitrary. Despite these indeterminate and indefinable aspects of drugs and drug taking we definitely know that addictions exist. The real problem is how to study them. Empirical science is dependent on statistically significant data gathered from so-called representative samples for its assertions.

This approach is therefore never in a position to address the relationship between drug (object) and addict (subject). A consequence of the empirical method is the assumption that drugs cause uniform effects which implies that the effects are only related to the drugs and indeed have nothing to do with the relationship between the object drug and the subject of the drug user. Empirical science is forced by its methodology to start from the point of view that toxicity and the effect of drugs are inherent to drugs. This conception fails because drugs are profoundly ambiguous in both their function and their effect. They can function as poisons or as remedies. Concerning their effect, it is a well-known fact that drugs and alcohol can affect people differently and can affect the same person differently at different times.[10] In other words neither function nor effect are uniform.[11] In Chapter 5 it was outlined that the cause of addiction is related to an effect (of drugs or alcohol); an effect that is specific to the subject of addiction. Addicts begin to depend on this effect and the signifiers and experiences that have marked them as subjects ultimately cause the specificity of this effect. It is important to state explicitly that the effect of drugs is not the cause of addiction, but the cause of addiction is precisely something in the effect that is subject-specific. To say the effect is the cause is to imply that drugs and alcohol cause addiction and that is obviously not the perspective put forward in this book.

Objective and empirical research fail in the area of addiction because the subject (yet again) throws a spanner in the works. Or perhaps it is better to say that the subject is not allowed to put in its spoke. Alain Delrieu published a very detailed study of more than 400 written texts on addiction published in the 19th and 20th century to which he gave the title *"L'inconstance de la toxicomanie"* (The Inconsistency of Addiction), in which he concluded: "Despite the multiplicity of scientific disciplines which are interested in this theme, it is actually impossible to respond in a straightforward way to two questions which obsess the adult world, 'why do so many young people take drugs?' and 'who are those who take drugs?'" (Delrieu, 1988, p. 101, my translation). In other words, addiction exists, but there is no such a person as the (typical) addict. This is precisely the point Markos Zafiropoulos refers to with his book title *The Addict Does Not Exist*.[12] Despite the uniform social, legal, and medical manifestation of addiction, the relationship between addiction and the subject is neither uniform nor predictable in any way. Listening to the discourse of addiction is perhaps a way out of the impasse. That means listening to the speaking subject who is addicted and that includes listening to the subject speaking about the specific effects of drugs and alcohol which implies a listening beyond a general symptomatology.

When Freud began to listen to his patients he started to realize that they all, irrespective of whether they were addicted or not, attempted to articulate something in relation to a conflict that apparently existed between their psyche and reality. However, one must immediately add that this does not imply that there is a fundamental opposition between the psyche and a so-called external reality. The conflict Freud heard in his patients was invariably situated in psychic reality and related to problems to do with pleasure. The psychic apparatus is primarily driven by pleasure (primary processes) and its relationship to external reality is established in a secondary movement (secondary processes). The relationship between the psyche and reality is of a precarious nature because it causes an incapacity for an unproblematic experience of pleasure for the subject. Freud and his patients were not the first ones to articulate this fundamental conflictual and paradoxical nature of human pleasure.

Rudiments for a differential diagnosis of addiction based on the mechanism of "administration"

The age-old problem of pleasure or why Epicures became stoic

In *Jokes and their Relation to the Unconscious* Freud analyses the technique of a joke about a dipsomaniac tutor. The joke goes as follows:

> A man who had taken to the drink supported himself by tutoring in a small town. His vice became gradually known, however, and as a result he lost most of his pupils. A friend was commissioned to urge him to mend his ways. "Look, you could get the best tutoring in town if you would give up drinking. So do give it up!" "Who do you think you are?", was the indignant reply. "I do tutoring so I can drink. Am I to give up drinking so that I can get tutoring?" (Freud, 1905c, p. 52).

Freud wrote that the technique of this joke is extremely scanty and therefore cannot explain its effectiveness. The cynicism here is open and direct: "Drinking is the most important thing for me". This dipsomaniac tutor wants to work only to be able to pay for his drinking. This joke and Freud's analysis of it touch upon a particular aspect of a certain kind of alcoholism: work is usually one of the first aspects affected in the lives of alcoholics, but at the same time the aspect they most need to hold on to in order to be able to continue drinking.

Further on in this book Freud continued with an interpretation of this joke. The joke corresponds to a conflict within people. On the one hand one wants enjoyment and it makes no difference how one gets it. This is exemplified in Horace's *Carpe Diem*, which according to Freud "appeals to the uncertainty of life and the unfruitfulness of virtuous renunciation" (Ibid., p. 109). At times one likes to hold on to this philosophy of life because one has stopped believing that renunciation will lead to satisfaction in the future since we might not be there to enjoy it. Freud wrote that this joke says "that the wishes and desires of men have a right to make themselves acceptable alongside of exacting and ruthless morality" (Ibid., p. 110). There will be always a voice in people which rebels against the demands of morality as long as healing has not made one's life safe and existing social arrangements do not make it more enjoyable. On the other hand, morality demands that one doesn't fulfil one's needs illegitimately because the continuance of the demands of so many unfulfilled needs can develop the power to change the order of society. Freud was referring here to a morality which is in the service of the common good. Freud concludes his interpretation by saying that there is no way out of this conflict (Ibid., pp. 109–110). And there is indeed no way out of this conflict unless one is prepared to commit oneself to a religion or an ideology. Both (in their own way) provide solutions to this conflict by demanding identification with—and adherence to—an ideal, which allows individuals and groups to renounce the satisfaction of their needs for the purpose of a greater good. It is perhaps not for nothing that addicted people often abstain from drugs and alcohol on the basis of the identification with an ideal.

This fundamental human conflict concerning the demand for satisfaction is reflected in two ancient schools of philosophy of ethics: Epicurism and Stoicism. Bertrand Russell quotes Epicures: "Pleasure is the beginning and end of blessed life. The beginning and the root of all good is the pleasure of the stomach; even wisdom and culture must be referred to this" (Russell, 1993, p. 252). Cyril Bailey made an interesting statement in relation to Epicure's conception of pleasure: "Absence of pain is in itself pleasure, indeed in its ultimate analysis the truest pleasure" (Ibid., p. 253, footnote 1). This is interesting because it is completely coherent with an apparent paradox inherent in Freud's pleasure principle, namely that pleasure and pain cannot exist independently of each other and that the former is built on a reduction of the latter.

In Stoicism, virtue is the only important thing and the sole good (Ibid., p. 262). Pleasure and satisfaction are of no importance in the light of being virtuous. One has to step back from seeking mundane desires and passions. Only then will man be completely free. Freedom in stoicism means to be subjected to reason: the reason to know what the difference is between a pleasure that is morally good and a pleasure that is morally bad. Pleasure is something that either comes your way or not, but it is not something that you actively pursue. Julia Annas writes the following about the stoic attitude to pleasure:

> The Stoics do not think that there are two fundamentally different kind of pleasure, but that pleasure can play either of two roles in our lives. If it simply supervenes on what we are doing, then it is morally neutral. But if our getting pleasure depends on our assent to some belief, then the pleasure itself is a pathos, and so bad. Pleasure is alright when it comes unbidden, as it were; but not if an impulse is required for us to have it (Annas, 1992, p. 112).

This seems paradoxical. Reason here concerns knowledge about an impulse and reason can only be attained through abstinence from acting on impulse. The Stoic idea of freedom through reason implies the following: not to have your self imprisoned by the demand for pleasures and passions of the body and the soul. The only position, which can ground this concept of freedom, is the ultimate moralism of virtue being the only common good. The paradox is that the freedom of true virtue implies a knowledge about what is bad in order to be good, and that in turn implies that in order to be good one has to be in touch with what is bad.

Epicurism and Stoicism seem to be completely opposed as ethical systems of thinking. On closer inspection of Epicurism however one comes to a surprising conclusion. It was mentioned before that the absence of pain is considered to be the highest good and one knows that overindulgence in all kinds of pleasures can lead to pain. This knowledge allowed Epicures to make the following statements: "The greatest good of all is prudence; it is a more precious thing even than philosophy", and "Sexual intercourse has never done a man good and he is lucky if it has not harmed him" (Russell, op. cit., p. 253). So even the high priest of pleasure and enjoyment preached the virtues of renunciation, refinement and moderation. It is the contradiction within Epicurism and its paradoxical relationship to Stoicism which illustrates and confirms Freud's aforementioned fundamental human conflict. Man finds himself in relentless pursuit of pleasure or avoidance of pain. But he finds this, at the same time, either unacceptable or else impossible to continue and therefore cannot allow himself to sustain it.

When Freud began to listen to his patients he realized that all of them, in their own peculiar way, were addicted to the principle of pleasure, but also curiously enough, its failure. The impotence for pleasure is caused by the fact that pleasure has to have a limit. In Lacan's thinking this limit is the automaton of signifiers. This automaton functions as the administrator of jouissance: it regulates, distributes, manages and dispenses enjoyment in culture. This limit is a necessity because too much of pleasure or enjoyment would annihilate culture. That is the very reason why people always experience enjoyment as lacking in something. The precarious nature of this situation is the cause of the failure of the pleasure principle and of man's inability for pure and unadulterated pleasure. Pain seems to be the destiny of humanity and discontent in civilization is man's lot in life.

Civilization and its toxicomanias

In the very last pages of *Civilization and its Discontents* Freud diagnoses the disorder in human civilization in a way that would not be acceptable to psychiatry. In his observation of civilization he has come to the conclusion that it is an irrefutable fact that man wants happiness, but cannot have it (Freud, 1930a, p. 145). In other words, man is destined to suffer. Earlier on in the article he wrote:

> But the most interesting methods of averting suffering are those which seek to influence our own organism. In the last analysis, all suffering is nothing else than sensation; it only exists in so far as we feel it, and we only feel it in consequence of certain ways in which our organism is regulated. The crudest, but also the most effective among these methods of influence is the chemical one—intoxication (Ibid., p. 78).

The connection, established by Freud here, between suffering, the regulation of our bodies and intoxication is extremely interesting and demands further exploration. The immediate context from which this quote is taken is crucial for our advancement of a psychoanalytic understanding of the problem of addiction. Hence, this context will be explored in some detail here. Freud indicates that suffering threatens us from three directions: our bodies, the external world and our relations to others (Ibid., p. 77). This last source causes most suffering. Isolating oneself from others is thus one solution to one's problems. Drugs and alcohol can provide people with pleasure, but they can also render them incapable of "receiving unpleasurable impulses". These two effects appear to be intimately connected with each other. Both the pleasure these "foreign substances" can generate and the halt they can call to unpleasurable impulses, whether they come from within or outside the organism, are independent of the Other. Freud wrote:

> The service rendered by intoxicating media in the struggle for happiness and in keeping misery at a distance is so highly prized as a benefit that individuals and peoples alike have given them an established place in the economies of their libido (Ibid., p. 78).

Implied in this statement and its wider context one already encounters the rudiments for a possible differential diagnosis of addiction which is not based on observation of empirical material, but is based on a certain economy and distribution of pleasure and jouissance. The economy and distribution of jouissance result from the constitution of the subject in language (or the field of the Other). In Chapter 7, in the section called Jouissance of the body and the death-drive, it was argued how the constitution of the subject in language is able to represent "certain ways in which our organism is regulated", how different forms of jouissance result from this process, and how certain distributions of these forms can lead to toxicity and indeed cause suffering, pain and anxiety.[13]

Addiction as a social symptom

Another important aspect of addiction, which Freud made quite explicit in *Civilization and its Discontents* is his insistence on the fact that addiction is a social symptom. He wrote:

> We owe to such media not merely the immediate yield of pleasure, but also a greatly desired degree of independence from the external world. For one knows that, with the help of this "drowner of cares" one can at any time withdraw from the pressures of reality and find refuge in a world of one's own with better conditions of sensibility. As is well known, it is precisely this property of intoxicants which also determines their danger and their injuriousness (Ibid.).

Addiction as a social symptom creates a specific social bond and forms a particular structure. All three clinical structures of the subject in psychoanalysis form social bonds and are relational in nature; they orient the subject in relation to the Other. These three positions in language represent three different ways in which subjects can manage with—or orientate themselves to—the original structural trauma or lack. If it is permissible to define the clinical structures (and addiction) with only a few words, based, not on the results of psychological measurement, but on a structural conception of the relationship between the subject and Other, then one can say the following: Neurosis addresses the Other with a question. That means that the subject has unconsciously accepted symbolic castration and its consequence; it takes responsibility for the lack, it renounces primordial real jouissance, puts up with ordinary pleasure and with the inevitable guilt and anxiety.

Perversion dresses the Other with an object. That means that the subject sometimes acknowledges the lack and at other times refuses this. The mother is not lacking and in order to disavow this fact (and ultimately symbolic castration), the subject replaces the lack with an object. Primordial real jouissance is given up, but a particular jouissance related to a specific object comes in its place. Anxiety and guilt are often hidden and therefore less obvious in this structure.

Psychosis is being or not being the Other. That means that there is no relationship to the Other for the subject. Language has been foreclosed; symbolic castration and the lack have not been accepted. Primordial jouissance is not given up and the subject is either overwhelmed by it, or else protected from it, by delusions and hallucinations. Anxiety and guilt are all or nothing in this structure.

Addiction is an independence of the Other. That means that if the relationship between the subject and the Other is one thing, addiction is something else (and somewhere else). In other words, symbolic castration and lack can be accepted (but repressed), disavowed or rejected (foreclosed) by the subject, but one way or another, addiction seeks administration. Anxiety and guilt are hidden at times, but paradoxically maintain an "obvious" (hidden) presence.

Towards a differential diagnosis of addiction via the administration of jouissance

Administration refers to an important concept whose theoretical value and clinical application might not be immediately obvious. I put forward here the thesis that addiction, in its various forms, is based on the mechanism of administration. I also propose to consider the possible wider application of this concept, namely that administration can be considered as a mechanism for the symptom in general. All symptoms—and it does not matter whether they function in the real (such as the addictions) or whether they are symbolically structured—are all particular and subjective forms of administrating joussance. However in this work only (the symptom of) addiction will be investigated (with respect to the clinical significance and applications of this concept of administration). One aspect of its clinical significance is that it allows for the designation of how the symptom functions in relation to the Other. This function is related to the position of the subject: administration, as a mechanism of the symptom, is determined by the structure of the subject (this will be demonstrated shortly) and is therefore, in the way it functions, dependent on the different mechanisms that belong to the different clinical structures, (repression, foreclosure and disavowal). To put this differently: the mechanism of administration does not determine how the subject is constituted in the field of the Other, but it is an indication of how the symptom functions in relation to that field. The proposal that addiction maintains an independence of the Other, means that it is an attempt to administer a jouissance independently of the Other. Jouissance here refers both to the ordinary pleasure that makes life coherent, and to the pleasure that subverts coherent life and is not curtailed by the normal limitations of human culture or social life. The dynamic tension between these two human tendencies has been described as being fundamental to human nature. It lies at the heart of (the human problem of) addiction.

Administration, as an organizational function, is an important aspect of society. Without administration there is neither organization nor a society. On the basis of administration it is possible to acquire usufruct from goods, objects, and services that circulate in society. Administration organizes life; it is the economic equivalent of Lacan's concept of the symbolic order. Administration functions best when it can do its work automatically. However, when the subject is involved there is always the presence of disturbance and division. (A consequence of the existence of language and the subject is a constant dynamic between the automaton of structure and the tuché of eruption, for example the dynamic between speech and the slip.) The division is caused by the disturbance. To put this in the terminology of Lacan: the division of the subject (its structure) is a response to the trauma of the real (its constitution in language). This leads to the following question: is it possible to detect a division or structure in administration that is coherent with a structure at the level of the constitution of the subject in language? A positive answer to this question would imply that the distribution and regulation of jouissance can be related in a meaningful way to the different psychopathologies on the level of the subject. Etymology teaches us that administration is a threefold structure with three different functions: (1) to govern or regulate; (2) to manage as a substitute; and (3) to dispense or supply. Addiction can be related to the three clinical structures of psychosis, neurosis and perversion. But it can also be related to Freud's (often forgotten) clinical category of the actual neuroses, and this last possibility would make addiction a clinical entity which is separate from the other clinical structures and their symptoms. The clinical category of the actual neuroses is important for the development of a differential diagnosis of addiction.

In Chapters 2 and 7 the claim was made that from 1892 onwards Freud began to develop a structural psychopathology. Very briefly the following was stated there. On the one hand, he established the psychoneuroses (initially he called these the neuropsychoses of defence) and on the other, he developed the category of the actual neuroses. The actual neuroses are characterized by an anxiety against which the subject cannot defend himself. The psychoneuroses display a whole array of (hysterical and obsessional) symptoms, all of which appear to form a relatively successful defence system against anxiety. This defence is indeed relative because psychoneurotics also experience anxiety of course. In fact, to be anxious is even their hallmark. There is however a difference in quality: psychoneurotic anxiety is more curtailed and less overwhelming, and is contained on the basis of a psychic or symbolic processing of an original trauma that causes this anxiety. The cause of anxiety is the same for the actual neuroses, but the difference is that a symbolization or psychic processing of the original trauma never took place. Actual neurosis is the failure of a psychoneurotic development in the subject. The actual neuroses are an anxiety reaction to the direct confrontation with the real, because psychic processing is lacking in essential points. The psychoneuroses are a continuous processing of this traumatic real with signifiers and symptoms (i.e., symbolically structured formations of the unconscious). The psychoneuroses are an attempt to cure the original real trauma. The actual neuroses lack this type of cure because there is no pacifying symptom.

One way out of the actual neurotic impasse is by regulating the organism with drugs and alcohol. This solution of the toxic route via the body, which manages to avoid the encounter with the Other, is foolproof. Any solution that is able to avoid the detour of language is guaranteed foolproof. The problem is that the subject will have to pay a heavy price. In order to maintain the solution the price will be addiction, because it is a solution without the possibility of a resolution: chemical intoxication is not a symptom that can be analysed and it can therefore not be resolved. Some chronic addictions have their roots in actual neurosis. Addiction can be found in all three clinical structures and therefore addiction will acquire a function in relation to the Other in each of these structures. The chemical processing of actual neurosis is a fourth form of addiction and it is a form of addiction that has its own relationship modality vis-à-vis the Other. This relationship modality is characterized by the independent administration of jouissance which functions as the *governing* or *regulating* of an unbearable real; a real that threatens to annihilate the subject in actual neurosis.

In psychosis the foreclusion of language (or symbolic castration) results in a position of the subject as an object or "Thing" for, or in, the Other. The lack, which is produced by the constitution of the subject in language, is not produced for the psychotic subject, precisely because he or she is foreclosed from language. This psychotic subject will be confronted with a massive presence of the real; an unbearable "too much" of something. The defensive reaction of the subject against this massive immediate presence of real jouissance, can take the form of a "suppletion symptom" or what Lacan calls a "synthome" in Seminar XXIII (Lacan, 1976, lecture of 18–11–1975).

The other solution available to the psychotic subject is to develop a delusion against the massivity of the real. A delusion is constructed on the basis of language; it is a signifying system. But language functions differently for the psychotic subject than for the neurotic (or perverse) subject. For the latter, language contains a structural lack which makes the signifiers continually shift as the subject tries to find certainty about a truth that always seems to escape. For the psychotic, language (which is the material for the delusional system) has to be complete in order to form a defence against the real. Language functions as a protective wall which is meant to be impenetrable. That is why psychotics "know for sure". It is a protection that must provide absolute certainty for psychotics, but it is also something that can make them paranoid as there is no doubt about the fact (only neurotics doubt) that it can always be taken away by this Other. These forms of psychosis are delusional (megalomania) or paranoid. When there is no "synthome", paranoia or delusional system available, the psychotic subject and his or her body will be completely at the mercy of the real; they will be overwhelmed or invaded by jouissance. This is the schizophrenic (catatonic) form of psychosis. Here one finds the connection between psychosis and addiction. In the event of the signifier being unable to function as a protection against the invasion of jouissance, the subject always has recourse to the route of the body via drugs and alcohol. Addiction here is a form of *management* (of jouissance) *by substitution* with drugs and alcohol as forms of self-medication. Also here one encounters some of the chronic addictions.

In neurosis and perversion the mechanisms of repression and disavowal result in a fundamental dissatisfaction due to a failure of the pleasure principle. What lies beyond this pleasure principle is always "too much" and yet the absence of this beyond creates a "never enough", a *plus-de-jouir* (more-to-be-enjoyed). Here we can situate one of the aforementioned references Lacan makes to addiction: "everything which permits the escape from this marriage (to the phallus) is clearly very welcome, that is the reason for the success of drugs, for instance; there is no other definition for drugs than this one: it is what permits to break the marriage to the little Willie" (Lacan, 1975c, pp. 263–270, my translation). Lacan indicates here that addiction is an attempt to break away from phallic jouissance and an attempt to turn the pleasure principle into a successful operation through the refusal of symbolic castration. It takes the form of the subject *dispensing* with the failure of the pleasure principle by *supplying* himself with an additional jouissance. The drug or alcohol here functions as an "object-cause-of-jouissance" which allows the subject to avoid the always problematic encounter with the desire of the Other and sustains in him or her the illusion that he or she is able to attain the lost "object-cause-of-desire". This implies direct access to jouissance for the subject, enabling him or her to avoid the long detour via the Other because it can be administered at will. It is therefore essentially oral in nature and drowns the symbolically structured "formations of the unconscious" in a sea of toxicity.

Despite the attempt of neurotic (and perverse) addicts to break away from phallic jouissance in an act that takes place independently of the Other, it is undoubtedly the case that this act is, at the same time, an appeal to the Other as it was the encounter between the subject and the Other that produced the dissatisfaction of having to put up with limited pleasure and desire. In other words, the act of neurotic and perverse addicts is an appeal to the Other in the form of a complaint.

The discourse or speech of addicts is full of complaints. A complaint is a question, a demand directed at an Other. It is a demand to be relieved of suffering; a demand for help, a demand for a solution to the problem of desire. The complaint as an expression of pain and suffering also contains an accusation or an attribution of the cause of this pain and suffering to an external source. This external source is the Other. The human dilemma is that the Other is indeed the cause of the subject's suffering, but the subject will always have to take responsibility for dealing and living with this fact. Addiction, based on neurotic or perverse structures, attempts to avoid this problematic and fundamental human dilemma, by repeating this dilemma at a different level and in a way which is ultimately utterly destructive. On the one hand, addiction functions independently from the Other for the subject, whilst on the other hand the subject is dependent on the act of repetitive drug taking. In terms of treatment, this act should be interpreted as an appeal for help and as an analysable symptom. The problem is that the independent function (vis-à-vis the Other) of addiction creates complications for the transference. Addicted subjects will tend to escape the encounter with the desire of the Other (which the therapeutic or analytic relationship provokes), by taking drugs or alcohol in order to avoid the anxieties and uncertainties that are inherent in the therapeutic process.

The toxicity in addiction, when one considers addiction as a separate clinical entity (by being related to actual neurosis), concerns a jouissance of the body which threatens the subject when the phallic or sexual jouissance of the signifier is unable to contain it. In Chapter 7 it was argued that in the case of a threat of the real of the body, addiction can function as a kind of "floodgate" which governs or regulates the lethal attraction to the jouissance of the Other and that the floodgate of addiction replaces the function of the signifier. As such a barrier is formed against an anxiety when something of the body cannot be psychically processed or symbolized. This form of anxiety belongs to actual neurosis. Addiction as a separate clinical entity is not a matter of "not-having-enough", but a matter of trying to get rid of a "too-much".

It is without a doubt the case that these different addictions have implications for the direction of treatment. That is the reason why a diagnosis of addiction, which includes the subject, is of crucial importance for intervention in the field of addiction. It is essential to know what one is dealing with and to that effect one needs theory to guide a clinic that includes addiction. This is a clinic which allows the subject to find or create a different orientation towards jouissance and the real, via the object and signifier of the transference. The only problem is that the real of psychoanalysis (the real on which it operates) is not the only real. It is not the real of modern science, nor the real of human science.

The real of science and the real of psychoanalysis

The real of psychoanalysis is a real pain and the real of science is positive

In their book *Intellectual Impostures*, Sokal and Bricmont accuse Lacan and his disciples of being theoretical at the expense of observations and experiments (Sokal & Bricmont, 1998, p. 34). They insist on the absolute necessity of empirical evidence in order to be able to say something scientifically about the natural and human world: "Throughout this book, we have defended the idea that there is such a thing as evidence and that facts matter" (p. 197). Why not look at some of the facts of human existence and nature that can be easily observed? At times people are at war and kill each other. There is no doubt about that and this is a fact that didn't escape Freud. Towards the very end of *Civilization and its Discontents* he writes:

> Men have gained control over the forces of nature to such an extent that with their help they would have no difficulty in exterminating one another to the last man. They know this, and hence comes a large part of their current unrest, their unhappiness and their mood of anxiety (Freud, 1930a, p. 145).

It was stated before that man wants to be happy but cannot be happy. This is a fact observed by Freud and something for which he obviously had ample evidence. But his explanation of this irrefutable fact is theoretical. The reason why Freud wants to explain this fact theoretically is that the existence of evidence is not sufficient to explain this fact. Freud's point of departure is that there is an irreducible real element in human nature or existence that causes pain and suffering. This real element is not the kind of real that is at stake in science. This real escapes the methodology of human science (statistics do not help here in order to explain the evidence by giving the observed data some validity), but it also differs from the real produced by modern science (in the form of products of industry). The real in science is either related to a general kind of knowledge or else it is something that is produced as an object in the real. But neither scientific real can be equated to the real of the human subject which causes symptoms and discontent in civilization. Lacan says: "It is clear that the knowledge imputed to something in the real, whether one calls that God or something else, has in no way anything to do with the knowledge which articulates itself especially from this, that there is a being who speaks" (Lacan, 1998, p. 21, my translation).

Knowledge imputed to the real in science is not the knowledge related to the real of the unconscious of the subject. The real of the unconscious has a relationship to meaning, because it wants to find an expression of an inexpressible jouissance. It is interesting to note that this idea also applies to the drug experience. Drug users and addicts often want to express what they experience, but they can't find the words to say it. Effects of drugs are in the real and the subject cannot express their differences in language. However—and this is very important—the causes of the effects are related to language and can as such be approached by the subject. It was mentioned before that effects of drugs and their differences find their ultimate cause in language. The cause of the different effects of drugs in the subject is an unconscious "knowledge in the real". This "knowledge in the real" are the signifiers that have affected the subjects from the very beginning and without their knowledge. It is this unconscious effect (or affect) of the signifier that ultimately led to particular effects of alcohol and drugs in the subject. The earliest encounters between the subject and the signifiers of the Other are of the utmost importance in the cause-and-effect relationship between drugs and their subject-specific effects.

Nevertheless, it is not sufficient to say that the particular effects are determined by the "knowledge in the real". They are also determined to a certain degree, and at a later stage, by the form of administration. It was described before that the form of administration is a function of the clinical structure of the subject. The clinical structure is a consequence of the constitution of the subject in language in a (later) stage in the encounter of the subject with the signifier of the Other. There is a universal aspect to the form of administration because it functions within a structure (its function is to some degree the same for everyone within that structure). But, paradoxically, the effects that are produced throughout and within the different forms of administration are radically particular and thus diverse. The only limit to the particularity of drug effects at this level is determined by the cultural elements that are part of any field of language and experience. The form of administration is another limit on the diversity or particularity of the effects, but it is a limit that is much more radical and it is situated at a different level than the more primordial one of culture or the mother-tongue. Effects of drugs are like (mathematical) sets whose limits are (also) defined by the different forms of administration. It will be demonstrated in the conclusion that this has important consequences for treatment. The real of psychoanalysis is the radically particular aspect of life which needs the universality of administration. It is essential to make a distinction between this real of psychoanalysis and the real of science. To paraphrase Laurent—it is extremely important to convince science of the fact that there is another form of real than the one of science (Laurent, 1998, p. 42). This is the fact that man has to be torn from his place of origin which causes a differentiation in—and problematic distribution of—jouissance in the subject. Civilization is an attempt to regulate this distribution; it is in that sense "a mode of jouissance, and even a common mode of jouissance, a systematic distribution of the ways and means to jouir" (Miller & Laurent, 1998, p. 25). There is no doubt about the fact that the products and gadgets of modern science are very effective ways of producing, regulating and distributing jouissance.

The neurosis of our time: En(d)joy!

Freud's theoretical explanation for man's incapacity to be happy is that man is caught between an egoistic urge for happiness and a cultural urge for unity in human kind. Man is unhappy because the latter urge has pushed the former into the background (op. cit., pp. 142, 143). These two opposing urges represent the individual and cultural superego (pp. 141, 142). Freud's diagnosis that mankind has become neurotic was based (as stated in the beginning of this chapter) on the influence of the cultural urges. In other words, man's neurosis and lack of happiness are based on the dominance of the cultural superego over the individual superego. Freud's cultural superego is one that forbids, restricts, sets ideals, provides rules, and so on. It causes unhappiness because the demands of the cultural Other force the subject to renounce its claim for individual happiness.

This does not seem to tally with today's preoccupation with happiness, enjoyment, (extreme) pleasure, individual lifestyles and success. J.-A. Miller and E. Laurent write:

> Can we speak today of a major neurosis of our times? If one was able to do it, one could say that its principle determinant is the existence of the Other—in so far as it rivets the subject to the pursuit of surplus-jouissance. The Freudian superego produced things like prohibition, duty and indeed guilt—so many terms which make the Other exist. These are the semblants of the Other. They suppose the Other (op. cit., p. 26).

Has the cultural superego (which Freud diagnosed as being the cause of our unhappiness) been replaced by another superego, one perhaps that puts more emphasis (or even pressure) on the individual superego thereby demanding more happiness in the process? This would be a superego closer to the spirit of our civilization. Miller and Laurent argue that the Lacanian superego with its imperative to enjoy is the superego of our times (Ibid.).

If a change of superego has taken place, this change should also be reflected in the development of modern science. Subjects in modern times are more sub-jected than ever to gadgets and non-linguistic apparatuses of enjoyment. An increasingly significant aspect of modern science has to do with the accumulation, control, and distribution of material objects. These objects are objects in the real. Lacan says that we have access to an aspect of the real via gadgets and that we attribute these gadgets to the real because we do not construct them without the enormous scientific apparatus which in itself has nothing to do with these gadgets (Lacan, op. cit., p. 12). Once initiated by the subject, science can produce objects in the real in an automatic and sometimes accidental fashion, that is to say, in a way that is detached from the desire of the subject. This has an important consequence that was remarked on by Marc Strauss when he claimed that the foreclusion of the subject in science leads to the object running its own course, outside signification of desire, but not without jouissance value (Strauss, 1994, p. 29).

In the 1950s such objects of jouissance value were produced more or less accidentally. These are the psychopharmaca and they are a scientific means to jouissance and the regulation of jouissance. The psychopharmaca are extremely effective and in that sense the use of psychopharmaca supports the subject in terms of his or her complaint about the Other which allows him or her to avoid exploring his or her own unconscious choices and responsibilities. They are a promise of happiness by the Other of civilization. The subject is not only ready to believe in the fulfilment of the promise of happiness, but in fact feels that science owes him or her this happiness. The psychopharmacologist Peter Waldmeier put it as follows:

> So death or illness had another value for people a hundred years or more back from now and they accepted illness and they accepted death. Whereas when the treatments became available, some hopes were raised and people expected more and more from medicine and drugs. So in one way or another, people expected that whatever happens to them someone can help them and they can be terribly disappointed if they learn that in some cases this is not possible. I think this is something new. The roots are probably in the availability of treatments and the raising of hope (Healy, 1996, pp. 578–579).

The distinction between the real of science and the real of psychoanalysis does not imply that one is without consequences for the other; it does not imply that there is no relationship between these two forms of real. The scientific production of objects of jouissance in the real can have a real effect on people. They can become overwhelmed by this jouissance and they might have to create different ways of responding to it. Esthela Solano made a very interesting remark in relation to this. She said that medical intervention is an intervention which forces the real of the symptom to respond differently and when one forces the real of the symptom to respond differently, that is never without consequences (Solano, 1998, pp. 51–52). In order to illustrate this point it might be helpful to quote again from David Healy's book of interviews with famous and outstanding psychopharmacologists. These quotes illustrate Solano's point nicely and they sum up concisely the arguments put forward in this chapter regarding the problems of diagnosis in psychiatry.

Pichot: Panic disorder was created in its present sense by Donald Klein on the basis of differential responses to drug therapy. He has written down in detail how he came to the idea that there were two distinct disorders in the anxiety neuroses, one of them, the acute episode he named panic, reacting to the anti-depressant therapy, while the other component, basic permanent anxiety, did not. It is true that the importance of a new disorder was later increased by world-wide trials of drugs, the result of which tended to influence key people. At the beginning, many French psychiatrists considered it as an uncommon disorder. But of course one finds a condition if one searches for it (op. cit., p. 12).

Ban: I had been engaged in research in which we induced psychopathology with drugs, and later on in research in which we controlled psychopathology with drugs; and since it was possible to do it both ways, I felt that finally we could meaningfully talk about mental illness because what we were talking about was no longer just a matter of belief, but was accessible and demonstrable experimentally (Ibid., p. 591).

So how do we respond to the neurosis of our times? By giving a voice and not fuel (psychopharmaca) to jouissance. If our "enjoyment-demanding" cultural superego has forced the real of our symptoms to respond differently, perhaps then it is possible to conclude from this that some of the symptoms of the neuroses of our times tend to move in the direction of addiction and toxicomania. That makes the ethical response of giving voice to jouissance even more pertinent today.

Psychoanalysis is a discourse and a theory but not a science

Psychoanalysis is not a science. There is nothing to observe and nothing to prove. The unconscious is not conscious. There is little evidence outside speech and language that can prove that what is conscious came from the unconscious. Yet, the facts of psychoanalysis are irrefutable: pleasure, anxiety, suffering, joy, pain, desire, unhappiness, and so forth. For most of his life, Lacan was exclusively interested in locating and defining the essence and function of psychoanalysis. What is the psychoanalytic act? What is a psychoanalyst? What kind of knowledge does psychoanalysis concern itself with? What is this knowledge related to and can this knowledge be transmitted? If there is a question about the transmission of psychoanalytic knowledge, then that raises the question as to whether indeed that knowledge is scientific. Scientific knowledge is positive, transparent, general, cumulative, and transmittable. The language of science is clear; it refers immediately and unproblematically to the object it has constructed. Its ideal would be to do without theory, so that nothing needs analysis or interpretation, but only verification, falsification or measurement to predict whether what we do or choose next time will be right.

Psychoanalysis is a clinical practice accompanied by a theory which functions as a guide to that practice. The theory has to be there so that analysts know what they are doing. This does not take away from the fact that the clinical practice and the produced theory do not form a science. The fact that psychoanalysis is not a science does not mean that it can permit itself to function without verification. Psychoanalysis has a real problem: the verification of psychoanalysis cannot be dependent on its *raison d'être*, namely the fact of the improvement (or not) of the patient. The reason for this is that the verification of that fact is always dependent on the speech of the patient. In other words, the establishment of the effectivity of analysis or therapy is dependent on the subjective experience and articulation of that experience by the patient. And that kind of verification is extremely unsatisfactory for obvious reasons. So what verification is possible for psychoanalysis?

The treatment of any psychopathology without theory is the equivalent of sending someone to sail the ocean in a boat without a map or compass; one will get lost and then, sooner or later, one drowns. This example of navigation is very appropriate to illustrate the function of theory in psychoanalysis. It is an example of the analyst Jean Paul Gilson (1987, pp. 41–42). He compares an analysis or a therapy to the old trajectories of colonial sea-routes which traversed oceans via dark continents. The idea is not to return empty handed, but like the old navigators and discoverers, to come back with herbs and spices whose smell and taste were not yet known. The knowledge, which emerges from this kind of therapeutic trajectory, is like a map which was created by cartographers through the transcription of oceans and continents. It is knowledge or theory as a transcription of the speech of the subject. The navigator needs a map. Without it he is lost and doomed to roam the oceans aimlessly, directed by currents and winds rather than his aim. How does a map actually function? For instance, does it support the navigator's navigation? Not really because it is the water which carries the ship (Ibid., p. 41). Is the map a metaphor for maritime circulation? One can't say that either because a map is not a representation of reality. In other words, the map looks entirely different from what the navigator sees around him at any point in time in his travels. It is not a metaphor for the reality of his travels and it bears no resemblance to that reality. The map has been created on the basis of mathematical calculations and it has become a thing in itself. If it is a form of writing, it is not a representation of reality, but rather the absolute minimum which is necessary in order not to wander aimlessly or to get lost. This kind of writing can guide us in a traversing of the seas and lands of the world. It is a writing which structures a chaos.

Lacan called this a "writing in the real". With this writing one can maybe approach some of that real. Theory, logic, and mathematics, as forms of writing in the real, constitute, as it were, a map for navigation in an analytic cure. They are not a representation of the reality of the subject, but a necessary beacon or landmark which allows the clinician his or her way in an analytic voyage which can lead to discoveries and prevent them at the same time from getting lost. The theory in psychoanalysis should situate itself between the symbolic and the real. Or to put it more simply: it should be the kind of theory that tries to do away with imaginary, intuitive and descriptive knowledge or content. This latter kind of knowledge or content already exists in the subject of the clinician (or scientist) and it has nothing to do with the particular truth that structures the symptoms and suffering of the patient. It is important to mention this here, because it is precisely this kind of knowledge that is so avidly pursued by addicts and the reasons for this will be explored in Chapter 9.

A possible verification for psychoanalysis is dependent on the rigour of those elements of theory, logic, and mathematics that are a "writing in the real". These elements form an approach to those aspects of humanity that psychoanalysis considers to be essential. Psychoanalysis operates upon these aspects with words in a social bond or discourse that were specifically designed by Freud in order to have a maximum effect in the real. The discourse of analysis was designed to establish an effect in the real of jouissance with the signifier of language. Psychoanalysis is a discourse or a particular social bond between people. There are different social bonds. Each bond allows for the production of a specific effect that speech can have on the people implied in that bond. Lacan specified four different discourses. Aspects of these discourses will be considered in some detail in Chapter 9 with the aim in mind to show that the discourse of analysis is in a better position to establish an effect in the subject's relationship to jouissance than the discourse of science. The discourse of analysis is also in a better position to say something, or produce something, about the pathology of patients; although it will be demonstrated at the same time that the discourse of analysis is not without its dangers when confronted with addiction.

However, before concluding this chapter on science and diagnosis, another source of verification for psychoanalysis should be briefly mentioned, especially because it is relevant to some of the ideas put forward in this book. A possibility for verification for psychoanalysis arises from a relatively new alliance between theory and (empirical) science. The connection established in this work between subject-specific effects of drugs and the signifiers that have marked the subject from the very beginning (i.e., unconscious "knowledge in the real") suggests the possibility of (empirical) research on the relationship between language and neurological variations or changes (this was already hinted at in footnote 11 of Chapter 5). These neurological changes can perhaps explain (amongst other things) the variations in the effects of drugs in people. It is interesting to note that this kind of research would not only include a psychoanalytic conception of the subject, but also leave room for an ethics of speech. If it is possible to establish, scientifically, a relationship between language, neurological changes (for instance the movement of neurotransmitters), and variations in the effects of drugs, then there is support from an unexpected corner for the inclusion of the speaking-subject in the treatment of addiction (and indeed other psychopathologies). It looks increasingly certain that the empirical aspect of neuro-psychoanalysis is another possibility of verification for psychoanalytic hypotheses. For more detail on this recent scientific alliance the reader is referred to the work of Karen Kaplan-Solms and Mark Solms (2000).

Notes

1. This quote was first found in P. Verhaeghe (1994, p. 56).
2. In 1916 Saussure's *Course in General Linguistics* is published. In this book he makes a distinction in language between a layer of signifiers and a layer of signifieds. Neither layer is static, but they flow in no particular direction. The implication is simple: the relationship between signifiers and signifieds, or words and their meaning, is arbitrary. No word or concept refers naturally to a particular object or meaning. Arbitrary means that the relationships between signifiers and signifieds have been agreed by convention. Saussure also said that what characterizes signifiers is their difference from one another and a meaning can only be generated contextually, that is, through the context of other signifiers on the basis of this difference. Language is a moving material and it is set in motion by a lack that is inherent in the functioning of language itself, i.e., the lack of ultimate meaning.
3. Verhaeghe writes: The lack of object, that is to say, object a, is the necessary condition for every symbolic system, therefore also for science. In other words, no epistemology will ever succeed in reaching the "thing", because it would dissolve itself. But there is more: science, as a symbolic system, produces ever more of this lack-of-object. That is what we would like to call the constructive misconception at the basis of every science: the more one conducts science, that is to say, the more symbolisation takes place, the more one moves away from the object (1994, pp. 59–60, my translation).
4. Pierre Pichot, a professor in psychiatry, founder member of the Association for European Psychiatry and a renowned researcher in psychopharmacology, said the following in an interview: "The work done by neuroscientists is extremely impressive. I don't dispute that, but until now very little comes out of it in psychiatry in terms of concrete clinical applications" (Healy, 1996, p. 17).
5. Although it must be acknowledged immediately that his intentions with this remark might have been entirely different than what is suggested here. Hughes also says that he recognizes that "there are those out there that do pose the questions and go about it in a logical way." However, he does not consider himself to be one of those. He knows that delusions are dangerous, but a good scientist should be able to recognize that (Ibid., p. 545).
6. Foucault writes that "the great break in the history of Western medicine dates precisely from the moment clinical experience became the anatomo–clinical gaze. Pinel's Médecine Clinique dates from 1802; Les Revolutions de la Médecine appeared in 1804; the rules of analysis

seem to triumph in the pure decipherment of symptomatic totalities. But a year before, Bichat had relegated them to history: 'for twenty years, from the morning to night, you have taken notes at patients' bedsides on affections of the heart, the lungs, and the gastric viscera, and all is confusion for you in the symptoms which, refusing to yield up their meaning, offer you a succession of incoherent phenomena. Open up a few corpses: you will dissipate at once the darkness that observation alone could not dissipate'" (Foucault, 1997[1963], p. 146).
7. The preference for this kind of unity in psychiatry (and psychopharmacology) was expressed very well by Tom Ban, Professor of Psychiatry at Vanderbilt University, when he said: "The only reason to have concepts is to be able to communicate, and if we have problems using a concept in communicating, we might just as well throw out such a concept. And if the dismissed concept leaves a void one should replace it with one which corresponds more with the real world" (Healy, 1996, p. 595).
8. As an illustration of the failure to establish a coherent diagnosis and an uniform explanation for addiction the reader is referred to an excellent and detailed summary of the psychiatric classifications of addiction by Mary McMurran (1994, pp. 19–21).
9. The following joke (quoted from an article by Nicholas Warner) is a good illustration of that ambivalence: In their book *Drinking in America* Mark Edward Lender and James Kirby Martin tell the old story of the American Congress man who was asked by a constituent to explain his attitude towards whiskey. "If you mean the demon drink that poisons the mind, pollutes the body, desecrates family life and inflames sinners, then I'm against it", the Congressman said. "But if you mean the elixer of Christmas cheer, the shield against the winter chill, the taxable potion that puts needed funds into public coffers to comfort little crippled children, then I'm for it. This is my position, and I will not compromise" (Warner, 1994, p. 299).
10. In a footnote to the *Confessions of an English Opium Eater* De Quincey wrote: "...the varieties of effect produced by opium on different constitutions are infinite. A London magistrate (...) has recorded that, on the first occasion of his trying laudanum for the gout, he took forty drops, the next night sixty, and on the fifth night eighty, without any effect whatever: and this at an advanced age" (De Quincey, 1986, p. 92).
11. In chapter 1 we demonstrated that Freud was already aware of this lack of uniformity with the drug cocaine in 1887. In Craving for and Fear of Cocaine he connects the irregularity of the cocaine effect to individual variations (Freud, 1887d, p. 175).

12. The original title in French is: "Le toxicomane n'existe pas" (Zafiropoulos, 1988, pp. 1–106).
13. For the convenience of the reader here is a brief summary of that argument. The confrontation of the subject with language is a confrontation between the total vitality of immediate experience and an order that mediates and differentiates. Language causes a differentiation in the realm of total vitality which results in different forms of jouissance. Language also causes the subject to speak and further provides it with a body made from the organism it once was. Both subject and body are incomplete because language itself is incomplete (there is no real victor in the confrontation between the subject and language). The introduction of language separates the subject from the experience of total jouissance, but paradoxically threatens to confront the subject with the return of this experience at the level of the body. Both the return of this experience at the level of the body and the confrontation with the lack at he level of the subject lead to anxiety, pain and suffering, albeit in different ways. This subject is divided because it always desires more, whilst something of the body often feels too much. Drugs and alcohol can function as providers of something more or indeed as barriers against that something too much. This very minimal distinction in the function of drugs and alcohol is nevertheless an indication that their function or effect are not necessarily a universal given, but instead can serve a purpose that is particular to the subject.

CHAPTER NINE

Addiction and discourse: a moral question and the ethics of treatment

"Before the effect one believes in causes different from those one believes in after the effect."

F. Nietzsche, The Gay Science, 2001, p. 144.

"Education is an admirable thing, but it is well to remember from time to time that nothing that is worth knowing can be taught"

O. Wilde, "A few maxims for the instruction of the over-educated", 1989, p. 570

Addiction as a discourse

Addiction as a violation of the social bond

It was stated in the previous chapter that addiction as a social symptom engenders (or implies) a particular social bond that is characterized by a specific structure; is this a fair claim? A social bond is a relationship of a typical nature between at least two people. In the same chapter another statement claimed that addiction (at least in the form of toxicomania) is an attempt to create a particular form of independence from the Other and that it tends to smother the symptoms and formations of the unconscious. Symptoms and other formations of the unconscious find their cause—and acquire their significance—in the relationship between subject and Other. The constitution of the subject in the field of the Other—the moment of symbolic castration—is a traumatic confrontation with a lack and a desire of the Other. A very first representation of this constitutive moment is immediately repressed (primary repression) and that inaugurates the unconscious and the possibility of further repression (secondary repression). The formations of the unconscious are symbolically structured manifestations of repetitive unconscious attempts of the subject to undo the failure to find an adequate protection against the trauma of lack and the desire of the Other.

The subject of the unconscious is always in conflict. The ethical responsibility of the subject is to come to terms with this fact and that implies the assumption of lack and desire via the medium of words. To go there and assume responsibility (*"wo es war, soll ich werden"*) is a matter of moral courage. It is obvious that many prefer any solution other than the long detour of language. Suffering is always in the real and experienced as immediate. When (for whatever reason) the symbolic route is not the preferred choice for reconciliation with this real, there are two other categories of solutions open to the subject. The first of these is the imaginary realm of fantasy as a protective layer against the real. The second category of solutions avoids the symbolic/imaginary realm altogether and confronts the immediacy of a real with the immediacy of another real. A solution that belongs to the last category is the toxic route of the body in addiction. In that sense, addiction is a stepping away from the confrontation with the desire of the Other in the illusion that, by doing so, lack and castration can be avoided. The addict avoids desire and opts for unmediated jouissance. The Other (including the Other as culture) is not needed and addiction, as such, forms a real threat to the group and indeed to society at large. Reactions against this uncurtailed jouissance (no Other is allowed in to limit it) rarely fail to occur and they usually take the form of moral panic and different forms of punishment.

This attempt at independence seems to indicate a violation of the social bond or a severance of the Other by the subject who is addicted to toxic substances. The time has come to put this idea of independence in addiction into a theoretical framework. The violation of the social bond in addiction does not make it less of a social bond: it only provides it with its particularity. The severance of the Other in addiction does not affect the structural dependence of the subject on the signifier of the Other: it only concerns the independent administration of particular distributions of jouissance which come as a result of this structural dependence. This is precisely what sets addiction apart from most other psychopathologies. As a symptom addiction does not represent the subject for another signifier, but eclipses the signifier that does. Addiction, as a psychopathology, functions (mainly but not exclusively, as will be seen) outside the signifier and yet it operates within a violating social bond. In order to provide a theoretical context to these remarks, and in order to explore some of their social and clinical implications, Lacan's theory of the four discourses and some of its background and applications will be considered in some detail. In seminar XVII, *L'Envers de la Psychanalyse*, (1969–1970), Lacan develops his theory of the discourses (1991).[1] Over the last number of years some excellent material has been published in English on this aspect of Lacan's work. For example, Mark Bracher (1994), Bruce Fink (1995) and Paul Verhaeghe (1995, 1997) provide detailed information on the discourse theory. The information presented here will hopefully allow the reader to follow the remainder of this chapter, whilst the difference with the other authors is the emphasis on those aspects of science and knowledge that are particularly relevant to the problem of the subject of addiction.

What is discourse?

Discourse in the Lacanian sense is not a matter of communication. In communication theory, an agent sends a message to a receiver, in whom an effect may be seen after the message has been decoded. The aim of communication theory is to establish a communication system in which messages can be sent, received or returned in a manner that is effective, clear and unproblematic. A perfect communication should be without "noise" (or interference) and should also not fail in the aim to establish a specifically desired effect. It is on this point that Lacan fundamentally disagrees with communication theory. In his thinking there is no such thing as a communication without failure. We talk and we continue to do so because there is always something that cannot be said or communicated. If everything could be said (if communication was perfect), there would be no need for communication.

Lacan agrees with communication theory in so far as there is an agent who speaks to another in whom an effect might be produced. That provides us with the following places:

$$\frac{\text{agent} \rightarrow \text{other}}{\text{product}} \downarrow$$

What Lacan disagrees with is that the effect the agent hopes to produce in the other can indeed be established. The reason for failing to establish this hoped-for effect is simple: the desire that fuels this hope cannot be entirely known by the agent, the cause of this desire is unconscious. Freud made it quite clear from the very beginning that we don't always know what we say and why we say it. We are not masters in our own home. The truth that drives us (as agents) to speak to others in order to produce an effect is something that evades us largely. It can, as Lacan said, only be "half-spoken"; it can never be fully articulated.[2] It belongs to the realm of that which is primordially repressed. The cause of our desire is the object we had to give up from the moment of our introduction into language. This cause (or object a) is the driving-force behind our speech. Communication is a consequence of the failure of the symbolic to retrieve this lost cause in the real. Now we have the four places of discourse:

$$\uparrow \frac{\text{agent}}{\text{truth}} \rightarrow \frac{\text{other}}{\text{product}} \downarrow$$

The product of the discourse, which comes as an effect of communication between the agent and the other, is unable to reach the truth. Discourse is something that tries to turn around in circles, but it actually fails to do so. Speech and communication are attempts that fail in coming to terms with the lack via the Other of language. What is produced in the other (as the recipient of speech) can never compensate for the total jouissance that was lost through symbolic castration. Considered in terms of formal logic, the relationship between product and truth is a disjunction of impotence (//). This disjunction is a reflection of the failure of the pleasure principle: it is not possible to reach a level of pleasure or enjoyment that is totally satisfying. The consequence of this failure is that one desires something more. This brings us back to the relationship between the agent and the other and the attempt to fulfil an impossible desire. The relationship between agent and other is a disjunction of impossibility: the desire of the agent cannot be fulfilled through the acts of communication and speech. This provides the following structure:

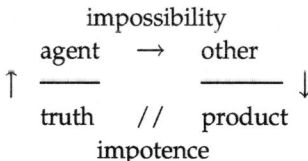

The inability to produce an effect that can reach the cause of desire results in a continuation of desire. The structure of discourse and the dynamic between the two disjunctions are extremely interesting and serve an important function. Discourse is a form of protection: it protects against the death-drive. Discourse prevents the subject from being annihilated on the irresistible path to total jouissance. What stops the subject from being annihilated is the safeguard of the continuation of desire. Desire keeps jouissance at a distance. As long as one continues to desire one will not be swallowed up by the jouissance of the real. Desire will always continue when the incompleteness of language causes a failure in communication.

The four discourses are four ways of social bonding that are centred around four impossible desires which are based on four ways of avoiding the realization of the death-drive. It is important to mention that a discourse does not start with the communication of an agent. The agent is always only an apparent agent. As said before, the real driving-force of discourse is rather the cause of the desire to communicate, and that cause is an effect of the signifier.

Before the agent communicates there is already a desire and a demand to do so. In other words, language and the signifier are involved from the very beginning. Language is the precondition for discourse and discourse exists prior to any form of communication. This is fundamental to Lacan's thinking on the nature of the speaking-subject and the relationship between desire, demand and their connection to anxiety.

It was stated before that the constitution of the subject in language confronts this subject with a lack or a desire of the Other. The first Other is the mother and the confrontation with her lack is so anxiety provoking that it is untenable. Lacan provides us with an excellent illustration of the relation between anxiety and the desire of the Other in his Seminar X *Anxiety* (1963, lecture from 14–11–1962). He asks his audience to imagine being confronted with an enormous female praying mantis who has the unfortunate tendency to kill the little male after sex. He then asks his audience to imagine that they are wearing a mask which displays the identity of either a male or female praying mantis and further that they (the audience) don't know which mask they have on. Presuming that sex is on the cards, you can imagine that the situation is rather precarious. In the case you know what mask you wear you will either have no sex (when you wear a female mask) or you will experience fear of being gobbled-up after having had a good time. This is ordinary fear because it has a specific object, namely death. You mightn't like it, but at least you know your destiny. Not knowing what mask you wear, i.e., not knowing what to expect, leads to the experience of something that is infinitely more disturbing than fear, namely objectless anxiety. Lacan indicates that the enormous female praying mantis is a metaphor for the desire of the m(Other). When the subject is confronted with the desire of the Other it has to do something in order to transform the overwhelming anxiety into something that can be negotiated. The subject will cover the abyss of not knowing with the texture of language and as such provide itself with an orientation in relation to the (unknown) desire of the Other. Through naming it desire becomes a demand and a demand can be negotiated. Bruce Fink:

> Once it is named, once you conclude that this is what the Other wants of you—to stay out of the way, for instance—the angst

abates, and you, can set about trying to make yourself scarce. The jumping to conclusions transforms the Other's desire—which strictly speaking has no object—into something with a very specific object. In other words, it transforms the Other's desire into a demand ("Stay out of my way"), a demand addressed to the subject who does the naming. Whereas desire has no object, demand does (Fink, 1997, p. 61).

Discourse is a conclusion that has been jumped at in the past and in that sense it is a foregone conclusion. The jump has been made a long time ago in the form of the subject's demand as a response to the Other's desire. The demand of the subject is not necessarily to be considered as something concrete the subject wants from the Other, but it is primarily to be taken as the interpretation and pacification of the desire of the Other on the basis of language. The very foundation of the social bond between subject and Other is therefore language. Without language there is no bond and, without this bond, speech and communication do not make sense.

All speech takes place on the basis of—or in relation to—a demand or an expectation. For instance, it is ridiculous to presume that one can give a paper or a lecture without the context of a demand or expectation of an audience. Likewise, it is ridiculous to presume that someone would go to a doctor without the expectation that the doctor knows something about medicine and without the demand that this knowledge be used in some form or other. Speech and communication are predetermined by the expectations that are imposed by specific situations, which in turn, have their effect on the meaning and sense of speech and communication. Discourse, according to Lacan, is the necessary structure which should be taken as something that goes far beyond more or less occasional speech (Lacan, 1991, p. 11). This structure is necessary because one needs more than the context of other words and language to make sense of speech. An act of speech outside the context of a discourse is meaningless. Discourse is the very basis for the interpretation of speech. It exists and functions without concretely spoken words. "Through the instrument of language a number of stable relationships are established, inside which something that is much larger, that goes much further, than effective utterances can of course be inscribed" (Ibid.). On the basis of the internal logic of his theory, Lacan was able to reduce all human discourse to four basic structures.

The four discourses

The crucial factor in the process of identification is the role of the signifier. The very first identification with the father happens on the basis of the function of what Lacan calls the master-signifier (S1).[3] Freud called the signifier of this identification the ego-ideal. This is a signifier which on its own is completely non-sensical. It is like the first acknowledgement of something of the father that indicates a "no", an intervention or a prohibition of sorts; something for which there is no ground (yet) to negotiate it: this master-signifier has to be obeyed. This master-signifier is a trait from the symbolic which causes the subject to exist and it comes to represent the subject. In this sense the subject is strictly speaking not a human essence and it is to be distinguished from the living individual which is nevertheless its locus and reference point (Ibid., p. 12).

The master-signifier (S1) causes the subject to come into existence. From here on, the subject will have to function in relation to a chain of signifiers (or a symbolic order). In order to be able to speak in a name (S1) that represents the subject, and in order to exist in a world of reality, the subject needs access to at least one other signifier. This other signifier is the minimal condition for language being a functioning structure. This signifier is written as S2 by Lacan and it stands for the rest of the chain of signifiers. The subject is represented by the master-signifier in relation to the rest of the chain of signifiers (the signifier represents the subject for another signifier). This process of representation leads to the kind of subject who is divided and torn between signifiers, and who never really knows which one to choose in order to come up with a definitive answer. What answer is the subject looking for? The subject is looking for its true essence beyond the material substance of the signifier. This true essence is jouissance and it is lost forever (object a) because the subject is doomed to look for it with the only material available to him or her: the signifier.

This produces four terms of Lacanian theory that have to be read in a particular order: the subject ($) is divided over the chain of signifiers (S$_1$→S$_2$) which produces an object of jouissance (a) that will forever remain something potential. There are also the four aforementioned fixed places of discourse: truth, agent, other and product. Putting the fixed sequence of terms on the fixed places produces the possibility of four discourses on the basis of four rotations. The discourses can be written as follows:

$$\text{master discourse}$$
$$\begin{array}{ccc} S_1 & \rightarrow & S_2 \\ \uparrow - & & - \downarrow \\ \$ & // & a \end{array}$$

$$\text{hysterical discourse}$$
$$\begin{array}{ccc} \$ & \rightarrow & S_1 \\ \uparrow - & & - \downarrow \\ a & // & S_2 \end{array}$$

$$\text{analytical discourse}$$
$$\begin{array}{ccc} a & \rightarrow & \$ \\ \uparrow - & & - \downarrow \\ S_2 & // & S_1 \end{array}$$

$$\text{university discourse}$$
$$\begin{array}{ccc} S_2 & \rightarrow & a \\ \uparrow - & & - \downarrow \\ S_1 & // & \$ \end{array}$$

The discourse of the master demonstrates that the constitution of the subject ($\$$) in the chain of signifiers ($S_1 \rightarrow S_2$) produces an object (a) which the subject cannot reach (impotence). The subject can only relate to this object in the unconscious through the medium of fantasy (written by Lacan as $\$<>a$). The discourse of the master represents the desire to master knowledge ($S_1 \rightarrow S_2$). The other is a slave to the master and the slave works in order to produce something: a surplus-value, (a), that the master can enjoy. Whatever it is the slave produces, it does not make the master happy, because it is ultimately not what he wants. However, it is the slave who gets to know something (S2) in relation to the jouissance of the surplus-value and not the master. In fact, the master does not even want to know. Not wanting to know is not incommensurable with wanting to master knowledge. What is important to the master is that he possess knowledge so that he can maintain his position in order to master the situation. Lacan writes: "A real master, as we have seen in general until a recent era, and this is seen less and less, a real master desires to know nothing at all—he desires that it work" (Ibid., pp. 23–24, unpublished translation by Russell Grigg). The discourse of the master is not something that can represent scientific activity. It represents rather the activity of the act of the philosopher as master. The slave has some knowledge and in classical philosophy this knowledge was extracted from the slave and transmitted to the master. Philosophy is "the theft, the abduction, the removal from slavery of its knowledge, through the operation of the master" (Ibid., p. 21). The master doesn't actually pay for his knowledge (and residue of jouissance) with his own work, because that would demonstrate that he is lacking in some form or other. The master has to deny (repress) being castrated ($) in order to maintain the power to keep the slave working for him. The discourse of the master is a discourse of unification: the master attempts to unify and control a field of knowledge. The other has to collaborate with the illusion that the master is in control by incarnating knowledge (S2). The master functions as the ego-ideal for the other. One of the outstanding features of this discourse and the reason for its power is that it works and sustains itself independently of the subjectivity of the agent and the subjectivity of the other (Clavreul, 1978, p. 165). The discourse of the master objectifies through the repression of subjectivity and it takes place over and beyond the desire of the subject. An example that typifies this kind of discourse is medical practice: it is a discourse that disconnects the subject from his or her illness.

The discourse of hysteria represents the desire to master the master ($→$S_1$). Every speaking being who functions in language finds him or herself in a hysterical position. This subject stands divided ($) in relation to the object-cause-of-desire (a). Desire is the very foundation of hysteria. Desire, translated and expressed in language, becomes a demand which often takes the form of a complaint and it is always addressed to an other. The other has to be a master (S1) who knows a thing or two (S2). However, what the master knows, or what he produces as knowledge in response to the demand, is never really it. She demands this knowledge, she even enjoys this knowledge, but she cannot accept this knowledge as truth. This knowledge fails her in terms of an answer to the question of the cause of her desire and her suffering. This failure results in more pressure on the master for a knowledge which he duly produces. This discourse is very productive in that it results in the accumulation of knowledge (S2). Hence, Lacan likens this discourse to a discourse of science in *Television*. He says:

> I conclude that scientific discourse and the hysteric's discourse are *almost* (his italics) the same structure, which explains our error, induced by Freud himself, in hoping that one day there would be a thermodynamic able to provide—within the future of science—the unconscious with its posthumous explanation (Lacan, 1987[1974], p. 23).

Lacan immediately adds that, indeed, he can't see it happening that the unconscious will be explained in terms of modern science which would imply the death of the unconscious. The important thing is that Lacan makes clear that this has to do with precisely the difference between the structure of hysterical discourse and the structure of scientific discourse. They are almost identical. First, their similarity has to do with the fact that both produce knowledge and that this knowledge, for different reasons, is structurally incomplete (S2). In hysteria this knowledge cannot reach the truth of what causes the division of the hysteric (a).

But what about their difference? The difference between hysterical discourse and scientific discourse is that the agent or power in scientific activity has to be the rationality of reason. The agent of scientific endeavour cannot, and indeed, should not be the subjectivity of neurosis or hysteria. Science would not progress in that way. It would immediately descend into the imaginary and obscurity of fantasy and science fiction.[4] However, the reason why modern science cannot explain and undo the unconscious is precisely because of its exclusion of the subject as a viable source for information and data. Hysteria and the subject are a problem and they cause problems all around them. That is why it is in many ways much easier to avoid them: although often that proves not to be so easy. Hysterics will either find a master or else erect one. They typically invite others to work and study their symptoms. The question of what is tearing them (a)-part is addressed at someone who is in a master position (S1): a doctor, a priest, an analyst, etc. They need to identify someone (or something) who represents an ideal and of whom a solution can be expected. The knowledge that is demanded of these masters has to function as a barrier against the horror of castration. However, in the end even that does not work. The hysteric will push the master to the limit of his knowledge. It is nearly as if she wants to say to him: "you were wrong and this is where your knowledge is lacking!" Hysterical discourse demonstrates the essence of the human condition, namely the impossibility of desire as expressed in the domain of relationships between people.

The discourse of analysis represents the desire to master the subject (a→$). But this must immediately be qualified by the statement that the desire to master in the discourse of analysis is not the desire of the discourse of mastery. The desire of the analyst does not concern a desire for unity in a field of knowledge, nor the desire to control people, but the desire to produce difference. This is a desire for a knowledge that can only be produced one by one (S1). This knowledge sets each subject apart from the other and it sets the subject apart from the analyst. Hence, the aim of Lacanian analysis could never be the identification with the analyst. The truth that drives this discourse is a knowledge of the analyst (S2) concerning his or her desire (for instance, to be an analyst) and his or her jouissance. This is a knowledge that has nothing to do with the knowledge (including "knowledge in the Real") that is particular to the subject (S1). Not that the subject does not desire this knowledge. The analyst is supposed to know. However, the analyst also knows that it is important to keep his or her knowledge (S2) in the right place so that he or she can listen to something else. Knowing that this knowledge cannot be generally applied allows the analyst to function as object (a) or agent provocateur of the desire of the subject. In that position it (the analyst as object) tries to move the signifiers of a treatment in such a way that it does not direct the subject. The relationship between object (a) and subject ($), i.e., the relationship of unconscious fantasy ($<>a), is pushed to the forefront of this discourse into a domain where it can be explored in an inverted way. This is the opposite of the discourse of the master where this relationship remains repressed in the unconscious. The position of the analyst in the discourse of analysis provokes the transference and maintaining that position allows the transference to develop. Transference is the transportation, translation and concentration of the neurosis of the patient into a space between the analyst and the subject. Inviting the subject to speak freely within this space can result in the production of a knowledge that is the sister of truth. This is a knowledge regarding the modes of jouissance (and suffering) of the subject and that includes a knowledge regarding the cause of the subject-specific effects of drugs.

The discourse of the university represents the desire to master the object ($S_2 \rightarrow a$). General and objective knowledge (S2) is generated in order to grasp the object that so far has escaped science. It is certain that one does not wish to research and accumulate knowledge about things that are already known, and once one gets to know something new, one is immediately confronted with the limits of this knowledge and therefore with new objects of study. General and objective knowledge is built up in research institutes, university departments, hospitals etc. However, the more knowledge and signifiers are generated in order to grasp the object, the further this discourse moves away from reaching its aim. It is precisely this lack of grasp that seems to create the desire for an even firmer grip, i.e., the subject (of the scientist) wants more and more (S). The discourse of the university can be used as an explanation of the remarks made by John Hughes on the reason why scientists are often deluded (see Chapter 8). His remarks were introduced there by saying that the further the object of science retreats, the more the subject of science tends to step forward. In other words, the more one realizes how little one knows, the stronger one's (subjective) desire to know. The discourse of the university demonstrates that the blind will of a systematic and objective knowledge produces a desiring subject. However, this is a subject that is excluded from any knowledge about the object that causes his or her desire (a). In the discourse of the university, knowledge (S2) is a misunderstanding of the object of jouissance (as lacking) and it functions as a justification for this misunderstanding. Hence, the extraordinary emphasis on methodology in the human sciences. In concentrating on methodology, it compensates for not being able to step beyond language in order to grasp the truth of the matter. In the discourse of the university, the other is at the receiving end of knowledge. But why is the other as recipient an object (a)? Universities as teaching institutions (and not as research institutes) provide a clear answer to this question: the students are the passive objects or recipients of a knowledge that can be taught. The command in this discourse is "keep on knowing" (Lacan, 1991, p. 120). The discourse of the university is the discourse of science (Ibid.). Indeed, science is a drive to keep on knowing more. In fact, it is a death-drive, because it keeps on knowing without regard for anyone. Lacan wonders what the status of the other is in the human sciences in the discourse of the university (Ibid.). He coins a new word and calls the student an "astudied". The student is someone who feels "astudied" and that leads him or her to experience more unease ($). It is important to note that what is not being produced in Lacan's conception of human science as an university discourse, is precisely what characterizes human science, namely a general knowledge about people (S2). That is why Lacan was not correct in saying that human science shows the structure of university discourse. This has interesting implications for understanding addiction as will be demonstrated further on. It will be contended that a structure that represents human science has to incorporate elements of the structure of hysterical discourse as well as elements of the master discourse. The truth that drives university discourse is the fact that it is the master (S1) who guarantees its knowledge. The truth of this discourse is that without the discoveries of the master, it would not be able to function. The master here functions as an insurance policy against the inevitable failure. When the failure arrives—and this is inevitable, because knowledge or the chain of signifiers is lacking—one can depend on the masters. That means one begins to pay one's insurance policy by paying homage to these masters in the form of quotes and references. This knowledge of the master (S1) helps to justify the existence of objective knowledge (S2), but it is not accessible to the subject ($).

The discourse of addiction and the discourse of analysis: a dangerous encounter and the necessity for a "small" difference

What gives addiction as a social symptom its sense of uniformity, is the fact that an object is in command, but surprisingly also, what it commands. For the drug addict, the alcoholic—and in the cultures of addiction—everything centres on the object. At a conscious level, that is to say, at the top level of the discourse, one cannot speak of addiction being a matter of choice for the addict.[5] The object (drug or alcohol) is in the place of agent. What is the effect of this object in command? The effect is an eclipse of the signifier which represents the subject for another signifier. The object tries to absorb this master-signifier (a→S_1). This relationship represents the (impossible) desire to unite an object with the master-signifier.[6] In other words, this is an attempt to put the object and the ego-ideal in the same place, when one considers the latter to be the symbolic identification with the master-signifier of the Name-of-the-Father (S1). The peculiarity of this desire not only creates a sense of uniformity (at least from an outside perspective), it also creates a group.

What binds people together in a group (for instance, a self help group) is a process of identification. People seek to identify with

ADDICTION AND DISCOURSE 249

each other in a group. It helps them to resolve a problem: it resolves the problem of a lack in identity. Group formation helps to complete an Oedipal development that remained, for structural reasons, incomplete. The resolution of the Oedipus Complex is the identification with the Name-of-the-Father. This is the moment when the law intervenes between child and mother; the moment when the child is forced to take up a position in the symbolic world. This is also the moment when the dual unity with the mother has to be given-up. The Oedipus Complex, as structuring moment, allows people to recognize themselves as they are. It is the creation of the possibility of the social bond based on the identification with the father-figure. The effect of this identification is a sense of community, but also a tendency to form groups.[7] The latter tendency is there to compensate for the structural lack of identification provided by the father figure. The group identity functions as a barrier against the anxiety generated by a lack of identity. In *Group Psychology and the Analysis of the Ego* Freud wrote: "A primary group is a number of individuals who have put one and the same object in the place of their ego-ideal and have consequently identified themselves with one another in their ego" (Freud, 1921c, p. 116). He represents this as follows (Ibid.):

The human subject is always constituted in relation to an object. The ultimate object is lost, but one has access to some compensation for this loss, via the worldly objects of human reality. These objects can be other people, work, etc., but they can also be alcohol or drugs. Drugs and alcohol are important objects for addicts. In fact, they may become so important to them that other objects and relationships are excluded. Drugs and alcohol are an ideal or idealized object for addicts and their pathology dictates that they are in need of such an ideal. This ideal can lead to a group formation amongst addicts. The external object (drug or alcohol) functions as a common ideal, an ideal with which each group member identifies. The process of group formation takes place when people put their object in the place of a shared ideal. This process produces a common ego-ideal as something with which everyone in the group is subsequently identified. Any object can lead to group formation, providing it possesses a quality for idealization such that it can function as a point for identification. It is a well-known fact that heroin can execute these functions extremely well.[8] But so can ideas, ideals, ideologies, religions and 12-step programmes.

The conjoining of object and ego-ideal binds people together and this has consequences for addiction as a social phenomenon.[9] It can lead to all kinds of therapeutic difficulties, especially when the therapies are group and community based. Freud likens this conjoining to the hypnotic relationship. He writes that "(...) the hypnotic relationship is (if the expression is permissible) a group formation with two members. Hypnosis is not a good object for a comparison with a group formation, because it is truer to say that it is identical with it" (Ibid., 115). Lacan considers this definition of hypnosis, as the confusion between the object a and the ideal signifier, to be the most assured one so far (Lacan, 1979, p. 273).

In his article *Psychical Treatment*, Freud argued that the use of hypnosis tends to create a kind of dependency of the patient on the doctor (Freud, 1905[1890], pp. 298, 301). The patient becomes addicted to hypnosis. In the same article Freud compares the hypnotist to a mother feeding a child (Ibid., p. 295). In relation to this, Sylvie le Poulichet wonders: "Do the words of the hypnotist possess themselves than a similar statute as the one of the flow of mother milk?" She continues: "The hypnotist functions like an imaginary Other who is not lacking, an Other who does not let himself be de-completed so that the desire of the subject can take root in this gap" (Le Poulichet, 1987, p. 73). She suggests that a true toxicity in the field of psychoanalysis concerns words and especially those spoken in the relationship of hypnosis (Ibid.). This idea is extremely important because it is able to explain why abstinence from drugs or alcohol is often not problematic for addicts.

The proposal put forward here is that a detoxification can be easily maintained as long as a re-intoxication takes place in the form of a substitution. The therapists and therapeutic communities who demand total abstinence from their patients often need to compensate for this demand by positioning themselves as caring and complete others. That is to say, they seek to set themselves up as an ideal object of identification for their patients. The relationships tend to become hypnotic ones in this structure; the words acquire a "toxic" effect and are capable of re-intoxication. It is important to note that this substitution is not always successful. It will not always result in pleasant and docile behaviour. Sometimes patients react against this through for instance, "acting-out", other forms of behaviour, or indeed a relapse into what is called "active addiction". In therapeutic communities this structure can lead to, what Thierry Snoy calls, a "toxic space" (Snoy, 1993, p. 48). A toxic space can take many different forms in this context. There can be a bad atmosphere, an euphoric one, an aggressive one, a secretive one or what is called an "us-and-them" situation all of which is often labelled as "addictive behaviour" or "addictive thinking". Snoy argued that when the toxicity rises above a certain level the therapeutic work becomes impossible, even in an orientation of therapy in which these behaviours are considered to be symptomatic or avatars of transference (Ibid.). The "toxic space" in the therapeutic community is a manifestation of negative transference. Too much toxicity stops the work of transference. The level of toxicity has to be kept within certain workable limits, but it is very important to take it for what it is, namely the dynamic of transference has to be allowed to develop or else therapy is not possible.

A treatment centre or therapeutic community is set up in order to bring the pathology of addiction within its realm. That implies that addiction will meet its mirror image in the transference phenomena provoked by the treatment institutions which are positioned as "institution-supposed-to-know". The pathology of addiction will manifest itself in the transference and it is crucial that the transference is allowed to take place. Unfortunately, however, far too often these phenomena of transference lead to counter-transference and they are considered to be something that needs to be avoided.

Transference and counter-transference are paramount in the treatment of addiction and the reason for this is none other than that addiction touches upon an essential aspect of the human subject. Addiction was defined before as a relentless search for happiness through a pursuit of pleasure or enjoyment and indeed through the avoidance of pain and suffering. When this pursuit with drugs or alcohol is discontinued, for instance on entering a treatment centre, this pursuit will be continued at the level of the relationship with the institution. That means that the demand of clients on staff is going to be enormous. On top of that, these demand are impossible demands. To some degree all people identify with the ideals implicit in the pursuit of addicts and it is no doubt the case that some aspects of addiction "act-out" what non-addicts can only dream of, or indeed fantasize about. Addiction has the capacity to expose an unconscious fascination in the Other and once this is exposed, anxiety and even panic might ensue. This point characterizes the essence of counter-transference.

So far the discussion has centred on the relationship between the agent and the other in the discourse of toxicomania. What does this relationship produce in this discourse? It produces an increasing division of a subject, $, who suffers in the real when the effect of the intoxication has ceased.[10] The only route available for this subject to undo his or her mounting suffering and pain is to rush straight to the object which is in command. The phallic signifier, S1, is rendered idle, because it hangs apart from the rest of the chain of signifiers, S2, in this movement. The subject therefore has no access to a knowledge about his or her jouissance on the place of truth. This "knowledge in the real" is unconscious and remains unconscious. Now it is possible to represent the complete formula of the discourse of addiction or toxicomania as a social symptom in the way it was first presented and elaborated on by Charles Melman in a paper on toxicomania from 1989 entitled "Un héroisme populaire" (Melman, 1989, pp. 95–96):

addiction discourse

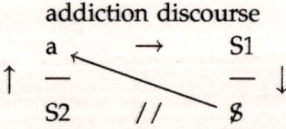

$$\uparrow \quad \frac{a \quad \leftarrow \quad \rightarrow \quad S1}{S2 \quad // \quad \$} \quad \downarrow$$

One immediately notices the similarity in structure with the discourse of analysis:

analytical discourse

$$\uparrow \quad \frac{a \quad \rightarrow \quad \$}{S2 \quad // \quad S1} \quad \downarrow$$

There is, however, an (apparently) small difference, in that the right antipode is inverted. This "small" difference makes all the difference, because, in the discourse of analysis the subject relates to his or her object-cause-of-desire and is positioned such that in this structure the relationship between the two can be openly explored. In the discourse of addiction the subject is excluded, or foreclosed, from any form of investigation. This exclusion is the element it shares with the discourse of science. It will be demonstrated shortly that this leads to a harmonious, but fruitless, encounter between these last two discourses. Before going into the encounter between the discourse of science and the discourse of addiction, it is important to situate toxicomania in relation to the disjunctions of impossibility and impotence in the discourses. First, a brief reminder of what has been said so far about the dynamic between the two disjunctions.

The disjunction of impotence represents the gap of the unconscious as something that is situated beyond the pleasure principle, namely, the total jouissance for which we are not eligible anymore and which is lost on us. This disjunction is therefore situated between product and truth at the bottom level of the discourse. It hides the disjunction of impossibility at the top level of the discourse which represents the impossible desires and failures related to the pleasure principle. The existence of, and the dynamic between, these two disjunctions shows that one is constantly duped. Toxicomania is one way of avoiding this, whilst psychosis is another. In psychosis the discourse comes full circle in the sense that the impossibility of the relationship between agent and other does not exist. The psychotic is not cut off from total jouissance. It completely overwhelms him or her and the relationship of impotence does not protect him or her from the real horror of being One or the Other. The result is that the psychotic is driven mad in a discourse from which there is no way out. The psychotic does not get a chance to tumble from impotence to impotence as an escape from one discourse to another.

In toxicomania there appears to be a lack of impotence which expresses itself in the relationship of impossibility. In reality, however, the sensation of omnipotence in the toxic state directly hides the relationship of impossibility. This leaves the subject with the illusion that there is the possibility of a complete harmonization of the relationship between agent and other. The implication of this for the domain of sexuality is that drugs and alcohol can function as objects that bridge the gap with the sexual other. In other words, they can provide the illusion of a proportion (or harmony) in sexuality. The movement of toxicity avoids, as such, the necessary and protective dynamic between the disjunctions of impotence and impossibility. Addiction avoids the detour of hiding the failure of the pleasure principle through our impotence for a lethal jouissance which lies beyond it.

To say that addicts have found a direct route to jouissance does not necessarily mean that they have successfully come to terms with the death-drive. It implies only that they have found a way of dealing with the death-drive. And this is a way that is different from the way of unconscious fantasy, which is situated at the bottom level of the discourse. It is as if addicts operate a system similar to the function of a conscious fantasy. Addiction is an immediate way of "dealing" with jouissance; it is a symptom in the real. Unconscious fantasy—in contrast—is a way of dealing with the real via the detour of the signifiers of the Other, which create the parameters of a particular subjective structure. Addiction is more akin to a conscious fantasy or illusion in the sense that the idea is openly upheld that alcohol and drugs can administer jouissance to an ideal level.

It is proposed here that most addictions intervene directly and openly on the relationship of impossibility at the top level of the discourse, by trying to establish a perfect communication between agent and other via the toxic route of the body. It is important to keep in mind that the success of establishing this illusion of a perfect communication is still dependent on the unconscious fantasy structure of the subject. In other words, it is still dependent on the particular effects that drugs or alcohol can have on the subject; effects that are determined by the "knowledge in the real". Exceptions to this are those forms of toxicomania for which the act of drinking or taking drugs is a (symbolically structured) appeal to the Other. The act, in this case, is an act committed in relation to, or with, a signifier which represents the subject for the other signifiers and it should be treated as a neurotic symptom. For instance, if a priest is addicted exclusively to a beer called "devil" or "forbidden fruit", one might fairly safely assume that there is a symbolic element involved.[11] In fact, one might even go so far as to say that what is really incorporated is a signifier with two horns and a tail which represents the priest as subject for God and which communicates to God that the priest wants some of his jouissance. This kind of act is eminently analysable.

Without this connection to the signifier, however, addiction, as a symptom, is not analysable (which, by the way, does not mean that it is not treatable by language). If addiction, as a symptom, functions entirely in the real, that is to say, if there is no indication of there being any formation of the unconscious involved, another intervention will have to be done first, before an analysis can start. This is a problem that requires further discussion, as there are important ethical questions involved. One of these questions is: why should one do an analysis or therapy if another intervention can separate the subject from his or her addiction? Some of these ethical questions and implications will be explored in the remainder of this chapter and in the conclusion.

Scientific discourse and addiction

A discourse of human science: for the love of knowledge

In a series of four lectures from his *Seminar* L'insu Que Sait de L'une-Bévue S'aile a Mourre which he entitled Vers un Signifiant Nouveau, Lacan says that mental illness is the unconscious and it does not wake up to the truth (Lacan, 1977, lecture from 17-5-1977). Science, he continues, is a kind of awakening, but a difficult and suspect one (Ibid.). When, in this context, he says that science and religion go well together, he seems to be suggesting that when science wakes up to something, it is to that which grounds it, namely the idea of God as a name for the Father (S1). This installs the master signifier—which represents God—in the place from which it can be woken up in the discourse of science. In a discourse where knowledge (S2) is in command, God or the master signifier (S1) is on the place of truth to ground this knowledge, $\left(\frac{S_2}{S_1}\right)$. Lacan also says here that the subject finds himself in an impotent position to justify what is produced by the signifier (Ibid.). What is produced by the signifier is the subject. This positions it on the place of product from where this subject is unable to grasp its own particular truth. Lacan implies here something which he said before in Seminar XVII: scientific discourse is a university discourse (Lacan, 1991, p. 119).

When looking at the structure of this discourse one notices that it does not produce knowledge, but a subject. On the basis of this, one must conclude that this discourse does not have the right structure for representing that form of science which produces knowledge. As a university discourse it represents the teaching and application of knowledge. How is it possible to represent the structure of a discourse of the kind of science which produces knowledge about people? How can one develop a discourse of human science? On several occasions in his later seminars, Lacan indicated that the four discourses can be twisted in such a way that they represent a more specific discourse. This is justifiable as long as the resulting discourses represent a particular praxis or are able to illustrate certain clinical phenomena within a system which is logically coherent. In this way, discourse theory does not lapse into a metalanguage.

In his article "Science and Truth", Lacan indicates that science implies the foreclosure of subjectivity from its practice by "suturing" the subject and avoiding, as such, its truth as cause (Lacan, 1989[1966], p. 17, 24). Scientific research generates knowledge and explanations (S2) over and beyond the subject. This is a generated knowledge which separates the subject from its cause and finds itself on the place of product. The scientist who wants to understand and unify the "material" is placed on the position of agent as a master in his field of research (S1). The "material" he or she objectively researches (a) is on the place of other. The subject of science (who is sutured) is on the place of truth because without this subject there would be no such science. This analysis produces a discourse of human science and it reads as follows:

$$\text{human science}$$
$$\uparrow \frac{S1}{S} \quad \begin{matrix} \rightarrow \\ // \end{matrix} \quad \frac{a}{S2} \downarrow$$

A first glance at this discourse immediately leads to the observation that a role reversal has taken place when one compares it to the discourse of addiction. Addiction is the mirror image of human science. Do these two have a relationship with each other that is of

ADDICTION AND DISCOURSE 257

an imaginary nature? This is the kind of relationship that, clinically speaking, does not lead to a resolution for the subject. It is the kind of relationship that inhibits a symbolic route to the unconscious of the subject by remaining stuck on the axis of imaginary identification and produces nothing but empty speech. This is the guessing in games that was referred to in Chapter 6 and it is represented by the ego-to-ego axis (player 1 to player 3) in the adjusted L-schema. Before coming back to the question about the nature of the relationship between addiction and human science it might be interesting to look at an encounter between the (aforementioned) writer William Burroughs and psychiatry. Something may be learned from this encounter with regards to the relationship between (human) science and addiction.

"Why do you need narcotics, Mr Lee?", is a question that stupid psychiatrists ask. The answer is, "I need junk to get out of bed in the morning, to shave and eat breakfast. I need it to stay alive" (Burroughs, 1977, p. 23).

This is how Burroughs displays his contempt for the need (of psychiatry) to understand the reasons why addicts become addicted. In the prologue of his book, *Junky*, he claims that addicts do not decide to become addicts for any kind of reason. He writes:

You become a narcotics addict because you do not have strong motivations in any other direction. Junk wins by default. I tried it as a matter of curiosity. I drifted along taking shots when I could score. I ended up hooked. Most addicts I have talked to report a similar experience. They did not start using drugs for any reason they can remember. They just drifted along until they got hooked. If you have never been addicted, you can have no clear idea what it means to need junk with the addict's special need (Burroughs, 1977, p. xv).

Burroughs' annoyance with those psychiatrists who want him to explain his need for drugs is probably derived from his own frustration at being stuck for a true answer that could satisfy them. The only explanation he can come up with is the one they do not want to hear—namely, that he does not want to die and that he needs drugs in order to survive. That is not a very satisfactory explanation. Burroughs seems to suggest that addicts become addicted because they do not have any desire for anything else in life; they lack motivation, encounter drugs, drift along and then it hooks them by default.

What is striking in Burroughs' description is that before one is addicted and completely dominated by this need or craving for drugs, there appears to be no subject of desire who is able to make choices along the way. It is as if potential addicts wander around, aimlessly and passively, until something which can provide them with a particular jouissance, hooks them. Indeed, this is very characteristic of the phenomenology of addiction. What "hooks" addicts to the world is a particular jouissance (enjoyment), rather than a desire, which is constituted in relation to a law that prohibits jouissance. However, it is interesting to note that whilst Burroughs' remarks are fairly characteristic of addicts, there is at least one aspect of his ideas which is not at all characteristic. Unlike most addicts and psychiatrists, Burroughs is not looking for meaningful explanations and obvious reasons for (his) addiction.

Addiction is a mental illness and it has an unconscious cause. In the discourse of addiction one finds not only that knowledge is its driving force and thus superimposed on the place of truth, but also that explanations are often openly and explicitly stated, whilst completely misrepresenting this truth. Both addicts and their therapists confuse cause and explanation. In the language of addiction treatment, one often hears therapists say to addicts that they shouldn't look for causes for their addiction because it will only justify their "addictive behaviour". What shines through these words is a moralistic perspective which can be condensed into the judgement: "Your behaviour is not justifiable!" It is an empirical fact that explanations are heavily sought after by addicts. This represents a true surge for knowledge which is valued like a precious substance (S2 // $).

Clinical work often exposes the attempt by addicts to understand the so-called "true cause" of their addictions. This attempt is successful in that it results in a series of explanations. These explanations are mostly plausible and based on an a priori established knowledge, a generally accepted viewpoint. Addicts seek and find explanations, but they search for them because they have a desire not-to-know. And their desire not to know—that the cause of their addiction concerns a "knowledge in the real" which particularizes their mode of jouissance—is precisely the reason why they find explanations. They find explanations as a means of not having to look any further. If one looks far enough, one always arrives at the traumatic point of the encounter with the real in the Other and that entails a return to the moment of subjective choice and responsibility, i.e., the response of the subject to this real.

The Freudian subject is the result of a traumatic encounter with things (such as real drives, jouissance, desire) that initially do not make sense and are therefore disturbing. It is not so easy to face subjective responsibility, especially when it concerns one's own choices in relation to suffering and neurosis. Avoidance of responsibility is a very characteristic feature of addiction. This clinical feature is often transferred onto relationships with others. Addicts are very adept at surrounding themselves with people who will take responsibility for them, such as spouses, friends or family members. In the jargon of addiction treatment these people are called "enablers", as an indication that this kind of conduct will enable addicts to continue their "addictive behaviour".

Another reason why addicts find what they seek is that there is plenty of material around to be found. Confronted with the real problem of addiction, the sciences have produced a vast body of knowledge and an enormous array of explanations. These scientific explanations traverse the whole spectrum of the sciences; from chemical substances in the brain, unemployment, poverty and deprivation, addicted parents and addictive personalities, to modern culture and its counter-culture. Some of these explanations contain an element of truth. However, the problem is that these truths and explanations are taken up by addicts (and others) as complete justifications for addiction. It is easier to hold on to a scientifically established fact than to look further at subjective choice and responsibility. In this sense, the knowledge of science functions as a barrier against knowing the truth about these subjective choices as responses to the traumatic real. This relationship between knowledge and truth prompted Lacan to comment that scientific knowledge "does not want-to-know-anything about the truth as cause" (op. cit., p. 22) and that it is not desire for truth which presides over knowledge, but horror against which knowledge forms a defensive barrier (Lacan, 1974, lecture from 9-4-1974). Aside from this, it is interesting to note that these scientific "facts" appear and disappear with remarkable regularity. The reason why these facts come and go is that they bear no relationship to the unconscious truth of the subject. These user-friendly and easily digestible "facts" concerning people are produced, over and beyond their subjectivity, in the form of disposable products.

Happiness through a meeting and confusion of minds

It was stated that the discourses of human science (such as psychiatry, clinical psychology, and the social and educational sciences) are characterized by their faith in the existence of relatively simple explanations for problematic human questions. The discourse of addiction is characterized by a similar faith. That is, most addicts seek, and indeed, often find, explanations or reasons for their clinical condition and symptoms. Addicts have a true passion for knowledge, in the form of (pseudo-) scientific explanations which permeate their discourse virtually all the time. Aspects of these explanations are often to some degree valid, but, as was said, the problem is that they begin to function as justifications for the addiction. However, it should be emphasized that the problems of this kind of justification should not be confused with another kind of justification that one often encounters in the field of addiction, namely justification of the so-called "addictive behaviours"; the bad or unacceptable behaviour of addicts committed by themselves and inflicted on others.

Transgressive behaviour is often part of the symptomatology of addiction. Justification of this behaviour simply leads to a clinical impasse, because this allows the subject not to take any responsibility for what he or she does or says. But, whilst it is ethically and clinically correct to refuse to justify "addictive behaviour", in practice this position is often translated into a moralistic judgement on the behaviour of the subject, into an attempt to keep behaviour within limits generally thought to be in the service of the "common good".

The jouissance pursued by addicts is decidedly not in the service of the common good; it exceeds all limits imposed by the Other. Freud compared addiction to masturbation because it circumvents the Other. Addiction and masturbation are a menace to society because they threaten to evade the limits set by castration. Unlike masturbation, the threat of addiction is real. The attempt to escape castration is to some degree successful because addicts have found an immediate route to jouissance. Society forbids people, as much as it can, to enjoy on their own. The incestuous nature of this mode of enjoyment produces the imagined threat (in the case of masturbation) or the real possibility (in the case of addiction) of going too far.

Moral judgement and insistence on conformity—in response to the problem of addiction—are, therefore, reactions against an anxiety-provoking jouissance which threatens the common good and disturbs the fabric of our society. Society is constantly up in arms about addiction because, at that level, addiction functions as a traumatic real which threatens to disrupt and derange the symbolic structure of society. Unfortunately, where anxiety is concerned, there is often an immediate reaction which is defensive and imaginary in nature, rather than a response which is well thought out and based on a structural analysis of the problem.

A similar reaction often takes place in the treatment of addicts. Moral judgement and conformity find their therapeutic instruments in confrontational techniques, which usually involve confronting the addicts with the reality and consequences of their behaviour. These techniques are a fairly extreme form of forcing subjects to adapt their behaviour to a given reality, which is usually defined in terms of a set of norms and ideals. This kind of therapy can only lead to an impasse because—as has been suggested—it completely ignores the particular and peculiar relationship addicts have with jouissance. It does not allow for any kind of exploration of this relationship, and it will therefore change nothing in the economy of this relationship. Most therapeutic techniques concerned with the treatment of addiction aim at changing behaviour to conform to reality in the hope that a jouissance, which threatens that reality, will be given up. This is a blind hope, as these techniques intervene precisely at the point where they do not make a difference—at least, they make no difference with regards to jouissance or "knowledge in the real".

Addicts confuse cause and explanation. Clinicians, therapists and counsellors also often confuse cause and explanation, but in different ways and for different reasons than addicts. Despite these differences they nevertheless find themselves in a most peculiar collusion. The addicts confuse cause and explanation by using the latter to allow themselves to ignore the unbearable real aspect of the former. Therapists who work in the field of addiction (more often than not) apply a clinic of re-education (university discourse), especially when treatment takes place in an institutional setting. They do not make a distinction between cause and explanation because their desire is to unite both ($S_2 \rightarrow a$). Also their desire is related to something unbearable; a horror which stares them in the face, like it does with those people who are attracted to the gory results of a car accident. The subject of addiction demonstrates a grotesque relationship to drugs as an object of jouissance, which exposes, as stated earlier, the illusionary character of every object, by dramatizing the horror for—and struggle with—a lack which ultimately no object can fill. Addiction confronts the subject with the truth of a terrifying chasm. This explains the fascination, horror and even panic which toxicomania can evoke in others. Therapists who work with addicts often protect themselves against this, at times, overwhelming abyss by basing themselves on an approach which is based in human science (or sometimes religion). The knowledge upon which this approach is based has a double function. It functions as a protective illusion between the subject and his cause, but also between the therapist and addict. The confusion of cause and explanation, or rather their collapse into one and the same thing, is based on the compulsion in human science and education discourse to attempt to conquer the world by teaching it a knowledge precisely at the points where knowledge emerges as lacking or indeed proves incomplete. This compulsion, in fact, any compulsion to repeat, is related to the real as lack in the symbolic.

This knowledge is usually (pseudo) scientific or sometimes even religious in nature. The so-called self-help programmes of Alcoholics Anonymous and Narcotics Anonymous exemplify the latter kind of knowledge. The knowledge in the former is, as stated previously, a knowledge produced by human science. It is essential to note that there is a similarity between the structure of the discourse of human science and the structure of the discourse of addiction. In both the subject is separated from a relationship with his object and this deprives him or her of the possibility of exploring it with the ultimate intention of trying to change something in its economy. In other words, in both discourses there is no symbolic way out of the imaginary impasse.

The marriage between human science and addiction is a happy marriage, but with "unresolved issues"—as they say. The encounter between them is a "happy" one because addiction produces a subject and at the same time blinds this subject to its cause in an attempt to avoid suffering and pain. In both discourses the subject is lured away from the possibility of an exploration of the problematic relationship to his or her cause, by the illusion or fantasy that this cause is unproblematic and attainable. Addicts look to cause a specific effect and human science believes that the general effect is the cause. Addiction produces a suffering subject who is blinded to the real cause of his or her pain and anxiety by the effects of alcohol and drugs. This is perfectly in accord with human science with its exclusion of the subject, and with the production of knowledge as a barricade of ignorance against the cause of the subject. Addiction and human science collaborate "happily" in a project to avoid life as it is—namely, knotted to the real and conjoined with death. Although the encounter is a "happy" one, the consequences can be disastrous. The least disastrous of these consequences is either an identification with the therapist as an ideal or with the group of addicts as one of its members. With regard to the latter identification, it is a well-known fact that addicts often present themselves as "I am an alcoholic" or "I am a drug addict". The more disastrous con-sequence is a relapse into the single-minded (or—bodied) pursuit of complete satisfaction and happiness thereby producing ever more suffering. This is one of the most disastrous ways of giving in to the death-drive.

Although the modern sciences are sciences of the real, and are thus related to the death-drive, this does not imply that they are better equipped to deal with a life which is grounded in the real and permeated by the death-drive. This is due to the irritating fact that—as Lacan says—"the modern sciences do not "speak", but only depart from the truth" (Lacan, 1974, lecture from 12-2-74, my translation). In other words, as sciences they do not aim at the truth, despite the fact that it is their starting-point. Modern science, like psychoanalysis, is based on "knowledge in the real", but unlike psychoanalysis, it does not presuppose a subject who is affected by this knowledge, and for who this knowledge might acquire a sense or meaning after the process of analysis. What do the sciences do? "They turn truth into an empty value—in that sense it means nothing" (Ibid., lecture from 9-4-1974, my translation). In order to deal with the truth of the real and of death, one requires the speech of analytic discourse. Lacan suggests that this is the only act which is able to approach this truth.

The human sciences, in contrast, speak loudly and clearly, in a transparent and unambiguous way. However, this is not the speech of analytic discourse. In analytic discourse, the analyst provokes the speech of the subject by taking up the position of analyst—that is, of object of desire for the analysand. The true speech of analytic discourse is the speech of the subject, which is able to approach the truth of the unconscious. The speech of the human sciences does not come from the subject but is, inversely, directed at him or her. The speech of the human sciences contains a knowledge about the subject which is constituted independently of him or her, and is therefore unrelated to his or her cause as unconscious truth. Knowledge produced by the human sciences separates the subject from his cause by not only ignoring the unconscious choices and responses of the subject to the real, but also by placing knowledge as an obstacle between the subject and his or her truth. In the discourse of human science, the subject is barred from his or her true cause by being spoken to in no uncertain terms of a knowledge that pretends to know without fail.

As stated before, addicts pursue precisely this kind of knowledge or explanation. The availability of this knowledge simply feeds their desire to know nothing about the truth of their addiction. It is interesting that analysis with addicts sometimes exposes this desire as a protection against a different kind of desire or search, a search which does not immediately lead to a finding. This is the search for another kind of knowledge, the kind which is related to the unconscious truth. This is "knowledge in the real" about the lethal jouissance which drives addicts. The problem is, however, that they cut themselves off from this painful search either by the physical means of toxicity, or by hiding under "explanations" about their symptom. If addicts cut themselves off from a "knowledge in the real" with the help of chemical toxicity or explanations provided by human science, and if a "science of the real" doesn't speak and only departs from this "knowledge in the real", what is one to do?

Ethical implications for a treatment of addiction

Moral reaction and ethical response

To claim that civilization and its institutions make people unhappy by repressing their freedom to pursue pleasure is to profoundly misunderstand the nature of civilization and the nature of the subject. Civilization is a consequence of repression; it is the external manifestation of the internal necessity for the prohibition of an incestuous jouissance. Civilization is the attempt to regulate the death-drive. Addiction causes moral panic, because anything that tries to escape from prohibition or castration causes trauma. The translation of this panic into the language of addiction treatment and policy demonstrates very clearly a moral judgement as an action against this panic. One need only read daily newspapers and government policy reports to be aware of this fact.

It is illuminating to juxtapose this idea of moral judgement as a defensive action with Lacan's concept of moral action. In Seminar VII, *The Ethics of Psychoanalysis*, he suggests that:

> ...the moral law, the moral command, the presence of the moral agency in our activity, insofar as it is structured by the symbolic, is that through which the real is actualized—the real as such, the weight of the real (Lacan, 1992, p. 20).

He continues by stating that moral action is grafted on to this real, whereby it introduces something new, and opens a path to a point which legitimizes the presence of the analyst (Ibid., p. 21). This point in the real is, he claims, the ethical limit of analysis, which coincides precisely with the limits of its practice:

> Its practice is only a preliminary to moral action as such—the so-called action being the one through which we enter the real (Ibid., p. 22).

This real is to be found beyond the pleasure principle and the established categories of "reality", at the point where it structures our psychic reality of the unconscious. This is, in Lacan's words, the opaque surface known as the death-drive. The death-drive points to the site of "the Thing". The Thing came into being as a consequence of the introduction of the primordial law of the signifier into the life of the subject (symbolic castration). This signifier, which says "no", designates the prohibition of incest between child and mother. From then on, unconscious desire becomes a drive for the "Thing" which is: "the maternal thing, of the mother, insofar as she occupies the place of that thing, of das Ding" (Ibid., p. 67). This drive is a death-drive because its realization or satisfaction would lead to the annihilation of the signifying chain, and thus the death of the reality of the subject, whose only presence is to be represented by this chain.

However, the structure of unconscious fantasy serves as our protection against the attraction of the death-drive. Fantasy is the response of the subject to the question of the real; it masks the real by turning it into the reality of life for the subject, via the long-winded route of sense and meaning. Fantasy is the imaginary means of orchestrating an impossible jouissance, by creating the illusion of a possible reconciliation between the real and the symbolic, truth and fiction, or "object a" and subject ($<>a). This illusion directs the compulsion to repeat, and hooks the death-drive (situated on the side of the object) to the subject.

If—as Lacan says—psychoanalysis can lead to moral action, through which we can enter the real, then what is the consequence of this for the subject's relationship to the death-drive and to drugs? In other words, how can psychoanalysis help us to live a life which is grounded in the real, penetrated by its presence, and thus permeated by the death-drive without having to have recourse to addiction?

According to Lacan, in his Seminar on Ethics, psychoanalysis is based on an ethics of speaking well. Speaking well can be defined as an attempt to come to terms with the absolute contradiction of a lethal attraction for the real (the death-drive) and its traumatizing or disturbing effect. Speaking well is extremely difficult because moral judgement and the universal good lure us away from it and, in that sense, function as strong barriers against it.

Lacan asks: "What is it what man wants and what does he defend himself against?" (Ibid., p. 240). As an answer, he proposes that man wants to enter the field of the death-drive—beyond the pleasure principle and beyond the signifier—but it is precisely this against which everything in him defends. He suggests that man defends himself against entering the field of the death-drive through illusions of what is good and beautiful (Ibid., pp. 218–240). To these it is possible to add addiction, as a third illusion.

Speaking well—therefore—is about speaking a truth which finds itself caught between what we can hope for (from the symbolic) and what we receive as an answer (from the real). Speaking well is near to impossible, because the relationship between the symbolic and the real is—in itself—impossible. It is impossible in the sense that the real and the symbolic cannot be reconciled with one another to the extent, for instance, that death can be conquered. The battle against the death-drive is a battle that is already lost. Does that imply that the war against drugs is lost? It certainly means that the war against drugs is a useless war. In fact, everyone knows that it is only fought because politicians and policy makers have to be seen to fight it. It would indeed be much better to surrender and find another way. There is no enemy (unless one wants to fight the subject) and there will always be toxicities and toxic substances. The questions that should be asked are: who will be affected by toxicities and who will abuse toxic substances? Those are not questions that pertain to an object that can be defeated, but they are questions concerning the subject of administration. The subject of addiction is not a matter of winning; it is a matter of responsibility regarding desire and that means accepting losing. It is important to give something up in order to gain something else. But it is important not to step into the trap of thinking that there is going to be a peaceful solution. A life permeated by the death-drive cannot be peaceful.

The necessity for being duped

The discourse of analysis provides the subject with an opportunity for exploring the fantasmatic relationship he or she has with his or her object-cause-of-desire. But it would be extremely naive to presume that this discourse is the only soul-saving one in the treatment of a subject who finds him or herself caught in the discourse of addiction. One only needs to look at the similarities in structure of these discourses to realize the inherent danger of an encounter between them. In this encounter, the analytical relationship can easily tilt over into a hypnotic relationship in which words can become toxic for a subject who looks for his or her cause in an effect. A general indication for a direction of treatment is that the therapist must prevent the subject from trying to fill the gap of his cause with an effect. That is to say, the therapist has to keep this gap open long enough to establish a demand so that eventually an analysis or a therapy is able to produce a change in the real.

The not-duped are mistaken! Yet they are happy! But at what cost? At the cost of their own organism? Or else, as Freud suggested, "at the cost of a large quota of energy which might have been employed for the improvement of the human lot" (Freud, 1930a, p. 78). What can psychoanalysis do? Psychoanalysis can apply its "know-how". That means a knowledge based on truth which does not know what is best, or even, what is merely good for the other. It is a "no-ing" which produces a particular knowledge, as it is supposed to the subject, in the discourse of analysis. Does that imply an abstinence from drugs and alcohol for the subject? That depends. It means definitely keeping a certain distance from toxicity, which is not quite the same thing. The ethics of psychoanalysis is maybe not without a relationship to the ethics of Stoicism. In Seminar XI, *The Four Fundamental Concepts of Psychoanalysis*, Lacan wonders: "Is it not strange, that echo we found (...) between the ethic of psychoanalysis and the Stoic ethic?" (Lacan, 1979, p. 254). But then he puts this immediately into perspective by rhetorically asking: "What does the Stoic ethic really amount to other than the recognition of the absolute authority of the desire of the Other, that Thy will be done! that is taken up again in the Christian register?" (Ibid.). What about the ethics of Epicurism in this context? Would you tell a chronic alcoholic who is stretched out on the pavement drunk and out of his mind to moderate his drinking, to refine his tastes, and drink an ironically labelled "appellation controlée"? That's unlikely!

Instead one should appeal for the intervention of the desire of the analyst which is a desire to obtain the absolute difference. This is the kind of difference that can include the radical particularity of a subjective "knowledge in the real". That implies that the object and the ego-ideal, which are conjoined in addiction, are placed at the greatest possible distance from each other in the discourse of analysis. The analyst, or therapist, who will find him or herself in an idealized master position to the enslaved subject, has to assume the responsibility for permitting him or herself "to fall in order to be the support of the separating a, in so far as his desire allows him, in an upside-down hypnosis, to embody the hypnotized patient" (Ibid., p. 273). That means that the analyst should embody the object and be in the position of agent, whilst the addict should come to be as subject in the position of other.

The question of how a clinical intervention can make the addict come-to-be as subject will be considered in the conclusion. By way of finishing this chapter it is absolutely crucial to state that it is an ethical imperative for any clinician working with addicts to begin any kind of intervention or treatment by making clear to the addict that he or she has to be duped and cheated out of something. It makes no difference how that is done, as long as it is done. Without this, there is no possibility of a treatment result that is different than making the general cause a general effect and vice versa.

Notes

1. In "Radiophonie" (1970), his unpublished seminar from 1970–1971, *D'un Discours qui ne serait pas du Semblant* (1971), and his seminar from 2 years later *Encore* (1975a), Lacan continues to work on and with this theory.
2. In *Television* Lacan starts his television appearance by saying: "I always speak the truth. Not the whole truth, because there is no way to say it all. Saying it all is literally impossible: words fail. Yet it's through this very impossibility that the truth holds on to the real" (Lacan, 1987[1974], p. 7).
3. In Chapter 7 reference was made to this very first identification and it was called an identification or incorporation of the unary trait. The unary trait is an earlier version of the master-signifier (S1).
4. It is obvious that there are many of those kind of discourses in existence. In the domain of helping people one only needs to refer to the various occult practices and mention such things as rebirthing techniques, aromatherapy and parapsychology.
5. The subject has a choice at the level of the unconscious. Addiction and neurosis are a responsibility of the subject. Even when the subject is not responsible for the cause of his or her suffering, he or she still has to take that responsibility. That is a fundamental (Freudian) dilemma which makes therapy and analysis so difficult. How do you get someone to take responsibility for something for which they are not responsible? Yet, we know it is possible to do so because that is the essence of the human condition. No one asked to be born, but one better accepts life as one's task (in the knowledge of course that one will die).
6. About the (social) effect opium had on him, De Quincey wrote: "For opium (like the bee, that extracts its materials indiscriminately from roses and from the soot of chimneys) can overrule all feelings into a compliance with the master key" (De Quincey, 1986, p. 81).

7. There is a difference between a sense of community and the tendency to form groups. The former is an awareness of oneself and others in terms of a shared responsibility for co-existence. The latter is an act of grouping together that takes place on the basis of excluding others.
8. With regards to the roles of an ideal object and object of identification that heroin can play, Ann Marlowe writes: "What I did mourn for the first year or so without the drug was the sense of identity and specialness it brought. Giving up the elements of minor outlawry meant renouncing certain claims to specialness, to exceptionality. Not that most people would have known the nature of my 'specialness', but I knew. It robed me with a mantle, however thin, of trangressive glamour" (Marlowe, 1999, p. 272).
9. A lot of addicts form groups with their own style and aesthetics and some (youth) cultures are centred around a particular drug. Take rave or dance culture and its obsession with ecstasy.
10. Withdrawals are manifestations of a suffering in the real. The mental and physical horror they engender are experienced as immediate and the possible effect of words is directly smothered by the agony.
11. These beers and priests do actually exist in Belgium.

Conclusion

Why should psychoanalysis contribute to helping people to live a life which is grounded in the real and penetrated by its presence? How can it help people to live a life that is permeated by the real, the death-drive and by toxicomania?

Lacan emphasizes that the analyst only intervenes with words and not with drugs on the body (Lacan, 1974, Lecture from 21-5-1974). If the real, the death-drive, and the bodily route of addiction (toxicomania) are situated outside the realm of signifiers and words, does that imply that the discourse of analysis is impotent when it comes to helping us live a life which is overwhelmed or troubled by this real? A hasty conclusion would be to say "yes". An alternative response, however, would be to turn the question around by rhetorically asking what the other discourses have to offer instead. It has been argued in this work that they offer a lot, but little with regards to the possibility of changing something in the relationship between the subject and the real or jouissance. At best, some of these discourses would offer knowledge as a life assurance against death. But who would put their trust in an assurance company whose only way of assuring people is by saying that it does not want to know anything about what people want to assure themselves against?

Science (including human science) does not want to accept the reality and real of the death-drive.

What can the discourse of analysis offer? The analyst can offer him or herself as an object cause of desire for the analysand. That does not mean that the analyst offers knowledge. It means only that the analyst has the respons-ability to cause the desire of the analysand and to keep this cause open for as long as is necessary, by not offering the knowledge which the analysand imputes to him or her. This structure evokes and provokes the transference. It will immediately bring to the forefront the fantasmatic relationship the subject has with his object-cause-of-desire; a relationship which (at least partially) organizes his or her jouissance. This is the very reason why psychoanalysis or psychoanalytic psychotherapy should contribute to the treatment of addiction. How the subject organizes his or her jouissance economy—the administration by the addicted subject of jouissance and toxicity—is to a large degree determined by his or her subjective position. An effective treatment of addiction has to relate the symptom or solution to the underlying structure. A differential diagnosis is possible precisely on the basis of what happens or develops in an analysis, namely the transference. The transference will eventually expose the unconscious jouissance economy of the subject as the cause of the addiction. The cause of addiction is not a general cause, but a cause that is specific to the subject, and this cause can only be approached through speech in a transferential relationship. That is why a treatment that is based on the transference is an absolute prerequisite in addiction treatment. The respons-ability of the analyst is to allow the transference to unfold, or take place, around his or her position as object. Through analytic work on fantasy and other solutions such as addiction, it is possible to establish a change in the subject's economy of jouissance. Braunstein writes:

> (...) the experience of analysis consists of the confrontation of the subject of the symptom with the impossible of jouissance and to offer to this impossibility the route of verbalization in the ideal and artificial conditions which are those of the psychoanalytic encounter, those of the transference (Braunstein, 1992, p. 278, my translation).

The human subject, as a speaking being, has access to the real via the signifier (Lacan, 1974, lecture from 21-5-1974). However, this is problematic, because every fantasy and illusion of the subject will fight against this penetration of the real by the signifier. The real penetrates life, but not if we can help it. This penetration of the real causes pain, anxiety, and trauma, whilst our illusions, fantasies and symptoms fight tooth and nail against it. Psychoanalysis allows the analysand to traverse the fantasies and break through the illusions, in the hope of being able to arrange a different relationship for the subject with the real of jouissance. These unconscious fantasies and illusions can be bits and pieces of knowledge built up as defences against the real drives and jouissance of the body; bits and pieces in the unconscious which are the effect of—in Lacan's words—"the copulation of language (as it is with this that I support the unconscious) with our bodies" (Lacan, 1976, lecture from 16–3–1976, trans. Luke Thurston). It is via analysis, via the transference, via working-through, that the subject can work on this unconscious knowledge. It needs to be worked on because it is, as Lacan says, like a cancer to him (Lacan, 1974, lecture from 11–6–1974).

This unconscious knowledge is a "knowledge in the real" which does not work for the subject, but rather works against him, as a death-drive. This produces symptoms as signs that something is not working in the real (Lacan, 1975b, lecture from 10–12–1974). These symptoms need to be analysed, but not by just "making sense" of them. As with the psychoanalytic treatment of toxicomania, it is not so much the act of comprehending the sense of symptoms, but rather the act of a very elaborate working-through or a deciphering of the effects of the jouissance of the real on the unconscious of the subject. In toxicomania, the unconscious of the subject is drenched by a jouissance of the real of the drives, because they never became inhabited and pacified by language. This elaborate deciphering comes down to the slow process of bringing jouissance within the realm of the signifier, in such a way that jouissance will bow to the law of desire and can be replaced by ordinary pleasure.

The end of analysis—as Lacan suggested—is constituted by a knowing how to cope (s'avoir-y-faire) with one's symptoms (Lacan, 1977, lecture from 16–11–1976). Or, as Ellie Ragland put it.

> Lacan gives us a new subject of lack, a new object of limit, and an injunction to live with less attachment to our symptoms because and this is crucial our masked suffering makes us harm ourselves as we harm others (Ragland, 1995, p. 179).

This harm is nowhere more obvious than in relation to toxicomania. That this harm in toxicomania can be curtailed by psychoanalysis is certain. That addicts would be prepared to take the long detour of language and speech is not so certain, because to do so, they would have to give up the shortcut of drugs and alcohol via the body. And it is precisely at this point that one encounters the crux of the problem in the treatment of addiction.

It has been demonstrated that it is essential that addicts should get the chance to bring a harmful toxicity within the realm of the signifier in order to be able to come to live with the facts of who and what they are. If they do not get, or indeed, take this chance, they will sooner or later relapse into either their previous addiction, or else another form of harmful administration. This raises three questions that need a proper response if addiction treatment is to get out of its impasse: (1) Where and when should one intervene in order to be most effective in terms of treatment? (2) How does one intervene with addicts such that therapy or analysis becomes a possibility? (3) How can the intervention with addicts be conducted in such a way that the end result will lead to the likelihood of therapy or analysis, in other words, how can the demand for analysis be stimulated?

Addicts are caught between two masters and in their period of so-called "active addiction", they have chosen the master that is the drug or alcohol. The danger of any intervention is that addicts might switch one master for another. It is very likely that they will look for an ideal to hold onto or be dictated by. Any intervention, any treatment, runs the risk of being positioned in that role by the addict. Every desire for a master is always matched by another's desire to be a master. This latter desire is, like the former, related to the desire to master the ultimate master. The addict's relationship to the death-drive, the jouissance of the real and thus, excess and transgression, often provoke a moral reaction to master the addict's behaviour, especially when he or she is faced with death.

A brief clinical interlude

This clinical fragment illustrates the dynamic between the transference and the desire of the therapist in an institution which presents itself as what is called a "caring community". More often than not, caring institutions behave like an authoritarian Other or a maternal superego. This fragment concerns an alcoholic who was in analysis. He stopped drinking many years ago and he chose to do an analysis because he wanted to explore his life in that way. He spoke about an experience in a "caring community", which took place a good while ago. It was something that had traumatized him, something he never had been able to overcome.

On being admitted to the "caring community", this man was given a guided tour through the building by the female therapist of his therapy group. She showed him traces left behind by group members who had been able "to get in touch with their emotions". The therapist told him: "I want you to leave something behind as well." He was also told that if he could do that he would be cured. He began his therapy group the next day. There was a rumour circulating that the therapist had a preference for men. He said that this rumour disappointed him for some reason (he didn't know exactly why). He immediately "opened-up" in the group and he spoke about a particular incident. He thought he had done his best with this "first step" in treatment. He thought he had been incredibly honest. The group reacted to what he said with, what is called, "feedback". One group member, who he didn't like, said to him that he had been totally dishonest. At this point it should be added that, on several occasions the therapist had encouraged him to "express his emotions"; "to let himself go". She had even said that he should not "hold back" because she was very well protected against a possible assault. Instead of complying with the hidden suggestion, he decided to attack the man who had given him "negative feedback". He grabbed him by the throat and "acted-out" his aggression. He said he didn't feel particularly angry and it had even given him some pleasure. He added that he did it just because he wanted to do it. That, of course, is important because it means that it was an act in the true sense of the word: something that produces pleasure (and therefore something that is not unrelated to addiction). His reaction was not instinctive. The therapist told him at the end of the session that "now he was going to be cured". The next day was family day (as it is called). Family members, friends and other acquaintances were present in the group. At a certain point he got extremely angry and he couldn't remember what the cause was. However, he could remember what he said: "the group was only interested in pleasing the therapist". He was so angry that he "saw red". He "felt strange and not himself at all". After this feeling disappeared he felt "bad and guilty". He spoke with the therapist and he apologized profusely. Apparently, that was sufficient, but not for long. The next day he was asked to leave the centre. He had gone too far in letting himself go and he had left behind too big a trace. It didn't last long before he was drinking again. When he apologized to the therapist she had told him that the group was in an impasse and she had been on the verge of dissolving the group.

A lot can be said about this fragment, but will be restricted here to a number of aspects. Transference always comes as a surprise, and that is extremely problematic for institutions, especially the ones who are not prepared for it. "Caring communities" are not prepared, at least not within their treatment philosophy, because "why should clients get angry with us when we are trying to help and care for them?" The "acting-out" of this man during group therapy was an act that took place in response to an institutional suggestion. It was an act committed in relation to an implicit ideal; it represented the desire to fulfil or satisfy a demand which took the form of an expectation. The transference surfaced the next day as a surprise. Precisely at that moment, a little piece of truth came to the surface as something that was unconscious and experienced as strange (he felt strange and not himself). The institution did not tolerate this piece of truth. The act (as opposed to "acting-out") in the first group was "dishonest" because he wanted to satisfy the desire of the therapist. The outburst the next day was spontaneous and indeed a more direct expression of the underlying truth. This truth is related to his "dummy" from the previous day, namely the expectations that rested on his shoulder. This "dummy" is an indication of his dependence on the master: the authority of the therapist or institute she represented. Something of the pathology of the addiction manifested itself in this fragment. For example, the dependency on the master hides a not-wanting-to-know about the unconscious cause of anxiety.

Most therapeutic communities are based on a master discourse. In that sense, it is possible to say that they form a barrier against the unconscious. Every manifestation of a lack or an unconscious desire (and it makes no difference whether this concerns the pathology of the patient or the unconscious aspect of the institute itself) is "too much" for the institution. It does not sit well with its rules. Institutions and their therapists will often show a reaction such as happened in this clinical fragment and this reaction happens when the "too much" cannot be incorporated. This is a "toxic" reaction with disastrous consequences for addicts; it is an institutional "acting out". The institution is reacting at the same level as the symptom or solution of addiction in this instance.

The addicted subject attempts to reach the object of the drive with a drug in order to obtain an ideal level of pleasure, satisfaction or jouissance. The institution attempts to moor a subject who has gone adrift, by putting the law and the object onto the same place. That attempt is exactly the same as trying to unite the ego-ideal with the object. For instance, the clinical fragment illustrates that everything has to fit into the expectations, ideals, and rules of the institution. When something disturbs the equilibrium of the institution, when something happens that transgresses its rules, ideals, and expectations, the unity is broken (the therapist had been on the verge of dissolving the group because it did not function anymore). The expulsion of the man was an attempt to reunite the group; a sacrificial offer to the ideal, in order to bring the group together. The unification of the ideal and the object (in an institution) creates an institutional hypnosis.

To give addicts a chance, it is absolutely essential that, from the very initial stages of intervening, they be given the chance to explore their subjective relationship to jouissance. Institutions have to conduct a clinic that includes the subject and not just focus on the addiction. It is therefore essential that the object and the ideal be kept as far apart from each other as possible. A treatment centre for addictions has to create a space between object and ideal. That is the precise definition of a therapeutic space in a treatment centre. Only this kind of space leaves room for a confrontation between the subject and the lack or desire of the Other. Institutions should function as a lacking Other. But if they function as an authoritarian father or a caring mother, that is, if they function without a lack, they have turned their ideals into objects of desire and jouissance.

Any institution or treatment centre functions, to a greater or lesser extent, on the basis of elements of a master discourse. No centre or institution can function without ideals, without a signifier that unites them. However, in the case of a treatment centre for addiction, it is crucial that the law, which represents these elements or ideals, is not a cruel law. A cruel law is a law which forces the ideal onto the subject. This implies a law which demands that the subject enjoys in a perverse way. To install a law that is not cruel is not an easy thing to do. Today's consumer culture has managed extremely well to bring the law and the object together in a cruel unit. Our institutions represent that culture. That is why it is an absolute imperative that exceptions are made to—and within—those units. The problem is that while our culture enforces the law of jouissance, it has a great need for strong prohibitions at the same time and this precisely in order to curtail the "too much" of jouissance. One of the strongest prohibitions is the one which makes the law itself an object of enjoyment. Quite often this characterizes the ideology and methods of addiction treatment. As asserted earlier, a detoxification of drugs is relatively easy via a reintoxification with the law. This was called a collective hypnosis.

"Addicts are victims". This is a statement one often hears. It is not the kind of statement that tallies well with the ethics of psychoanalysis. However, if one accepts that addicts are victims, then so are the institutions that deal with addiction. These institutions have the impossible task of marrying the ideal of consumer society—to enjoy as much as possible—to the installation of a law, because a very strong prohibition is needed to call a halt to the evoked jouissance. How can this be translated into the daily reality of addiction treatment? "Do as I do!"; "Follow the programme!"; "Forget the past!"; "Meet your needs!"; "Get in touch with your emotions and you'll get better!". "Forget the past" is something that one hears a lot in the world of addiction treatment. This is very interesting because the only a-historic aspect of the subject is precisely jouissance. This imperative of addiction treatment indicates a choice for jouissance and not a choice for creating a distance from jouissance through a symbolization of the past. The imperative "to get in touch with your feelings" is a classic example of the impossible and cruel order to enjoy. Treatment centres and institutions have accepted the impossible task of uniting the law with the object of jouissance because it is an attempt at preventing the disastrous consequences of the ideal of consumer society. The impossibility of this task is so frustrating that it often results in aggressive behaviour (such as happened in the clinical fragment).

In a general way one can say that addicts are dominated by a maternal superego which commands that he or she enjoy outside the phallic function or the symbolic law. Addiction is, as was already noted by Freud, a way of pacifying the superego. But the superego is (as is no surprise) egoistic. The more it is promised, the more it wants from the subject. This was Freud's original discovery in *Civilization and its Discontents*. Addiction can never be a solution for this discontent. Considered from the point of view of its relationship to culture, addiction always centres around an impossible dynamic between two solutions that exclude one another. It is an attempt to enjoy as commanded by the perverse superego, and it is an attempt to disarm this superego by drowning it in a sea of toxicity. Heroin culture reflects this impossible dynamic. Groups of heroin addicts often form a sub-culture in reaction to a dominant culture which commands that people enjoy in the way it wants them to. The effect of heroin and the effect of heroin culture obfuscate and disarm, by their very action, the effect of the command of culture. Heroin addicts install (in their own particular way) an ideal and this ideal is the exact mirror image (i.e., the reverse) of the ideal of dominant culture. Society is up in arms about this. (It is important to remind the reader at this stage that what is being talked about is addiction as a social bond. One should not lose sight of the fact that behind the manifest uniformity of addiction one encounters the complexities of the subject and addressing those should be the ultimate aim in treatment.) The war against drugs is a desperate attempt to fabricate a failing father function as a way out of the obvious impasse. It is especially in the context of this desperate attempt that psychoanalysis has to assume responsibility. Both society and addicts have to pave a way towards desire. This implies the necessity of a symbolic pact, not the command to enjoy.

An intervention can be done such that it leads to the possibility of an interrogation of the administration of jouissance by the subject. This requires that in the "intervention set-up" room is created between the ideal (or law) and the object. Another requirement is that therapists (and other clinicians) are prepared for the fact that the solution they offer is not 100% foolproof. If one demands from one's clients that they be duped, one has to allow for being duped oneself. Not every addict will recover. That is a fact. And anyone who does not accept that fact should not be allowed anywhere near an addict. However, once one is prepared to be duped, there is still a crucial question to be answered: when does one intervene in order to move most effectively from the specific effects of drugs and alcohol to the cause of addiction via the medium of articulation? An intervention should start with the initial point of transference, namely the demand of the subject of addiction, which is a demand that relates to, or will be particular to, the subjective position of the subject. Why should one start there? The specific effects of drugs (also those that lead to addiction) are determined by unconscious "knowledge in the real", but these effects are filtered through and co-determined by the subjective structure of the subject (his or her position). To put this into other words: the restrictions on the effects of variations in unconscious "knowledge in the real" (which also cause variations in drug and alcohol effects) are the limits set by the subjective structure of the subject (with the exception of the less delineated limits set by culture). That implies that the limit on variations in ways of dealing with jouissance is set by the different mechanisms of administration. Hence, it is possible to say the following: the effects of drugs and alcohol depend on unconscious "knowledge in the real", but they are shaped and restricted by the structure of the subject via the mechanism of administration. One should start an intervention with the demand, because that is the point where something of the real cause of addiction reverberates in language; that is the point where unconscious "knowledge in the real" makes itself felt linguistically, albeit in extremely veiled terms. The demand, also in the form of a complaint or an accusation, is the translation of the real into the language of the patient via the code of the mechanism of administration. The language of (addicted) patients is often defensive because translating the real is extremely painful. This requires a long working-through process in the treatment of addiction. The treatment of the subject of addiction implies a therapeutic movement starting from the demand to establish a change in the unconscious "knowledge in the real" with the hope for a change in the future regarding the effects of drugs and the effects of life. To say that the treatment should start with the language of the demand is coherent with the hypothesis put forward in this work that addiction is symbolically determined. The real complications arise from the problem that, despite the one source of determination (the symbolic order or the signifier), there are always ultimately at least two causes for addiction: (1) the cause of the constitution of the subject in language which installs a lack which the subject of addiction wants to undo, and; (2) the unconscious "knowledge in the real" as an effect of the cut of the signifier in the real which causes subject-specific effects of drugs and alcohol which can "hook" the subject. It is in the interplay between these two symbolically determined causes that addiction finds its cause. For instance, it is not sufficient to say that addicts cannot stand lacking anything. The complex interplay of causes is one of the reasons why addiction is such a complex pathology and why it is difficult to treat.

Finally, if treatment should start with the demand, then what is required to create a demand in addicts for therapy or analysis? The answer is simple: everything and anything that works. And it is clear what works and what doesn't work. What works is the lure of an ideal. What works is anything that incarnates the essence of addiction. What works is the scientific real of methadone. What works is the imaginary identification of therapy groups and self help groups. What works is the symbolic position of the master. Is it justified or ethical to use that lure? The answer has to be that it is. These are the only tools available unless, of course, one is prepared to incarcerate addicts or commit them to a hospital. Unfortunately, there are far too many people around who would be prepared to do just that. To lure addicts is both justified and ethical on the basis of a distinction that has to be made. One has to separate the position of agent provocateur from the way the agent is going to function. The agent should never function as lure or ideal. Making this distinction is perfectly coherent with the ethics of analysis: it is the lure of a promise that brings an analysand to an analyst and it is the function (as object of transference) that creates the possibility of an analysis. This is perfectly applicable to the treatment of addicts. Every initial encounter with addiction is an encounter that involves symbolic elements (especially, for instance methadone exchange programmes, but also doctors, family members, work, etc.) and that leaves room for a symbolic way out. Often that room is tiny, but it is a matter of knowing that it exists and indeed to seize the moment (carpe momentum) and act with words.

For most chronic addicts, the imaginary identification of a therapeutic community might be the only viable start of a recovery.

There are a number of therapeutic communities that incorporate a Lacanian ethics in their way of working (for instance, Enaden in Belgium and Communauté Zéro in Italy). However, a lot of therapeutic communities that treat addicts are based on a moral reaction to the problem of addiction. The majority of these types of treatment originate in North America (Synanon and Daytop) and they unite the law with the object in a way that leaves no room for the subject. Alcoholics Anonymous and Narcotics Anonymous also originated in the U.S.A., but they do not come from a moral tradition, and they are not therapeutic instruments or facilities. There is also a European tradition in therapeutic communities. Maxwell Jones is the father of what is called the Democratic Therapeutic Community. He started a community in Northfield Hospital during the Second World War. He had analytic training but did not consider analytic ideas to be of importance for his therapeutic work in communities. Harold Bridger trained analytically in the Tavistock Clinic in London. Bridger was inclined to incorporate psychoanalytic ideas into his way of working with patients in communities. He also worked with groups in the Northfield Hospital and he became a close associate of Wilfred Bion.[1] These European therapeutic communities have their roots in psychoanalytic thinking. The therapeutic intervention of these types of communities includes the subject. However, this is not made explicit because the English psychoanalytic tradition never developed a theory of the subject. But that certainly does not mean that there was no room for the voice of the subject. It is precisely the idea of a "transitional space" in the therapeutic community that leaves room for the subject. The transitional space is a concept that relates to Winnicott's transitional object. This object has a function for the subject in the encounter with the Other. The transitional space is a space that leaves room for the subject in the therapeutic community for an encounter with the Other.

The direction of the treatment of addicts is a matter of managing the transference in such a way that via speech within the transference the particular effects of drugs and alcohol on the subject can be influenced via an effect on the "knowledge in the real". The therapist creates the possibility for analytical work of the subject. In other words, the universal function of the therapist/analyst creates the possibility for the production of the very particular in the subject. However, classical analysis is often not a viable option in addiction treatment. That does not mean that addicts cannot "recover" through an analysis. It is possible when the analyst is able to replace the drug or alcohol as an object of transference. This is not possible in every case, and as indicated before, in chronic cases it is even extremely unlikely. In that case, all and everything is permitted, as long as the intervention contains the opening of a psychoanalytic ethics. This is an opening for the speaking subject.

Note

1. For an excellent overview of the traditions and history of the therapeutic communities the reader is referred to an article by Eric Broekaert: "Geschiedenis, filosofie en grondstellingen van de therapeutische gemeenschap" (1996).

REFERENCES

A.A. (1952). *Twelve Steps and Twelve Traditions*. New York: Alcoholics Anonymous World Services.

Abraham, K. (1927[1908]). The psychological relations between sexuality and alcoholism. In: *Selected Papers on Psychoanalysis* (pp. 80–89). London: Karnac.

Allouch, J. (1984). *Lettre pour Lettre, Transcrire, Traduire, Translittérer*. Toulouse: Eres.

Annas, J. E. (1992). *Hellenistic Philosophy of Mind*. Berkeley: University of California Press.

Anzieu, D. (1975). *L'Auto-Analyse de Freud et la Découverte de la Psychanalyse, Tome 1*. Paris: P.U.F.

Armstrong, T. (1994). Addiction, electricity and desire. In: S. Vice, M. Campbell & T. Armstrong (Eds), *Beyond the Pleasure Dome* (pp. 132–142). Sheffield: Sheffield Academic Press.

Belot-Fourcade, P. (1989). "Boire, dit-elle", *Le Trimestre Psychanalytique. Les Toxicomanies*, 4: 13–18.

Becker, E. (1973). *The Denial of Death*. New York: Free Press.

Berger, L. (1991). *Substance Abuse as Symptom*. London: The Analytic Press.

Bergler, E. (1957). *The Psychology of Gambling*. New York: Harper and Row.

Bracher, M. (1994). On the psychological and social functions of language: Lacan's theory of the four discourses. In: M. Bracher, M. W. Alcorn, R. J. Corthell & F. Massardier-Kenney (Eds), *Lacanian Theory of Discourse: Subject, Structure and Society* (pp. 107–128). New York: New York University Press.

Braunstein, N. (1992). *La Jouissance: Un Concept Lacanien*. Paris: Point Hors Ligne.

Broekaert, E. (1996). Geschiedenis, filosofie en grondstellingen van de therapeutische gemeenschap, *De Nieuwe Therapeutische Gemeenschap* (pp. 9–32). Leuven/Apeldoorn: Garant.

Burroughs, W. S. (1977). *Junky*. London: Penguin Books.

Burroughs, W. S. (1993). *Naked Lunch*. London: Flamingo.

Byck, R. (Ed.) (1974). *Cocaine Papers*. New York, Stonehill.

Charraud, N. (1986). Roulettes et lôteries, *L'Ane, 27* (pp. 44–45). Paris: Seuil.

Charraud, N. (1987). La theorie des jeux et la question du sujet. In: *Aspects du Malaise dans la Civilisation* (pp. 23–30). Paris: Navarin éditeur.

Clavreul, J. (1978). *L'ordre Médical*. Paris: Seuil.

Coleridge, S. T. (1993). In: J. Beer (Ed.), *Poems*. London: Everyman.

Crowley, R.M. (1939). Psychoanalytic literature on drug addiction and alcoholism. *Psychoanalytic Review, 26*: 39–54.

Declerck, F. (1997). Unpublished doctoral thesis, R.U.G. (State University of Ghent).

Delrieu, A. (1988). L'inconsistance de la toxicomanie, Paris: Navarin. *Analytica, 53*: 1–128.

De Quincey, T. (1986[1821]). *Confessions of an English Opium Eater*. London: Penguin Classics.

Derrida, J. (1981). The pharmakon. In: *Dissemination* (B. Johnson, trans.) (pp. 95–117). London: The Athlone Press.

Dollimore, J. (1998). *Death Desire and Loss in Western Culture*. London: Alan Lane The Penguin Press.

Dupont, J. P. (1984). Discours de la toxicomanie. *Quarto, Bulletin de la Cause Freudienne en Belgique, 17*: 47–56.

Ferbos, C. & Magoudi, A. (1986). *Approche Psychanalytique des Toxicomanes*. Paris: Presses Universitaires de France.

Fingarette, H. (1996). *Death: Philosophical Soundings*. Chicago: Carus Publishing Company.

Fink, B. (1995). *The Lacanian Subject*. New Jersey: Princeton University Press.

Fink, B. (1997). *A Clinical Introduction to Lacanian Psychoanalysis*. Cambridge: Harvard University Press.
Forrester, J. (1990). *The Seductions of Psychoanalysis*. Cambridge: Cambridge University Press.
Foucault, M. (1997[1963]). *The Birth of the Clinic*. London: Routledge.
Freud, S. (1884e). Über Coca. In: R. Byck (Ed.), *Cocaine Papers* (pp. 48–73). New York: Stonehill, 1974.
Freud, S. (1885a). Contribution to the knowledge of the effect of cocaine. In: R. Byck (Ed.), *Cocaine Papers* (pp. 96–104). New York: Stonehill, 1974.
Freud, S. (1885b). On the general effect of cocaine. In: R. Byck (Ed.), *Cocaine Papers* (pp. 112–118). New York: Stonehill, 1974.
Freud, S. (1885f). Addenda to Über Coca. In: R. Byck (Ed.), *Cocaine Papers* (pp. 106–109). New York: Stonehill, 1974.
Freud, S. (1887d). Craving for and fear of cocaine. In: R. Byck (Ed.), *Cocaine Papers* (pp. 170–176). New York: Stonehill, 1974.
Freud, S. (1888b). Hysteria. In: *The Standard Edition of the Complete Psychological Works of Sigmund Freud, Vol. I*. London: The Hogarth Press.
Freud, S. (1891d). Hypnosis. In: *S.E., I*. London: The Hogarth Press.
Freud, S. (1893a). On the psychical mechanism of hysterical phenomena: preliminary communication. In: *S.E., II*. London: The Hogarth Press.
Freud, S. (1893c). Some points for a comparative study of organic and hysterical motor paralyses. In: *S.E., I*. London: The Hogarth Press.
Freud, S. (1894). Draft E. How anxiety originates. In: J. F. Masson (Ed. & trans.), *The Complete Letters of Sigmund Freud to Wilhelm Fliess 1887–1904* (pp. 78–83). Cambridge: Harvard University Press, 1985.
Freud, S. (1894a). The neuro-psychoses of defence. An attempt at a psychological theory of acquired hysteria, of many phobias and obsessions and of certain hallucinatory psychoses. In: *S.E., III*. London: The Hogarth Press.
Freud, S. (1895). Draft H. Paranoia. In: J. F. Masson (Ed. & trans.), *The Complete Letters of Sigmund Freud to Wilhelm Fliess 1887–1904* (pp. 107–112). Cambridge: Harvard University Press, 1985.
Freud, S. (1895b[1894]). On the grounds for detaching a particular syndrome from neurasthenia under the description "anxiety neurosis". In: *S.E., III*. London: The Hogarth Press.
Freud, S. (1895d). Studies on hysteria. In: *S.E., II*. London: The Hogarth Press.
Freud, S. (1896). Draft K. The neuroses of defence. In: J. F. Masson (Ed.

& trans.), *The Complete Letters of Sigmund Freud to Wilhelm Fliess 1887–1904* (pp. 162–169). Cambridge: Harvard University Press, 1985.

Freud, S. (1896b). Further remarks on the neuro-psychoses of defence. In: *S.E., III*. London: The Hogarth Press.

Freud, S. (1898a). Sexuality in the aetiology of the neuroses. In: *S.E., III*. London: The Hogarth Press.

Freud, S. (1900a). The interpretation of dreams. In: *S.E., V*. London: The Hogarth Press.

Freud, S. (1901b). The Psychopathology of everyday life. In: *S.E., VI*. London: The Hogarth Press.

Freud, S. (1905[1890]). Psychical (or mental) treatment. In: *S.E., VII*. London: The Hogarth Press.

Freud, S. (1905c). Jokes and their relation to the unconscious. In: *S.E., VIII*. London: The Hogarth Press.

Freud, S. (1905d). Three essays on sexuality. In: *S.E., VII*. London: The Hogarth Press.

Freud, S. (1905e). Fragment of an analysis of a case of hysteria. In: *S.E., VII*. London: The Hogarth Press.

Freud, S. (1906a). My views on the part played by sexuality in the aetiology of the neuroses. In: *S.E., VII*. London: The Hogarth Press.

Freud, S. (1909d). Notes upon a case of obsessional neurosis. In: *S.E., X*. London: The Hogarth Press.

Freud, S. (1910c). Leonardo Da Vinci and a memory of his childhood. In: *S.E., XI*. London: The Hogarth Press.

Freud, S. (1911c). Psychoanalytical notes on an autobiographical account of a case of paranoia. In: *S.E., XII*. London: The Hogarth Press.

Freud, S. (1912d). On the universal tendency to debasement in the sphere of love. In: *S.E., XI*. London: The Hogarth Press.

Freud, S. (1912f). Contributions to a discussion on masturbation. In: *S.E., XII*. London: The Hogarth Press.

Freud, S. (1912–1913). Totem and taboo. In: *S.E., XIII*. London: The Hogarth Press.

Freud, S. (1913f). The theme of the three caskets. In: *S.E., XII*. London: The Hogarth Press.

Freud, S. (1914g). Remembering, repeating and working-through. In: *S.E., XII*. London: The Hogarth Press.

Freud, S. (1915b). Thoughts for the times on war and death. In: *S.E., XIV*. London: The Hogarth Press.

Freud, S. (1915c). Instincts and their vicissitudes. In: *S.E., XIV*. London: The Hogarth Press.

Freud, S. (1916–1917). Introductory lectures on psycho-analysis. In: *S.E.*, *XVI*. London: The Hogarth Press.

Freud, S. (1917d). A Metapsychological supplement to the theory of dreams. In: *S.E.*, *XIV*. London: The Hogarth Press.

Freud, S. (1917e). Mourning and melancholia. In: *S.E.*, *XIV*. London: The Hogarth Press.

Freud, S. (1919a). Lines of advance in psycho-analytic therapy. In: *S.E.*, *XVII*. London: The Hogarth Press.

Freud, S. (1920g). Beyond the pleasure principle. In: *S.E.*, *XVIII*. London: The Hogarth Press.

Freud, S. (1921c). Group psychology and the analysis of the ego. In: *S.E.*, *XVIII*. London: The Hogarth Press.

Freud, S. (1923b). The ego and the id. In: *S.E.*, *XIX*. London: The Hogarth Press.

Freud, S. (1924c). The economic problem of masochism. In: *S.E.*, *XIX*. London: The Hogarth Press.

Freud, S. (1925d). An autobiographical study. In: *S.E.*, *XX*. London: The Hogarth Press.

Freud, S. (1925e). The resistances to psycho-analysis. In: *S.E.*, *XIX*. London: The Hogarth Press.

Freud, S. (1926e). The question of lay analysis. In: *S.E.*, *XX*. London: The Hogarth Press.

Freud, S. (1927c). The future of an illusion. In: *S.E.*, *XXI*. London: The Hogarth Press.

Freud, S. (1927d). Humour. In: *S.E.*, *XXI*. London: The Hogarth Press.

Freud, S. (1928b). Dostoevsky and parricide. In: *S.E.*, *XXI*. London: The Hogarth Press.

Freud, S. (1930a). Civilization and its discontents. In: *S.E.*, *XXI*. London: The Hogarth Press.

Freud, S. (1933a). New introductory lectures on psycho-analysis. In: *S.E.*, *XXII*. London: The Hogarth Press.

Freud, S. (1937c). Analysis terminable and interminable. In: *S.E.*, *XXIII*. London: The Hogarth Press.

Freud, S. (1941f[1938]). Findings, ideas, problems. In: *S.E.*, *XXII*. London: The Hogarth Press.

Freud, S., & Bullitt, W. C. (1966). *Woodrow Wilson: A Psychological Study* New Jersey: Transaction Publishers.

Gay, P. (1988) *A Life for our Time*. London: Macmillan.

Geberovich, F. (1984). *Une Douleur Irrésistible: Sur la Toxicomanie et la Pulsion de Mort*. Paris: InterEditions.

Ghaffari, K. (1987). Psychoanalytic theories on drug dependence: a critical review. *Psychoanalytic Psychotherapy*, 3(1): 39–51.
Gilson, J. P. (1987). Het belang van de topologie voor de praktijk van de analyticus. *Rondzendbrief uit het Freudiaanse Veld*, 28: 41–54.
Glover, E. (1956[1928]). The Aetiology of Alcoholism, *On the Early Development of Mind* (pp. 81–90). London: Imago Publishing.
Glover, E. (1956[1932]). On the Etiology of Drug-Addiction, *On the Early Development of Mind* (pp. 187–215). London: Imago Publishing.
Gossop, M. (1993). *Living with Drugs*. Hants: Arena.
Gross, A. (1935). The psychic effects of toxic and toxoid substances. *The International Journal of Psychoanalysis*, XIV: 425–438.
Gunther, R. (1994). Alcohol and writing: patterns of obsession in the work of Marguerite Duras. In: S. Vice, M. Campbell & T. Armstrong (Eds), *Beyond the Pleasure Dome: Writing and Addiction from the Romantics* (pp. 200–205). Sheffield: Sheffield Academic Press.
Healy, D. (1996). *The Psychopharmacologists*. London: Chapman and Hall.
Heidegger, M. (1993[1954]). The question concerning technology. In: D. F. Krell (Ed.), *Basic Writings* (pp. 311–341). London: Routledge.
Jonckheere, L. (1987). Otto Gross (1877–1920): De fictie als geschiedschrijving van een afval verschijnsel. In: J. Quackelbeen (Ed.), *Psychoanalyse en Klinische Psychiatrie: Een Geschiedenis van Eigenheid of Verbondenheid?* (pp. 153–160). Ghent: Ides a.
Jonckheere, L. (1988). Angst als Reële in het Psychoanalytisch Discours. Aan de Praxis Voorafgaande Vragen, unpublished doctoral thesis, R.U.G (State University of Ghent).
Kaplan-Solms, K., & Solms, M. (2000). *Clinical Studies in Neuro-Psychoanalysis*. London: Karnac Books.
Kouretas, N. (1996). The development of the concept of the "borderline" in psychoanalytic diagnosis and treatment. In: J. F. Gurewich & M. Tort (Eds), *The Subject and the Self* (pp. 43–61). New Jersey: Jason and Aronson Inc.
La Rochefoucauld. (1959). *Maxims* (L. Tancock, trans.). London: Penguin Books.
Lacan, J. (1938). *Family Complexes in the Formation of the Individual* (C. Gallagher, trans.), School of Psychotherapy, St Vincent's Hospital, Dublin, unpublished.
Lacan, J. (1963). *Seminar X, Anxiety* (1962–1963) (C. Gallagher, trans.), unpublished.
Lacan, J. (1966[1946]). Propos sur la causalité psychique; In: *Écrits* (pp. 151–193). Paris: Éditions du Seuil.

Lacan, J. (1966). La place de la psychanalyse dans la médecine. *Cahier du Collége de Médicine*, 12: 761–774.
Lacan, J. (1970). Radiophonie. In: *Silicet* 2/3 (pp. 55–99). Paris: Éditions du Seuil.
Lacan, J. (1971). *Le Séminaire, Livre XVIII, D'un Discours qui ne Serait pas du Semblant, 1970–1971*, unpublished.
Lacan, J. (1972). *Le Séminaire, Livre XIX, Óu Pire, 1971–1972*, unpublished.
Lacan, J. (1973). L'étourdit. In: *Silicet* 4 (pp. 5–52). Paris: Éditions du Seuil.
Lacan, J. (1974). *Le Séminaire, Livre XXI, Les Non-Dupes Errent, 1973–1974*, unpublished.
Lacan, J. (1975a). *Jacques Lacan Le Sémimaire, Livre XX, Encore, 1972–1973* (texte établi par J.-A. Miller). Paris: Éditions du Seuil.
Lacan, J. (1975b). Le Séminaire, Livre XXII, "R.S.I.", 1974–1975 (texte établi par J.-A. Miller) *Ornicar?*, 2–5, 1975. Paris: Éditions du Seuil.
Lacan, J. (1975c). Cùlture aux Journées d'études des Cartels. In: *Lettres de L'École Freudienne de Paris* (pp. 268–270). April, 1976, nr. 18.
Lacan, J. (1976). Le Séminaire, Livre XXIII, "Le Sinthome", 1975–1976 (texte établi par J.-A. Miller) *Ornicar?*, 6–11, 1976–1977. Paris: Éditions du Seuil.
Lacan, J. (1977[1948]). Aggressivity in psychoanalysis. In: *Écrits* (A. Sheridan, trans.) (pp. 8–29). London: Tavistock Publications.
Lacan, J. (1977[1949]). The Mirror Stage as formative of the function of the I as revealed in psychoanalytic experience. In: *Écrits* (A. Sheridan, trans.) (pp. 1–7). London: Tavistock Publications.
Lacan, J. (1977[1953]). The function and field of speech and language in psychoanalysis. In: *Écrits* (A. Sheridan, trans.) (pp. 30–113). London: Tavistock Publications.
Lacan, J. (1977[1958a]. On a question preliminary to any possible treatment of psychosis. In: *Écrits* (A. Sheridan, trans.) (pp. 179–225). London: Tavistock Publications.
Lacan, J. (1977[1958b]). The direction of the treatment and the principles of its power. In: *Écrits* (A. Sheridan, trans.) (pp. 226–280). London: Tavistock Publications.
Lacan, J. (1977[1960]). The subversion of the subject and the dialectic of desire in the Freudian unconscious. In: *Écrits* (A. Sheridan, trans.) (pp. 292–325). London: Tavistock Publications.
Lacan, J. (1977). Le Séminaire, Livre XXIV, "L'Insu que sait de l'une bévue s'aille a mourre", 1976–1977 (texte établi par J.-A. Miller) *Ornicar?*, 12–18, 1977–1979. Paris: Éditions du Seuil.

Lacan, J. (1979). In: J.-A. Miller (Ed.), *The Seminar of Jacques Lacan, Book XI, The Four Fundamental Concepts of Psychoanalysis, 1964–1965* (A. Sheridan, trans.). London: Penguin Books.

Lacan, J. (1982[1952]). Intervention on transference. In: J. Mitchell & J. Rose (Eds), *Feminine Sexuality: Jacques Lacan & The École Freudienne* (J. Rose, trans.) (pp. 61–73). London: MacMillan Press.

Lacan, J. (1987[1974]). Television. In: *October* (nr. 40) (D. Hollier, R. Krauss & A. Michelson, trans.) (pp. 7–50). Cambridge: MIT Press.

Lacan, J. (1988a). In: J.-A. Miller (Ed.), *The Seminar of Jacques Lacan, Book II, The Ego in Freud's Theory and in the Technique of Psychoanalysis, 1954–1955* (S. Tomaselli, trans.). Cambridge: Cambridge University Press.

Lacan, J. (1988b). In: J. P. Muller & W. J. Richardson (Eds), *Seminar on "The Purloined Letter", The Purloined Poe* (J. Mehlman, trans.) (pp. 28–54). Baltimore: The Johns Hopkins University Press.

Lacan, J. (1989[1966]). Science and truth. In: *News Letter of the Freudian Field, Vol. 3, nrs 1&2* (B. Fink, trans.) (pp. 4–29).

Lacan, J. (1991). *Jacques Lacan Le Séminaire, Livre XVII, L'Envers de la Psychanalyse, 1969–1970* (texte établi par J.-A. Miller). Paris, Édition du Seuil.

Lacan, J. (1992). In: J.-A. Miller (Ed.), *The Seminar of Jacques Lacan, Book VII, The Ethics of Psychoanalysis, 1959–1960* (Dennis Porter, trans.). London: Routledge.

Lacan, J. (1995[1964]). Position of the unconscious. In: R. Feldstein, B. Fink & M. Jaanus (Eds), *Reading Seminar XI, Lacan's Four Fundamental Concepts of Psychoanalysis* (Bruce Fink, trans.) (pp. 259–282). New York: SUNY Press.

Lacan, J. (1998). Le phénoméne Lacanien. *Les Cahiers Cliniques de Nices*, 1: 9–25.

Laurent, E. (1986). Une seule règle vous manque, *L'Ane* (nr. 27) (pp. 43–44). Paris: Seuil.

Laurent, E. (1998). L'Attribution réelle du corps: entre science et psychanalyse, table ronde a Laussanne. *Mental*, 5: 41–58.

Lenson, D. (1995). *On Drugs*. Minneapolis: University of Minnesota Press.

Le Poulichet, S. (1987). *Toxicomanies et Psychanalyse. Les Narcoses du Désire*, Paris, Presses Universitaires de France.

Libbrecht, K. (1991). De problematische verhouding van het subject ten aanzien van het lichaam. *Rondzend Brief uit het Freudiaaanse Veld*, 48: 41–54.

Limentani, A. (1986). *On the Psychodynamics of Drug Dependence, Between Freud and Klein* (pp. 48–65). London: Free Association Books.

McGuire, W. (Ed.) (1974). *The Freud/Jung Letters* (R. Manheim & R. F. C. Hull, trans.). London: Routledge and The Hogarth Press.
McMurran, M. (1994). *The Psychology of Addiction*. London: Taylor & Francis.
Magoudi, A. (1986). Revue de la littérature psychanalytique sur les toxicomanies. In: C. Ferbos & A. Magoudi (Eds), *Approche Psychanalytique des Toxicomanes* (pp. 7–43). Paris: Presses Universitaires de France.
Magoudi, A. (1995). Freud: de la cocaine au complexe d'oedipe, Cliniques Méditerranées (nr. 47–48) (pp. 107–119). Aix-en-Provence: Centre National du Livre et L'Université de Provence.
Marlowe, A. (1999). *Heroin: How to Stop Time*. London: Virago Press.
Masson, J. (Ed.) (1985). *The Complete Letters of Sigmund Freud to Wilhelm Fliess 1887–1904*. Cambridge: Harvard University Press.
Melman, C. (1989). Un héroisme populaire. *Le Trimestre Psychanalytique*, 4: 87–102.
Melman, C. (1990). *On Depression*. Dublin, St Vincent's School of Psychotherapy, unpublished.
Melman, C. (1993). Essays in clinical psychoanalysis: the alcoholic. In: S. Schneiderman (Ed. & trans.), *How Lacan's Ideas are Used in Clinical Practice* (pp. 234–246). London: Jason Aronson Inc.
Melman, C. (1999). Addiction, *The Letter* (nr. 16) (C. Gallagher, trans.) (pp. 1–8). Dublin: CPS, LSB College.
Mijolla de, A., & Shentoub, S. A. (1981). *Pour une Psychanalyse de L'alcoolisme*. Paris: Éditions Payot.
Miller, J.-A. (1994a). La passe de la psychanalyse vers la science: le désire de savoir. *Quarto*, 56: 36–43.
Miller, J.-A. (1994b). "Extimité". In: M. Bracher et al. (Eds), *Lacanian Theory of Discourse* (pp. 74–87). New York: New York University Press.
Miller, J.-A., & Laurent, E. (1998). The other who does not exist and his ethical committees, *Almanac Of Psychoanalysis* (M. Julien et. al., trans.) (nr. 1) (pp. 15–35).
Morgenstern, J., & Leeds, J. (1993). Contemporary psychoanalytic theories of substance abuse: a disorder in search of a paradigm. *Psychotherapy*, 30(2): 194–206.
Nietzsche, F. (2001). *The Gay Science*. (B. Williams, ed., J. Nauckhoff, trans.). Cambridge: Cambridge University Press.
Nobus, D. (1994). De kreten van de ademloosheid: artikulaties van het perverse fantasma. *Psychoanalytische Perspektieven*, 24: 129–143.
Nobus, D. (1997). Psychoanalysis and clinical diagnosis. *Journal of the*

Centre for Freudian Analysis and Research, 8&9: 45–65.
Nobus, D. (1998). Life and death in the glass: a new look at the mirror stage. In: D. Nobus (Ed.), *Key Concepts of Lacanian Psychoanalysis* (pp. 101–138). London: Rebus Press.
Nunberg, H., & Federn, E. (1962). *Minutes Of the Vienna Psychoanalytic Society, I, 1906–1908.* New York: International Universities Press.
Nunberg, H., & Federn, E. (1967). *Minutes of the Vienna Psychoanalytic Society, II, 1908–1910.* New York: International Universities Press.
Nunberg, H., & Federn, E. (1975). *Minutes of the Vienna Psychoanalytic Society, IV, 1912–1918.* New York: International Universities Press.
Plato, (1927). *Laws II* (R. G. Bury, trans.). Cambridge: Harvard University Press.
Quackelbeen, J. (1991). *Zeven Avonden met Jacques Lacan.* Gent: Academia Press.
Radö, S. (1926). The psychic effects of intoxicants: an attempt to evolve a psycho-analytical theory of morbid cravings. *The International Journal of Psychoanalysis*, XII: 396–413.
Radö, S. (1984[1933]). The psychoanalysis of pharmacothymia (drug addiction). *Journal of Substance Abuse Treatment*, I: 59–68.
Ragland, E. (1995). *Essays on the Pleasures of Death.* New York: Routledge.
Roberts, N. (1994). Peter Redgrove: drinking as menses-envy. In: S. Vice, M. Campbell & T. Armstrong (Eds), *Beyond the Pleasure Dome: Writing and Addiction from the Romantics* (pp. 149–158). Sheffield: Sheffield Academic Press.
Rosenfeld, H. A. (1964). The psychopathology of drug addiction and alcoholism: a critical review of the psycho-analytic literature. In: *Psychotic States* (pp. 217–252). London: The Hogarth Press.
Rudgley, R. (1999). *Wildest Dreams.* London: Little, Brown and Company.
Russell, B. (1993). *The History of Western Philosophy.* London: Routledge.
Saussure de, F. (1916). In: C. Bally & A. Sechehaye (Eds), *Course in General Linguistics* (W. Baskin, trans.). Glasgow: Collins Fontana.
Sheridan, A. (1980). *Michel Foucault: The Will to Truth.* London: Tavistock Publications.
Simmel, E. (1929). Psycho-analytic treatment in a sanatorium. *The International Journal of Psychoanalysis*, X: 70–89.
Snoy, T. (1993). "Per via di Porre, Per via di levare". Psychoanalyse en therapeutische instelling, *Rondzendbrief uit het Freudiaanse Veld*, 54: 31–49.
Sokal, A., & Bricmont, J. (1998). *Intellectual Impostures.* London: Profile Books.

Solano, E. (1998). L'attribution réelle du corps: entre science et psychanalyse, table ronde a Laussanne. *Mental*, 5: 41–58.
Soler, C. (1996). The body in the teaching of Jacques Lacan. *Journal of the Centre for Freudian Analysis and Research*, 7: 6–38.
Strauss, M. (1994). Psychanalyse et science. *Quarto*, 56: 23–30.
Temmerman, K. (1994). Auto-erotische asfyxie: een "status quaestionis" van theorie en onderzoek. *Psychoanalytische Perspektieven*, 24: 109–127.
Thornton, E. M. (1986). *The Freudian Fallacy*. London: Paladin Books.
Trevarthen, C., Aitken, K., Papoudi, D., & Robarts, J. (1998). *Children with Autism* (2nd enlarged edition). London & Philadelphia: Jessica Kingsley.
Vera Ocampo, E. (1989). *L'Envers de la Toxicomanie, Un Idéal d'Indépendance*. Paris, Éditions Denoël.
Verhaeghe, P. (1993). Psychoanalytische diagnostiek: het symptoom tussen de aktualneurose en psychoneurose. *Psychoanalytische Perspektieven*, 18: 71–79.
Verhaeghe, P. (1994). *Klinische Psychodiagnostiek vanuit Lacans Discourstheorie: Impasses en Antwoorden*. Gent: Idesça.
Verhaeghe, P. (1995). From impossibility to inability: Lacan's theory on the four discourses. *The Letter*, 3: 76–99.
Verhaeghe, P. (1997). *Does the Woman Exist?* (M. Dury, trans.). London: Rebus Press.
Verhaeghe, P. (1999). Subject and body, Lacan's struggle with the real. *The Letter*, 17: 79–119.
Vigano, C. (1999). Les nouveaux symptumes et la question préliminaire: l'exemple de la toxicomanie. *Mental*, 6: 47–65.
Warner, N. (1994). Forbidden fruit: nineteenth-century American female authorship and the discourses of drink. In: S. Vice, M. Campbell & T. Armstrong (Eds), *Beyond the Pleasure Dome: Writing and Addiction from the Romantics* (pp. 299–308). Sheffield: Sheffield Academic Press.
Wilde, O. (1989). A few maxims for the instruction of the over-educated. In: I. Murray (Ed.), *The Major Works*. Oxford: Oxford University Press.
Wurmser, L. (1995). *The Hidden Dimension: Psychodynamics of Compulsive Drug Use*. New Jersey: Jason Aronson Inc.
Yalisove, D. L. (Ed.) (1997). *Essential Papers on Addiction*. New York: New York University Press.
Yorke, C. (1970). A critical review of some psychoanalytic literature on drug addiction. *British Journal of Medical Psychology*, 43: 141–159.

Zafiropoulos, M. (1988). Le toxicomane n'existe pas. Paris: Navarin. *Analytica*, 45: 1–106.

INDEX

AA, 57, 83 n.18, 282
Abstinence, 33, 52, 54, 62, 250, 268
Abraham, K., 100–101, 285
"Acting-out", 276, 277
Actual neuroses, 26, 168–73, 219
　and addiction, 31, 52–53, 102
　and lack of psychic processing, 219
　and masturbation, 26, 31
　and psychoneuroses, 56, 87, 169, 219
　and somatic factor, 26, 56
　and the real, 173
　and toxicity/toxic substance, 8, 52, 56
　psychoneuroses as a defence against, 56, 173
A-diction, xviii
Addiction
　and castration, 69, 260
　and craving, 104
　and displacement of energy by drugs, 120

and effects of drugs, 86
and empirical science (method), 209–210
and Freud's meta-psychological concepts, 122
and group formation, 249–250
and humour, 66
and knowledge, 258, 260, 262, 264
and loss/lack, 48, 262
and masturbation, 25–26, 30, 32, 52, 66, 70, 87–88
and oral drive/satisfaction, 37, 163
and pain, 51
and simplification, xviii, 115
and sublimation, 46
and symbolic insufficiency, 87
and transgression, 43, 260, 274, 277
as (violation of) social bond/discourse, 78, 136, 235–7
as "alimentary orgasm", 103
as a-diction, xviii, 127

as appeal, 80, 221
as choice (for jouissance), 136,
  236, 248, 258, 261, 269 n.5,
  278
as conscious fantasy, 254
as identification (with an ideal),
  80, 249
as independent of the Other, 32,
  36, 101, 217–218, 222, 236–
  237
as not a symbolic construction,
  110, 146, 147, 237, 255
as replacement of function of
  signifier, 222
as threat to culture, 260–261
as toxic presence, 45
as waste product (of psychoanalysis), 44, 122
difficulty of definition, 96, 209
drive-theory of, 97, 101–103, 111
ego-psychology and, 97, 103–104
fascination with, 252, 262
uniformity of, 248, 279
Addiction; Death
  and death-drive, 266–267, 274
  as flirtation with death, 158
  as mastery of death, 162
Addiction; Psychopathology
  and (oral) perversion, 101
  and actual neuroses, 102, 218
  and administration, 63
  and cause, 110, 11, 122
  and clinical structure/subjective
    position, 42, 135, 218
  and masochism, 106
  and narcissistic neurosis, 113
  and neurasthenia, 30, 52
  and neurosis, 218
  and perversion, 101, 218
  and psychosis, 1123, 218, 220,
    221
  and transitional state/
    borderline state, 112–115
  as compromise between per-
    version and compulsion
    neurosis, 127 n.2

as separate clinical entity, 218
as social symptom, 216–7
as solution, 43, 56, 110, 236, 279
as symbolically structured
  symptom, 80, 109
as/and (psychoanalytic)
  symptom, 109–110
diagnosis, 86, 209, 233 n.9
is cause and effect, 110
mechanism of, 112
Addiction; Sexuality
  sexual, 87
  as substitute for sexual activity,
    163
  and lack of sexual satisfaction,
    33
  and sexual relationship, 253–
    254
Addiction; Treatment
  counter-transference, 251–252
  and demand, 43, 267
  and dual treatment, 255
  and institution, 277
  and psychoanalytic treatment,
    266, 271–274, 281–282
  as Freud's first therapeutic
    failure, 10
Addictive behaviour, 259–260
Administration, 135, 217–23, 267
  and actual neurosis (to govern or
    regulate), 219–220
  and determination of effects of
    drugs (and alcohol), 224–225
  and neurosis/perversion (to dis-
    pense or supply), 221
  and psychosis (to manage as a
    substitute), 220–221
  and society, 218
  as determined by structure of
    subject, 217–218, 224, 272,
    280
  as indicator of function of
    symptom, 217
  as mechanism of symptom, 217
  etymology of, 135–136
  of jouissance, 237, 272, 279

the three functions of (to govern
   or regulate; to manage as a
   substitute; to dispense or
   supply), 218
Aggression, 76
Alcoholism/alcohol
   and choice of partner, 160
   and denial, 24
   and (de)sublimation, 100–101
   and escape from hardship, 66
   and homosexuality, 58 n.18, 100
   and intolerance, 111
   and jealousy, 24, 45
   and lack in the world, 162
   and lack of responsibility, 24
   and manic-depression, 111
   and (mastery of) death, 161
   and mystic experience, 159
   and paranoia, 24
   and perversion, 101
   and religion, 159
   and sexual difference, 100
   and sexual potency, 101
   and sexuality, 24, 100
   and The Woman, 161
   and working-class, 159
   as barrier against toxicity, 190
   as flight from reality, 111
   as secondary symptom, 25
   as sickness of death, 158
   fantasy of the One, 159–160
Alienation, 154
Allotrion, 8
Allouch, J., 11, 16, 18, 21 n.2, 285
Annas, J. E., 213, 285
Anxiety, 240
Anxiety neurosis, 26, 171–3
Automaton, 151
Anzieu, D., 5, 285
Armstrong, T., 169–170, 191 n.1,
   285, 290, 294–295

Bailey, C., 213,
Beard, G., 169–170, 191 n.1
Belot-Fourcade, P., 158, 165 n.13,
   285

Berger, L., 128 n.6, 285
Bergler, E., 115, 127 n.6, 164 n.7, 285
Bernays, M., 9, 21 n.4
Bion, W., 282
Body, 177–84
   and drives, 123, 177
   and image, 180
   and jouissance, 177–178, 182, 234
      n.13, 273
   and language, 53
   and mind, 121, 153, 174
   and organism, 182
   and subject, 123, 234 n.13
   and toxicity, 89, 135, 182, 185, 193
      n.12, 222
   as reality, 179
   real of, 184–185, 188, 190, 234 n.13
Braunstein, N., xviii, 176, 272, 286
Bricmont, J., 223, 294
Bridger, H., 282
Broekaert, E., 283 n.1, 286,
Brücke, E., 14, 18
Bullitt, W. C., 79–80, 83 n.14, n.16,
   289
Burroughs, W. S., 173–174, 185,
   257–258, 286
Byck, R., 12, 19, 21 n.3, 286

Campbell, M., 285, 290, 294–295
"Caring community", 274–276
Cause
   and effect (in addiction), 96, 110–
      111, 209–210, 224, 263, 267,
      269
   and explanation, 256, 258–262,
      264
   as particular, 126, 272
   as truth, 256, 259, 264
   efficient, 91 n.1
   final, 91 n.1
   formal, 86
   material, 86, 91 n.1
   of addiction, 33, 55, 110, 210, 272,
      280–281
   (of addiction) in subject, 86, 88,
      110–111, 126

of effect (of drugs), 86, 110, 121,
  126, 210, 224, 231, 280
Castration, 32, 64, 68–69, 89, 107,
  134, 154–155, 160, 164 n.10,
  175–176, 178, 183, 187, 189,
  216–217, 220, 236, 239, 245, 260,
  265
Charraud, N., 150, 152–153, 155, 286
Clavreul, J., 244, 286
Cocaine
  and addiction, 3
  and conversion of energy (into
    work), 13
  and difference between animals
    and humans, 11, 14
  and disposable energy, 13
  and euphoria, 12
  and inanimation, 14
  and (increased) capacity for
    work, 11, 15
  and individual predisposition, 16,
    20
  and its dependence on a (psychic)
    variable, 16
  and lack of uniform effect
    (individual variation), 11
  and morphine addiction, 17
  and motor power, 15
  and psychic reaction time, 15
  and "the third scourge of
    mankind", 19
  and (vital) energy, 13
  as anaesthetic, 7
  as Freud's fantasy object, 17, 21
  as panacea, 12, 24
  as remedy for a "weak psychic
    state", 17
  as source of savings, 13–14
  as therapeutic instrument, 10, 12
  as unpredictable object, 20
Coleridge, S. T., 144, 286
Communauté Zéro, 282
Compulsion to repeat, 65, 262, 266
Confrontational (behavioural)
  techniques, 261
Consumer culture, 278

Crowley, R. M., 95, 286

Daytop, 282
Death
  and aesthetics, 144
  and feminine figure, 143
  and illusion of choice, 141, 158
  and immortality, 140
  and pleasure, 135
  mastery of, 135, 142, 145, 157,
    161–162, 266, 274
Death-drive
  and addiction, 90, 135, 266–267
  and aggression, 75, 106–108
  and beauty, 266
  and ego, 106–107
  and ethics, 265–267
  and fantasy, 266
  and imaginary, 162
  and post-Freudians, 105–107
  and real (of body), 135, 266
  and symbolic, 162
  and the good, 266
  and toxicomania, 185, 254, 263
  as beyond pleasure-principle, 62,
    89, 266
  as mastery of death, 135, 162
Declerck, F., 178, 286
Delrieu, A., 210, 286
Demand
  of Other, 78–79, 183, 276
  to renounce pleasure/satisfaction,
    90
  and desire, 240
  and anxiety, 240
  for analysis/therapy, 54, 274, 281
  to enjoy, 278–279
  as point of intervention, 280–281
  as complaint, 286
Democritus, 204
Depersonalization, 58 n.20, 125, 188
Depression, 12, 16–18, 33, 71, 83
  n.14, 101, 104–105, 148, 153,
  156, 207
De Quincey, T., 35, 61, 165 n.15–16,
  185–186, 233 n.11, 269 n.6, 286

Derrida, J., 7, 167, 286
Desire
  as caused by object, 9
  as cause of suffering, 123
  and demand, 240
  and pleasure, 176
  and jouissance, 176
  of Other, 178, 240
  of the analyst, 246, 268, 274
Detoxification, 41
Differential diagnosis, 26–27, 31, 87, 116, 135, 190, 208, 211, 215, 217–218, 272
Disavowal, 116
Discourse, 230–1
  and communication (theory), 237–239, 240
  and death-drive, 239
  and demand, 241
  and determination, 122
  and disjunction of impossibility, 239, 253
  and disjunction of impotence, 239, 253
  and knowledge, 243–248, 255–256, 258
  and philosophy, 243
  and psychosis, 253
  and truth, 246
  as social bond, 230–231, 235, 239
  language as precondition of, 240, 241
  of addiction, 136, 248–55, 260, 262, 267
  of analysis, 136, 230–231, 245–6, 252–253, 263, 267, 268, 271–272
  of human science, 256–257, 260, 262
  of hysteria, 244–5
  of master, 243–4, 276, 277
  of science, 136, 231, 245–6, 252–253, 263, 267, 268, 271–272
  of university, 246–8, 255, 261
  theory, 237–41
Disease concept, 80

Displacement, 26, 34
Dollimore, J., 189, 286
Dora (case study), 56 n.2
Dostoevsky, F., 25, 66, 68, 148, 164 n.10, 289
Drive(s)
  and alcohol, 47
  and body, 123
  and ego, 123
  and object, 123
  and psychic representation, 102, 123
  and satisfaction, 47, 74
  as problematic, 102
  become toxic, 102
  is death-drive, 265–6
Drug(s)
  and (mastery of) death, 161–162
  and compulsion to suffer, 65–66
  and ego, 123
  and energy characteristics of individual, 119
  and escape from hardship, 66
  and lack in the world, 162
  and language, 122
  and Perception-Consciousness system, 118
  and pleasure principle, 65, 185
  and quantitative change, 118
  and reality principle, 65
  and religion xv
  and toxic action, 118
  as barrier against toxicity, 190
  as blind force, 119
  as function outside language, 124
  as object-cause-of-jouissance, 221
  classification of effects of, 122
  different functions of, 234 n.13
  difficulty with definition, 96, 209
  effects are in the real, 126–127, 224
  effects of, 86, 110, 112, 115, 231
  liberation of energy, 120
  no essence to/not essential, 122–123
  (toxic) action of, 119–120

types of, 104, 225
unpredictability, 118, 210
war against, 267, 279
Du Bois-Reymond, E., 14
Duped (to be), 89, 267, 269, 279, 280
Dupont, J. P., 134, 136 n.2, 286
Duras, M., 158–159, 165 n.13–14, 290

Ego, 104, 105
  and aggression, 106, 108–109
  and death-drive, 106–107
  and ego-psychology, 108
  and image, 123, 125
  and need for elation, 104
  and subject, 108
  and suicide, 106
  and superego, 66, 75
  as sick, 107
  (not) a conflict-free zone, 108
Ego-ideal
  and addiction, 78
  and superego, 78–79
  as compensation, 78
  as master-signifier, 242, 244
  merged with object, 248–250, 268, 277–278
Einstein, A., 198
Ellenberger, H. F., 191 n.1
Empty speech, 257
Enabler, 259
Enaden, 282
Energetics, 12–13, 19
Energy, 16
  and cocaine, 16
  and condensation, 119
  and constancy-principle, 34
  and displacement, 26, 118–121
  and jouissance, 58 n.22, 121
  and libido, 26
  and psychic processing, 26
  and q-hypothesis, 26, 33
  and soma, 26
  and source of drive, 117
  and surplus, 51
  as a calculation, 199

  as unpredictable factor, 118–119
  conservation of, 13
  expenditure of, 49
  psychic forms of, 51, 118–119
  toxic, 119
Entropy, 183, 186, 188
Epicureanism, 213–214, 268
Erlenmeyer., 19
Eros, 75
Ethics, xvi, 265, 266, 268, 278, 281–283
Extimacy, 192 n.10

Fantasy, 12, 14, 17, 19, 21, 23, 29–30, 46, 58 n.18, 67–68, 70–71, 82 n.7, n.10, 87, 102, 105, 111, 145, 153, 158–161, 164 n.4, 178, 236, 243, 245–246, 254, 263, 266, 272–273
Fechner, G. T., 14,
Federn, E., 56 n.3, 59 n.25, 69–70, 82 n.6–7, 294
Fingarette, H., 157, 163 n.2, 286
Fink, B., 237, 240–241, 286–287, 292
Fliess, W., 24–25, 27–30, 52, 171–172, 287–288, 293
Foreclusion, 116
Forrester, J., 148, 164 n.8, 287
Foucault, M., 202, 232–233 n.7, 287, 294
Freda, H., 133–134
Freud
  and alcohol, 4
  and cocaine, 5, 8–9
  and death-drive, 55
  and drugs, 4
  and lack of uniformity in addiction, 5
  and Oedipus Complex, 29
  and pessimism, 55
  and (resistance to) addiction, 4
  and science, 186
  and self-analysis, 28–29
  and toxic substance, 62
  and trauma, 27
  and trauma theory, 28

Gadgets, 225–226
Galileo, G., 199
Gambling
  and anxiety, 68
  and being as stake, 155
  and debt, 153, 156
  and Dostoevsky, 66
  and fate, 156–157
  and games of chance, 152
    game (of odd and even), 151
    bridge game metaphor, 149–150
  and guilt, 66, 68
  and imaginary, 151
  and imaginary castration, 154
  and loss (of loss) or lack (of lack), 153, 155–156
  and masturbation, 66–67, 70
  and mood swings, 153
  and Other, 151
  and psychoanalytic cure, 153
  and signifier, 151
  and strategy, 148, 152
  and subject, 151
  and symbolic, 151
  and toxicomania, 146–147, 157
  as artificial creation of lack, 156
  as short-circuit, 153
  as substitute for sexual satisfaction, 25
  description of, 147–149
  illusion of omnipotence, 156
  (mastery over) death, 157
  symbolically structural, 157
Games theory (and psychoanalysis), 149–150
Gay, P., 4, 5 n.1–3, 289
Geberovich, F., 8, 21 n.2, 144, 289
Ghaffari, K., 128 n.6, 290
Gilson, J. P., 229, 290
Glover, E., 97, 102–103, 107, 111–115, 290
Gossop, M., 161, 290
Greek mythology, 142
Gross, A., 103, 107, 111, 115–122, 124, 126, 290

Gross, O., 40, 41, 42, 43, 44, 45, 57 n.8–9, n.13–14, 88, 89, 97, 290
Gunther, R., 290

Hallucinations, 48–49
Happiness, 62, 72–73, 75, 223, 225–227, 251, 264, 267
Healy, D., 227, 232 n.4, 233 n.8
Heidegger, M., 198, 290
Heisenberg, W. K., 198
Helmholtz, H., 14, 18
Heroin, 279
"Higher power", 80
Hughes, J., 201, 232 n.6, 247
Humour, 66
Huxley, A., 161
Hypnosis, 24, 78, 250–251, 267, 277–278

Ideal, 78
  and addiction, 54, 74, 80, 249, 268, 274, 276, 279
  and abstinence, 250
  and superego, 66
  as compensation for loss/sacrifice, 80–81
  and ideology, 78
  and primal father, 83 n.13
  therapist/analyst as, 54, 263
  law as, 277–278
  and object, 277–278
  as cure for treatment, 281
  cultural, 75, 78
Incest (prohibition of), 47, 49, 64, 265
Independence (of Other), 217–218, 236

Jokes
  and conflict, 212
  and expenditure of energy, 38
  and nonsense, 39
  and pleasure, 38
  as pleasure-producing act, 40
Jonckheere, L., 45, 57 n.9, 171, 290
Jones, M., 191 n.7, 282

Jouissance
  and civilization, 225
  and desire, 176
  and energy, 121, 128 n.9
  and fantasy, 266
  and knowledge, 246–247, 252, 273
  and pleasure, 174, 273
  and signifier, 187
  and vital energy, 186
  as death-drive, 175, 177, 184, 265
  as toxic, 222
  different forms of, 121, 174, 176, 187, 234 n.13
  law as (object of) jouissance, 278, 282
  of the body, 184, 188, 192 n.11, 234 n.13
  of the Other, 129 n.9, 154, 179, 192 n.11
  phallic, 128 n.9, 174, 184
  prohibited by law, 175, 265
  surplus, 128 n.9, as surplus-value, 243

Kafka, F., 57 n.9
Kann, L., 5
Kernberg, O., 113
Klein, M., 90, 112, 292
"Knowledge in the real", 178, 198–200, 224, 231, 246, 252, 254, 258, 261, 263–264, 268, 273, 280, 282
Kohut, H., 113–114
Kouretas, N., 113–114, 290

Lacan
  on Freud's desire, 8–9
  on addiction and drugs, 133–134
Language
  and death, 140
  and devitalisation, 183, 186
  and distribution of energy, 38
  and effects of drugs and alcohol, 124, 224
  and neuro-biology, 129 n.11
  and pleasure, 88

  and subject-specific effects of drugs, 129 n.11, 224–225, 231
  as barrier in subject, 121
  determining effect on psyche, 119
  incompleteness of, 129 n.10, 134, 164 n.5, 183, 234 n.13
La Rochefoucauld, 137, 167, 290
Laurent, E., 147, 225–226, 292, 293
Leary, T., 161–162
Leeds, J., 128 n.6, 293
Lenson, D., 209, 292
Le Poulichet, S., 21 n.2, 193, 250, 292
Libbrecht, K., 191 n.6, n.8, 192 n.8, 292
Libido, 19, 26
  and jouissance, 19
  and satisfaction, 77
  economics of, 77
Limentani, A., 95, 127 n.6, 292

Mack Brunswick, R., 5 n.1
Magoudi, A., 4, 5 n.3, 95, 122, 127 n.6, 286, 293
Mania, 49, 50–51
Marlowe, A., 144–146, 270 n.8, 293
Masochism, 65–66, 105–106, 174,
Masson, J., 25, 27, 171–172, 191 n.7, 287, 293
Master-signifier, 242, 248
Master-slave, 243
Masturbation
  and addiction, 25–26, 30, 32, 52, 66, 70, 87–88
  and anxiety, 72
  and damage/harmful, 69–70, 82 n.6, 82 n.7
  and depression, 33, 71
  and fantasy, 70
  and gambling, 66–67, 70–71
  and "inadequate disburdening" of sexual energies, 26, 30, 69
  and incapacity for pleasure, 88
  and incest, 68
  and independence of others or external world, 32, 69
  and infantile sexuality, 68, 70

and intellectual inhibition, 71
and neurasthenia, 30, 32, 152, 170
and pain, 71
and prohibition, 71
and (psycho)neurosis, 68, 70, 82 n.5
and unlimited pleasure, 71
as short-cut between desire and satisfaction, 69, 89
(not) auto-erotic, 79
McGuire, W., 41, 57 n.8, 293
McMurran, M., 233 n.9, 293
Melancholia, 50–51
Melman, C., 58 n.20, 156, 159, 164 n.11, 252, 293
Methadone, 281
Mijolla de, A., 3–4, 95, 127 n.3, n.6, 293
Miller, J.-A., 192 n.10, 197, 199, 225, 226, 291–293
Mirror stage, 83 n.11, 180
Morgenstern, J., 128 n.6, 293
Morphine, 3
Mourning, 50
Moralising, 260, 262, 265–266, 274, 282
Moral panic, 32, 262, 265

Narcissism, 101, 105, 108
Neurasthenia, 26, 169–71
 and addiction, 30, 52
 and depression, 31–32
 and lack of tension, 170
 and masturbation, 30–32, 52, 170
Neuro-psychoanalysis, 231
Neurosis (definition), 216
Newton, I., 200
NIDA (American National Institute of Dug Abuse) vii
Nietzsche, F. vii, 235, 293
Nobus, D., 203, 209, 293, 294
Northfield Hospital, 282
Nunberg, H., 56 n.2, 59 n.25, 69–70, 82 n.6–7, 294

Object a, 150, 232 n.3, 238, 250

Object relations, 111, 113, 115, 122
The One, 163 n.3
Opium, 35, 40, 42, 61, 144, 159, 165 n.15, n.16, 185–186, 233 n.11, 269 n.6
Other as lacking, 150

Pain, 51
Perversion (definition), 216
Phallus, 58 n.20, 128 n.9, 134, 178, 221
Pharmacogenic pleasure-effect, 104
Pharmacology, 12
Pharmacothymia (drug addiction), 99
Plato, 7, 136 n.3, 294
Pleasure
 and death-drive, 174
 and desire, 176
 and drug-use, 46, 251
 and humour, 66
 and jouissance, 174–176, 273
 and (lack of) happiness, 62
 and language, 88
 and mastery of death, 135
 and masturbation, 71
 and pain, 51, 118, 169, 213, 251
 and reduction of tension, 62, 169, 174
 and virtue, 213–214
 impotence for, 72
 regulation of, 74
Pleasure principle, 19, 47, 61–62, 65–66, 70, 73–74, 81, 89, 108, 110–111, 117–118, 141, 169, 171–172, 174–175, 183–185, 187, 193 n.12, 213–214, 221, 239, 253–254, 265–266
Poe, E. A., 151, 292
Popper, K., 201
"Principles of multiplicity", 117
Protagoras, 205
Psychopharmaca, 227
Psychosis (definition), 217

Quackelbeen, J., 14, 199, 290, 294

Radö, S., 97, 99, 102–111, 127 n.4, 294
Ragland, E., 273, 294
Ratman (case study), 82 n.5
Reality principle, 65, 70
Redgrove, P., 160, 165 n.17, 294
Reductionism, xvii, 115
Reintoxification, 278
Relapse, 274
Religion, 78, 91 n.1, 159, 166 n.18, 212, 250, 255, 262
Repression, 116
Roberts, N., 160, 165 n.17, 294
Rosenfeld, H. A., 95, 127 n.6, 294
Rudgley, R., xv, 294
Russell, B., 213–214, 294

Sachs, H., 127 n.2
Saussure de, F., 232 n.2, 294
Schreber, D. P., 24
Science, 195–201
  and addiction, xv
  and death, 138, 161, 263, 272
  and death-drive, 197, 247, 263, 272
  and discourse, 243–246, 248
  and exclusion of the subject, 81, 206, 226, 253, 256, 263–264
  and jouissance, 227
  and knowledge, 229, 259, 262–264, 271
  and pleasure, 88
  and progress, 74
  and psychoanalysis, 64, 223–31
  and reductionism, 204–205
  and religion, 74, 255
  and retreat of its object, 201, 204, 247
  and the real, 190, 223–228
  and truth, 45, 91 n.1, 255, 256, 259–260, 263–264
  as process of symbolization, 201, 232 n.3
  human, 138, 195, 197–199, 201, 223, 247–248, 255–257, 260, 262–264, 272

  modern, 195–201, 223–226, 245, 263
"Science of the real", 199, 264
Self-esteem, 114
Self-help groups, 80
Self-medication, 113
Self-psychology, 113
Separation, 155
Shakespeare, W., 141
Shentoub, S. A., 3, 4, 95, 127 n.3, n.6, 293
Sheridan, A., 202, 291–292, 294
Signifier
  as access to cause of addiction, 122, 272, 282
  as cause of subject, 255
  as sluice-gate, 121
Simmel, E., 115, 127 n.6, 294
Snoy, T., 251, 294
Sokal, A., 223, 294
Solano, E., 227, 295
Soler, C., 179, 180, 182, 191 n.6, 295
Solms, M., 231, 290
Stern, A., 113
Stoicism, 213–214, 268
Strauss, M., 226–227, 295
Subject
  and body, 123, 234 n.13
  and clinical structure, 207, 216
  and death, 163 n.1
  and diagnosis, 222
  and discourse of the Other, 125
  and effect of cause (of drugs and alcohol), 110–111, 124, 263
  and ego, 108
  and false self, 125
  and knowledge about drugs, 86–87
  and particular modes of jouissance, 246, 261, 271–272, 277
  and place of object (drug), 122–123
  and psychopathology, 206
  and specific effects of drugs, 116, 126, 210, 224–225, 231, 246, 263, 280, 281–282

and theory of addiction, xvi
as effect in material (of language), 125–126
as exception or limit of Other, 125
as link between cause and effect (of drugs), 126
as "missing link" (in story of addiction)121, 123–124
as necessary assumption, 125
as represented (by signifier)123
as split between object and unconscious, 125
excluded from treatment, 261, 262–263
of science, 198, 199, 200–201, 247, 256
toxicity in, 89, 190
Subjective responsibility, 64, 259, 260, 264, 267, 269 n.5
Superego, 75, 79
and aggression, 75
and death-drive, 81
and ego, 75
and guilt, 75
and happiness, 75
and humour, 66
and ideal, 81 n.1
as perverse, 279
cultural, 75, 141–142, 225–226, 228
maternal, 274–275, 279
Symptom
and pleasure, 30, 110
as appeal to the Other, 146–147, 254
as barrier against (desire of) Other, 155
as structured like language/ symbolically structured, 109
in psychoanalysis, 83 n.17, 109
in the real, 254–255
Synanon, 282

Temmerman, K., 209, 295
Thanatos, 75
Thermodynamics, 12, 20, 86, 186

The "Thing", 265
Thornton, E. M., 21 n.1, 295
Thumb-sucking, 36
Toxicity/toxic (effect), 27, 38, 53, 116, 267, 268, 274, 279
toxic action (of drugs), 117, 118; psychoanalytic theory of, 115, 120, 185, 192 n.12, 250–251
"primary toxic process", 117–118
Toxicomania and (other) addictions, xvii
Toxic space, 25
Toxic substance (as cause of suffering), 62
Transference, 42
and addiction treatment, 43, 222, 251, 272, 276, 280, 282–283
and counter-transference, 43, 251–252
and dependency, 54
and desire of therapist/analyst, 45
and discourse, 246, 272
and toxicity, 251
onto drug, 43
Transitional space, 282
Trevarthen, C., 129 n.11, 295
Tuché, 153

Unary trait, 181, 269 n.3

Vera Ocampo, E., 10, 21 n.2, 295
Verhaeghe, P., 27, 154–156, 171, 173, 182, 191 n.6, 203–204, 207, 209, 232 n.1, n.3, 237, 295
Vice, S., 136 n.1, 295
Victims, 278
Vigano, C., 295
von Fleischl-Marxov, E., 3

Waldmeier, P., 227
Warner, N., 233 n.10, 295
Wilde, O., 235, 295
Willpower, 80
Wilson, W., 78–80, 83 n.14, n.16, 289
Withdrawal, 10, 41, 44, 270 n.10

Wittels, F., 8
The Woman, 143, 161, 163 n.4
Working through, 280
"Writing in the real", 230
Wurmser, L., 128 n.6, 295

Yage, 173

Yalisove, D. L., 128 n.6, 295
Yorke, C., 4, 85, 95–96, 127 n.1–2, n.6, 295

Zafiropoulos, M., 210, 234 n.13, 296
Zweig, S., 66–67, 71

① Agenda
② New Term of Reference
③ 6 copies of Plan.